Praise for Matt R. Vance and The Review Cycle

A must read for business owners.

Matt Vance is one of the great review management leaders of this century. His knowledge comes from years of working in the trenches driving business growth by means of reviews. In The Review Cycle, he provides in-depth actionable insights that will instantly increase sales and customer satisfaction in any business. Any small business owner could directly impact their bottom line by simply implementing a fraction of the suggestions in this book. It has completely changed my view on the importance of reviews.

*— **Isaac Parkinson**, CEO, Skin Grip*

Comprehensive, insightful, and extremely helpful guide

What might have been boring research, Matt transforms into well-explained and even entertaining chapters that ease the reader into his expertise. After harnessing user-generated content to ethically benefit business for years, he presents his experience using graphs, illustration, and creative story. Any business would profit by implementing his strategies.

*— **Danielle Palmer**, Employee and Consumer Feedback Specialist, iFIT*

Relevant, Concise, Proven Formula, Quick Success

Matt has nailed an industry proven Review Cycle formula, which will provide systematic and rapid benefits to the bottom line. Every organization should immediately put these principles and processes into practice and realize measurable increases in product satisfaction and significant increases in profits!

*— **Roy Rasband**, Owner & Chief Technology Officer, BlueStep Systems*

Insightful and Actionable

The Review Cycle takes a deep dive into every aspect of review management. The tried-and-tested principles, compelling case studies, and step-by-step action items make this an incredible resource for anyone wanting to implement or improve their online reputation.

*— **Jaimee Marlette**, Digital Marketing Virtual Assistant, Marlette Marketing*

Enlightening and essential!

In just six weeks, we've improved certain online review metrics by better than 50% thanks to the application of a few of Matt's simple strategies. When it comes to reviews and brand reputation, Matt may just be the top authority. Simply put, his recommendations work.

*– **Sean Kelly,** CEO, Caroo*

A fun informative look into reviews.

The Review Cycle clearly demonstrates how reviews can change how a product is viewed and change how we think. It does it in a simple fun way that doesn't require a marketing degree to understand. I would highly recommend it to anyone interested in improving their reviews or wanting to understand product reviews as a consumer.

*– **Thayne Williams,** Software QA Engineer, iFIT*

In today's competitive consumer and talent markets, managing your online reviews is no longer a nice-to-have, it's key to survival. The Review Cycle is the kind of comprehensive resource all businesses need at their fingertips.

*– **Ursula Mead,** Co-founder and CEO, InHerSight*

Important information for every growing business

Matt is an expert when it comes to effective strategies for online reviews. He has built strong, review based profiles for multiple companies that has helped increase revenue and employee retention. In a tight labor market, a strong online rating from your employees is critical to attracting top talent.

*– **Jeremy Winn,** Vice President - Custom Sales, Denik*

A must read for business owners.

Matt Vance is a master of managing online reviews. He has significantly raised the average rating for several large corporations and can do it for you as well. I have not met anyone who knows this topic better than Matt. Read his book, apply what you learn, and watch your ratings and sales improve. This book is essential reading for all business owners.

*– **Michael Glauser,** Executive Director, Center for Entrepreneurship, Huntsman School of Business, Utah State University*

Enlightening, thorough, informative

Great book encapsulating all the key elements to understanding reviews, how to respond and when.

— **Jill Helander,** Human Resources Generalist - Benefits & Compliance, Medela LLC

Reputation management to an exact science

The Review Cycle demonstrates Matt's mastery of building both a product-brand and employer-brand reviews program. The playbook now exists. Do yourself a favor and give it a read. And then read it again. Your bottom line will thank you.

— **Stephen Moffitt,** Strategic Account Executive, Trustpilot

Matt does a fine job of qualifying and quantifying the power of customer reviews. From engagement with the reviewer to measurement of the results, this book provides a well-rounded view of this dynamic stream of influence.

— **Paul Kirwin,** CEO, Channel Signal

A critical marketing channel revealed

Matt is the perfect person to write this book. He has his pulse on where reviews can help drive business results whether through employer branding mechanisms and hiring or sales driven avenues. Matt has developed a great system and approach while always trying to learn how he gets better and shares that knowledge without hesitation in this book.

— **Mike Sheridan,** COO, Comparably

Five stars for this insightful analysis

As the founder and CEO of a startup consumer product company, this book is exactly the kind of guide we needed to understand the world of reviews and the effects they have on our success. The 3QPD (cupid) rule seems so obvious, but in looking back at our responses as a company, we were falling short. This book not only has great ideas but is backed by thorough analysis of the world of reviews. I highly recommend this book to anyone who cares about your business's reputation.

— **Stephen Colvin,** CEO, Bobelo

THE REVIEW CYCLE

Matt R. Vance

Library of Congress Cataloging Data

Name: Matt R. Vance, author

Title: The Review Cycle : The four-step model to mastering your online reviews. / Matt R. Vance.

Other titles: The Review Cycle

ISBN: 979-8-9861203-0-0

e-ISBN: 979-8-9861203-1-7

Disclaimer

The information provided in this book is for informational purposes only and is not intended to be a source of advice or business strategy with respect to the material presented. The information and/or documents contained in this book do not constitute legal or business advice. Additionally, no consultant-client relationship is formed from the sale of this book.

The publisher and the author do not make any guarantee or other promise as to any results that may be obtained from using the content of this book. To the maximum extent permitted by law, the publisher and author disclaim any and all liability in the event any information, commentary, analysis, opinions, advice and/or recommendations contained in this book prove to be inaccurate, incomplete or unreliable, or result in any financial losses undesirable to business outcomes. The publisher and the author are providing this book and its contents on an "as is" basis. Your use of the information in this book is at your own risk.

While the author has made every attempt to provide accurate website addresses at the time of publication, it is not unusual for some sites to have closed or have otherwise changed. The author and publisher assume no responsibility for author and third-party websites or their content.

For my wife Crista. You're a winner in my book.

TABLE OF CONTENTS

CHAPTER 1:
REVIEWER TENDENCIES

CHAPTER 2:
THE REVIEW CYCLE

CHAPTER 3:
ASKING FOR REVIEWS

CHAPTER 4:
RESPONDING TO REVIEWS

CHAPTER 5:
HARVESTING INSIGHTS

CHAPTER 6:
MARKETING WITH REVIEWS

Foreword

Online reviews are one of the most significant factors that determine why people decide to engage with a product, service, app, movie, restaurant – you name it. Marketers, entrepreneurs, employers, and anyone dealing with customers need to understand the enormous value of consumer feedback and how it impacts everything from sales to employment. The Review Cycle framework is a powerful way to visualize, understand, and influence the customer engagement journey.

I first met Matt in 2017 when he requested a demo for REVIEWS.ai, a company I co-founded to monitor and analyze consumer feedback data. At the time, Matt was the Reputation Strategy Manager at Malouf, a rapidly growing furniture and bedding manufacturer. During the demo, it was immediately apparent that he knew more than most clients about reviews. He asked insightful questions and even made suggestions to our system right on the call. This was unusual but something I love to see, because clients who recommend improvements to the system provide the most valuable feedback you can get.

After that demo, we stayed in touch, chatting about news related to Amazon reviews and sharing thoughts on the impact that reviews have on customers' purchasing intent. It became clear that we shared a passion for reviews and consumer feedback.

A few months after we met, Matt suggested that we should meet in person at Malouf's headquarters in Logan, Utah so I could meet the team and see how they were using our review analytics tool. It's rare that clients invite you to see their whole operation, so I was eager to see how a company that genuinely valued consumer feedback approached it. Matt showed me around Malouf's headquarters, introduced me to the CEO and founder, and invited me to dinner with his team. I was pleasantly surprised by how much I learned, observing the role that reviews play in the cycle that impacts the design, production, and marketing of Malouf products.

I also gained a greater understanding of Matt's impact at Malouf. I learned that he was instrumental in increasing the Malouf product catalog's average rating from 4.15 to 4.3 stars across 245,000 reviews. Using insights from reviews, he helped propel Malouf to many long-term #1 bestseller rankings on Amazon, Walmart, Overstock, Wayfair, and other sites. His methodologies helped Malouf win the 2019 Gold Stevie Award for Best Customer Feedback Strategy.

It was clear that Matt had developed a finely-tuned system for product reputation management. He was able to recognize and take care of negative trends before they became large-scale issues. His experience with review management led him to the employee side, as company reviews are just as influential for job seekers. He realized the importance of employer reputation and how it affected hiring and company culture. In the first two years of applying his approach shared in this book, Malouf won seven national best place to work awards, including being ranked nationally on Glassdoor.com, InHerSight.com and Comparably.com.

Our correspondence continued after Matt was recruited to lead the reputation efforts at iFIT. There, he replicated and enhanced his strategies at a global scale. In less than one year, iFIT's Google rating improved from 2.0 stars to 4.2 stars while Glassdoor increased by 1.3 stars. Over 500 product listings and 100 brand and company profiles were optimized with significant increases.

When Matt shared the news that he was planning to write a book, my reaction was, "What are you waiting for?" He has always talked about the practical impact of his ideas and how they could help more businesses collect more reviews and use them to fuel better experiences. I had the opportunity to read an early draft and was hooked by The Review Cycle framework, which is a structured, actionable and measurable approach to review management.

I'm thrilled that more people and businesses will be able to benefit from Matt's expert insights thanks to this book.

Julius Kurushko
Founder, REVIEWS.ai

Acknowledgements

Nearly five years after starting this project, I have many individuals to thank for their support and encouragement. No one has put in more time and energy than my wife Crista. She inspired me to start and complete this book. She went to great lengths supporting me and our family as I committed many early weekday mornings and Saturdays researching and writing. She read and edited the manuscript through multiple drafts. Thank you Crista. You are my world! My four children, Ruby, Greta, Bridget and Todd have all cheered me on with smiles and hugs. I love each of you. My parents, in-laws, brothers, sisters and all my family have kept me accountable and engaged over the years of working on this book. Thanks to each of you.

To Steve Douglas and Sam Malouf, thank you for supporting me individually and encouraging me to pursue this project in conjunction with the work we did together at Malouf. Thanks to Brian Blotter for the many laughs and opportunity to work on employee feedback together. Brian Child, the thoughtful conversations we shared about business success and life inspired me. Thank you for your friendship. To Kyle Hess, thank you for teaching me I need to slow down to go faster. To Nate Obray, thank you for your friendship and passion for innovation. A special thank you goes out to all my team members at Malouf throughout the years. Stephanie, Alecia, Isaac, Cade, Aniko, Amy, Spencer, Aani, Afi, Amanda, Sarah and Jared. Thank you for your shared passion for creating positive experiences. And to Donald Scott, thank you for your bright ideas and sharing your photography skills for the author photo.

To Nick Rasband for being the brave soul to read the first (and very rough) draft of this book. Seeing your feedback comments helped me keep going. Mike Sheridan, Co-Founder of Comparably, not only listened to me talk about my book but gave me multiple opportunities to share my work with others. Your early belief in my work is appreciated. In the first year I started writing, one acquaintance took genuine interest in my work. That was Julius Kurushko. Julius, your ongoing encouragement, friendship and feedback has meant so much. Even though I never had a class from Professor Michael Glauser while attending the Jon M. Huntsman school of

Business at USU, he mentored me as an author himself. Thank you Michael. A shoutout goes to Zach Kristensen of Juxtabook. Your insights about the book publishing process were very helpful.

I'd like to thank my clients, friends and business owners through the years who allowed me to be a small part of your journey. A special shout out goes to Saboor, Melinda, Norm, Lael, and Gary. To all those who took time to review the pre-release copy of this book, thank you! Your support means so much.

I appreciate the support of David Watterson, Eric Watterson and Joel Dewberry for the opportunity to join iFIT. The empowerment and trust you extended me allowed me to further solidify some of my work. Thank you to Jennifer Clark, Mark Watterson and Steve Barr for the chance to learn from you and collaborate on enhancing employee experiences through feedback management. Thank you to all the team at iFIT for your encouragement and friendship, especially my team—Cathy, Alecia, Soup, Danielle and Tonie. Tonie Rogers, your added time sharing feedback about the book and our many conversations about online reviews through the years has meant a lot. Danielle Palmer, your keen editing eye and exceptional writing experience is impressive. Thank you for sharing your insights. And to Colby Anderson, your creativity with the book graphics and cover is truly inspiring. Thank you.

To all my friends and family who are too many to name, know that I genuinely appreciate you. Thank you for your encouragement along the way.

Introduction

I missed what she said. It was almost 11:00 p.m. on a Sunday night. My family and I were driving home through Sardine Canyon after a weekend trip. With the kids asleep in the back of the car, my wife and I were in the middle of a deep discussion about career planning and roadblocks at work.

"Are you listening? What do you think of that idea?" my wife said. "Wait, um.... Tell me again," I replied.

This is where my excuse for missing the glorious epiphany moment comes in. It was early fall and the typically captivating mountain colors were concealed by a thick darkness. Even though the conversation was highly engaging, the subtle flickering under the headlights of branches and bushes along the road held my attention. Earlier that year we had come inches away from hitting two energetic deer that bolted in front of our vehicle. It was an experience I did not want to repeat.

"Sorry, I was watching for deer, dear." Now I was just trying to recover. She patiently responded, "I think you should write a book. You know. A book about what you do. That would help."

"I don't know. It would be a big project," I retorted. "We have a lot going on right now. Besides, who would want to buy a book from me?"

"Just think about it for a sec," my wife continued, "you just told me that research helps you learn. You also just told me that you like teaching other people. It helps you remember stuff. The book would be for you. It doesn't matter if people buy it or not."

"Yeah but I'm not going to do something like that just for a research project. It better sell if I'm going to do that...if I do that."

"Okay. Then make it good enough to sell."

Such a simple solution to a complex problem. Write a book, she said.

On October 13, 2014, three years prior to this pivotal conversation I reported for my first day of work at a small start-up called Malouf. They manufacture and sell exceptional bedding products like mattresses and pillows. With about 35 employees at the time, I was hired on the ecommerce team to "figure out reviews". Onboarding consisted of sitting in a two-day meeting with Sam, the CEO, my boss and a couple other managers. Every Monday and Tuesday they would go through every product listing in the catalog and discuss needed changes. This would include things like price adjustments, ordering inventory needs, category competitiveness and—you guessed it— reviews.

Soon I had a list of products to research and respond to reviews for. At the time, there were just over 100 product listings to manage. I started an excel sheet to track review stats and the quantity of reviews responded to.

Two years into my role, the company's product catalog had more than doubled and had expanded to several new websites. Our total product listing count was over 500. Our department of two had grown to ten people.

At this point, I had written responses to thousands of reviews. Due to the sheer workload increase, two new hires joined my team. They began following the review response best practices I had developed and documented. We also had a product-sampling program. At the time, it was not only allowable to give away products in exchange for reviews on Amazon, but also highly effective at boosting sales.

On October 3, 2016 everything changed.

Amazon banned incentivized reviews. For years, they had received negative press surrounding the untrustworthiness of reviews. This announcement represented a bold and unprecedented move.

For me personally, this announcement destroyed half of what my job was all about. I was responsible for ensuring the effective launch of new products with the placement of some customer reviews. I went home that day deeply concerned. What could be done?

Days turned into weeks. The product sampling program was stopped for Amazon and we started focusing on some other sites. Amazon review needs still existed.

Weeks turned into months. I was still stuck. What could we do to move forward on Amazon ethically and legally? We didn't want to risk doing things that could jeopardize our seller account.

Finally, my boss had a conversation with me. He challenged me to be creative. He reminded me of past successes and confirmed his belief in me while also reminding me of the key responsibility I held for the company. My mind kept going back to a Marissa Mayer quote I heard in a marketing class: "Creativity loves constraints."

I realized there were things I could try. I could research what companies existed to help businesses with their reviews. I could find a business conference and learn more about review management. I could go read a book about online reviews.

I looked for a conference about review management. There were none. I searched for a book about reviews. Nothing existed at the time. I searched for some review management companies and luckily found several. I read many of their blog posts and articles. There were a few gold nuggets of info, but nothing truly groundbreaking. It seemed many of these vendors were also pivoting with Amazon's big announcement.

These findings led me to the next idea—first hand research. I proposed a few different concepts to my boss, one of which included ordering dozens of products to observe what they do to collect reviews. That is where we started making gradual progress. If I could not learn secondhand from someone else, I could learn firsthand by myself and with my team.

Over the next year, I found quite a few ways to move things forward while still being compliant with the landmark banning of incentivized reviews on Amazon. Still, these many changes took more effort and often had smaller results than the old way of just giving away products for reviews. More innovation was needed.

By the fall of 2017, a year after the Amazon announcement, I was starting to feel stuck again. I thought a lot about how things were operating and the roadblocks in our way. I continued talking with my boss about our challenges and working with my team to be creative. Little wins brought fleeting relief.

Then one night my wife had this crazy idea. Write a book she said.

The more I thought about it, the more I realized my wife was right. This was the best next move. Write a book about review management. Sure, I'd written some best practice guides for my team, but writing a book would be more in-depth and complex. It would require better understanding of the consumer behaviors underneath our processes and developing new strategies.

Writing a book would facilitate the learning I desperately needed.

The first Saturday morning I sat down to start, it felt foreign. I had been conditioned my whole life to relax Saturdays, or at least go on a run or work in the yard. Gradually, it felt more and more natural spending this time investing in my own knowledge. Weekday mornings before work became a new prime time for research.

Writing continued while work progressed. The product catalog I managed with my team grew to 1,500 product listings across more than 50 ecommerce sites by 2018. We successfully ranked dozens of products as category-specific #1 best-seller across most of these sites. I started doing consulting on the side, testing my review management principles in other industries and applications. To my pleasant surprise, I found much success in these efforts. I began speaking at a few conferences, which fostered more learning.

At Malouf, I also opened employer review profiles on Glassdoor, Comparably, InHerSight and others. Leaning on my knowledge of customer reviews, I used the same principles of soliciting, responding to and harvesting insights from employee reviews.

Between 2018 and 2020 I was able to deploy similar methodologies used to gain good reviews on products for company reviews written by employees. Malouf then ranked seven times as a national best place to work, including a top ten ranking on Glassdoor out of over 1.3 million employers.

My methodologies were recognized nationally with a 2019 Gold Stevie Award for Best Customer Feedback Strategy above runners-up including Bank of America, Delta Airlines, DHL, IBM, Intuit, and VIZIO Inc. This award was important validation that I was doing something right.

Then in the fall of 2020, an opportunity presented itself to join iFIT, the world leader in interactive fitness. I was offered a role to direct global feedback and reputation strategy. I knew this would lead to even more growth and development of my research. I accepted the offer.

Malouf and iFIT are very different. At Malouf, I had the luxury of slowly building the review program to match company growth. iFIT is a global business with decades of history. Minimal efforts to manage iFIT's reviews had been made. Getting started felt like jumping in white water rapids, especially in the middle of the COVID-19 pandemic when the home-fitness industry was exploding.

I started building a team, tracking reviews and defining processes. The plans I had pitched in my interview started to produce the expected results. The absence of review management efforts were being corrected in months, driving 2.0-star ratings to 4.0+-star ratings. Customers who would have written negative reviews were contacting us before doing so as they found our public review responses helpful. Content and product feature enhancements were being identified and shared with the correct internal stakeholders.

It was working.

Beyond the consulting I'd done, this was significant. The evidence of these processes working now at a global industry leader not only brought me personal confidence, but the assurance that these principles should be shared with the world.

This is where you come in. This book represents years of early mornings, late nights and epiphany moments in my life. I want to share it with you. I've always defined success as a rate of improvement. This book can give you the knowledge to improve even faster and find success sooner in your business endeavors.

I wish you the highest rate of improvement possible.

Navigating The Review Cycle

I get it. Reading a book about online reviews isn't as exhilarating as your favorite fantasy. No offense taken. You have a lot to accomplish to help your organization succeed and I've made this easier for you. This book has been designed in a modular fashion. You don't have to read the entire book from front to back to gain value. Reading any single chapter or section will provide insights to you. Here is an overview of what to expect from the book so you can know how to approach it with your goals in mind:

Chapter 1: Reviewer Tendencies
This chapter focuses on consumer behavior. It will teach you why consumers use reviews and why they share them online.

Chapter 2: The Review Cycle
Chapter two introduces The Review Cycle and sets the stage for the rest of the book. This is a consumer behavior model I've developed with four phases a consumer follows before and after a purchase decision. The model is an evolution of the traditional and modern sales funnel. Sales funnels depict a path to purchase. In today's online world, this linear view neglects many ways consumers make purchase decisions. The Review Cycle accounts for these differences and outlines specific methods to positively influence consumers in each phase.

Chapters 3 through 6:
Each of these chapters focuses on one of the four phases of The Review Cycle. Consumer actions at each phase are paired with elements of influence you can have on the consumer's decisions and behaviors. Specific action items will be given to you that will drive increased sales and customer satisfaction.

Chapter Sections:

Primary principles within each chapter topic have their own dedicated section. The table of contents lists the several sections for the chapters. Each section within the chapters will have a description as well. This structure will help you navigate to topics of interest.

Chapter Questions:

Every chapter will start with a list of thought-provoking questions. The answers will be found as you read that chapter. Thinking of these questions first will help guide your discovery and learning process.

Chapter Summaries:

To increase your recall of key principles, every chapter has a summary at the end. This summary will include all the chapter questions and abbreviated answers for your convenience.

Foundational Knowledge Paired with Current Event Insights

Like many areas in business, things change over time. The same is true for the review management space. Community guidelines on specific platforms get updated. New adaptations of laws and algorithms force adjustments. The way people interact and shop online evolve.

For this reason, I've made a concerted effort to focus on foundational principles and concepts that are most likely to be applicable long term. Writing a book that included every possible tip for every review platform would not only be very long, but it would get outdated.

To achieve the highest level of success in your review management endeavors, I would recommend you pair your reading of this book with industry current event info from a diversified source of review management sources.

What I'm about to share is a powerful tool. It's one way I stay up to date with industry trends and you can apply this principle to any topic of interest. I call it "spoon-feeding". This is a type of passive research. It is a set-it-and-forget-it way to stay informed about any topic.

First, you identify companies, individuals, and groups on LinkedIn that are good resources on the topic you care about. You then follow all of them. You'll see all their content in your LinkedIn feed. They are now "spoon-feeding" you research, insights, and current events each time you open LinkedIn. Instead of searching for specific things that relate to your industry each day, a quick scroll through LinkedIn is likely to deliver relevant knowledge.

If you want to set up your "spoon-feed" on LinkedIn for Review Management, do this:

1. **Identify the most trusted industry players.**

   - G2 Crowd and Capterra are both software review sites. You can read reviews of all types of software there. If you search for "review management" on either platform, you'll find an up-to-date list of the dozens of companies in this space.

   - Here are some of my personal favorites:
     - REVIEWS.ai
     - Channel Signal
     - Power Reviews
     - Bazaarvoice
     - Podium
     - Yotpo
     - Birdeye
     - Trust Pilot
     - Reputation
     - Shopper Approved
     - Bright Local
     - Review Trackers

2. **Follow these trusted players.**

   - Follow them on LinkedIn.

   - Subscribe to their blogs and email newsletters for even more content.

3. **Share what you learn.**

   - The act of sharing and teaching what you read not only benefits someone else, but it will increase your retention of that knowledge.

CHAPTER ONE

REVIEWER TENDENCIES

Decode how consumers use reviews and why they post them

QUESTIONS TO CONSIDER:

How does the current review-focused marketplace compare to the past?

What consumer decisions are impacted by reviews?

How influential are reviews in today's marketplace?

Why are reviews trusted so much?

How do consumers engage with reviews while shopping?

What types of review biases affect the purchase journey?

What motivates people to write reviews?

How do people assign star ratings?

What prompts the posting of a review?

Why do these insights matter?

Section 1.1: Dollar Signs in Disguise
Why reviews precede profits

Your friend's graduation party is this weekend. You know they enjoy outdoor activities but don't know what to get them as a gift. So, you pull out your phone and start browsing ideas. Lists like "10 Essentials for Your First Camping Trip" and "27 Awesome Gadgets for the Outdoors" pop up in your search. Naturally, all these items have links to Amazon, making it easier to buy.

A few items catch your eye, and you start comparing them. Price is an easy qualifier. This is a good friend, and you'd be willing to spend more on them. You have now narrowed your list to three items: a mega-bright headlamp, a camping mess kit or a multi-tool with a compartment holding waterproof matches.

Each item is within your budget. What's your next step? You honestly have no clue what type of camping gear they already have. You say to yourself: "If I buy the one that has the best rating, then my friend is more likely to like it, too." With that reasoning you believe to be so unique; you compare reviews. The headlamp has 4.9 stars but only 14 reviews. The mess kit has 4.2 stars and 1,842 reviews. Not bad. The multi-tool has 4.6 stars and 973 reviews. Decision made.

Now it's party time. You hand your thoughtful gift to your friend. They open it and say, "Wow, nice! A multi-tool! This is the same one I bought on Amazon." Surprised, you ask them, "Do you like the one you have?" "I haven't used it yet, but it's in my camp bag", your friend replies. At the same time, the two of you nod your heads and say, "Well, it certainly had good reviews."

As many as 97% of shoppers are influenced by online reviews.[1] Do you consider yourself to be part of that 97%? Think about how reviews impact you on a daily basis. Have you ever purchased something or visited a restaurant based on reviews? If you're shaking your head no, I know some good restaurants you may enjoy.

Consumers are influenced by online reviews, but what does that mean? Simply put, it means consumers trust reviews enough to make real decisions, especially purchasing decisions, based on those five stars. Here's a powerful comparison. What would you guess is the most trusted professional? An accountant? An athlete? According to a research study by Hubspot, the most trusted professionals are doctors, with 49% of consumers agreeing they are trustworthy. Marketers and sales professionals were tied near the bottom, with 3% of consumers saying they were trustworthy.[2]

Naturally, you may be wondering what percentage of consumers trust online reviews compared to these figures. The number is 85%. Yes, 85% of consumers say they believe online reviews as much as personal recommendations.[3] This means most people trust a stranger's opinion more than any one professional, regardless of certification, experience or prestige. Reviews are the collective voice of the online community, which is expected to be more reliable. After all, if everyone believes that way, it must be true, right?

If you're feeling a little hesitant at this point, let's try a little experiment. Open the Amazon app or your preferred shopping app and visit your order history. How many of your 10 most recent purchases were influenced by reviews? I asked my personal network this same question. Of over 50 respondents, on average, 7.3 of 10 purchases were influenced by reviews. Convinced yet? Considering 8 out of 10 Americans now shop online,[4] it's clear the majority of consumers trust reviews enough to use them to make purchasing decisions.

Because consumers rely on reviews so much, a star rating can translate into big changes in revenue. The connection between reviews and revenue impacts local retailers, service industries, higher education, non-profits, ecommerce and beyond. Let's consider some examples. For restaurants, a 1-star increase of a displayed Yelp rating can increase overall revenue by 5-9%. You can guess the opposite is true as a star rating drops.

A higher star rating on TripAdvisor means better search results. A study by SiteMinder, a cloud platform for hotels, revealed that a 10% increase in excellent reviews on TripAdvisor resulted in an 11.3% improvement in search results.[5] Additionally, studies have shown that listings with higher ratings also achieve a higher revenue per transaction, meaning people will pay more for something because of its higher rating. This effect further supports the idea that online reviews influence the success of a business.

On Amazon, a product can experience a 100% upward or downward swing in sales volumes with a 0.1-star change. When the star average changes from 4.2 to 4.3 stars and vice versa, the star rating image associated with a product changes by a half star. This rounding typically doubles the sales rate or cuts it in half.

Figure 1.1: The difference in sales with rounded star ratings[6]

Amazon also rewards well-reviewed products with improved search results. A higher star rating and more verified purchase reviews means better search rank position, and as a result, more sales.

Maybe you're starting to see a pattern. If so, you're one step ahead of me. If not, I'll show you the pattern now. There are two primary correlations between reviews and revenue: the first is the review volume or total, and the second is the star rating.

Take a look at the following graph from Bazaarvoice, a leading review management firm. The Bazaarvoice customer network provides millions of online reviews to study and analyze. Their research shows the increase in conversions (or sales) as review volumes go up. The first review increases sales by an estimated 10%. It takes nine additional reviews to achieve an estimated 20% lift. From here, the impact of review volumes follows the law of diminishing returns, each review increasing sales but at a lower increment than the prior review. When launching a product or profile with reviews, a foundational goal is to get 100 reviews.

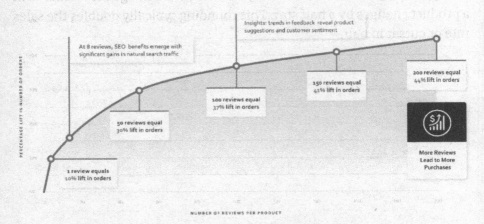

Figure 1.2: The change in conversion rates compared to review volumes[7]

The impact of a star rating is similar to the relationship between increased sales and review volumes; as a star rating rises, your sales increase. However, it's not exactly alike.

The following study was performed at KTH Royal Institute of Technology in Stockholm, Sweden. A total of 80 online products with different star ratings and their respective sales were compared against each other. In the next graph, the sales volume is extremely low until about 3.7 stars. From about 3.7 stars to 4.4 stars, sales volumes are grouped fairly close at viable volumes. The highest sales volumes occurred between 4.5 and 4.7 stars.[8]

As a rating rises above 4.7 stars and approaches 5.0 stars, sales decrease sharply. Products with average ratings of 4.8 to 5.0 stars have sales as low as those with 3.5 stars. Why would there be such a sharp decline in sales at near perfect ratings? Near-perfect ratings are sometimes believed to be faked, manipulated and unreliable. Most consumers see some negativity in reviews as a sign of authenticity. Having managed 1,500 product listings across more than 50 ecommerce marketplaces, I can confirm these trends generally hold true. With this in mind, there are some bias anomalies we'll take a look at in the next section.

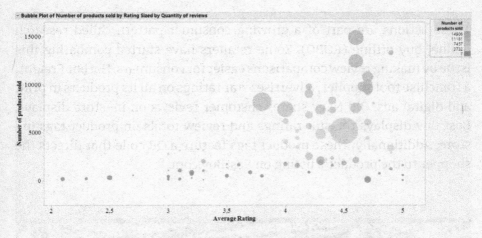

Figure 1.3: The change in sales volumes respective to star ratings[8]

The connection between ratings and review volumes isn't limited to online product sales. Let's consider how online product reviews impact brick-and-mortar shopping experiences.

First, consumers use devices to find basic information about places they'd like to visit. About 76% of consumers who search for a nearby store visit that location in less than 24 hours.[9] Have you ever visited a store the same day you searched for it online?

Consumers now expect a standard set of information (e.g. company name, profile picture, price indicator, star rating and review count) when browsing retailer profiles on Google and other review sites. If a profile-viewer is satisfied with the information they see, that 76% of consumers are more likely to visit your store rather than a competitor.

Once in the store, most shoppers consult their phones for reviews and price comparisons. Ok, now that's just crazy, right? Not really. Google research shows that 82% of consumers check their phones for product information while shopping in-store.[10]

These actions are part of a growing consumer pattern called research online, buy offline (ROBO). Some retailers have started combating this issue by making review comparisons easier for consumers. Harbor Freight, a franchise tool supplier, advertises star ratings on all its products in print and digital ads. Old Navy shares customer reviews on in-store displays. Best Buy displays the star ratings and review totals on product tags in-store. Additionally, these product tags feature a QR code that directs the shopper to the product's listing on BestBuy.com.

Figure 1.4: Harbor Freight displays review totals and star ratings for every product in its catalog. These catalogs are conveniently placed at the front of the store for quick reference when shopping[11]

Figure 1.5: Old Navy shares a customer review on an in-store display[12]

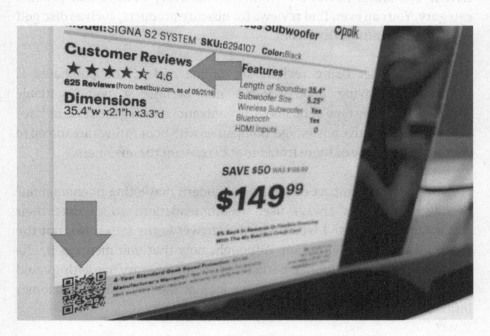

Figure 1.6: Best Buy regularly updates product tags with review totals and star ratings from BestBuy.com. A QR code also takes shoppers directly to the respective product listing[13]

Reviews are the currency of online success and their impact is spreading to all industries. For example, did you know you can rate college professors on RateMyProfessors? The site has been live since 1999 and has over 19 million reviews across more than 8,000 universities. How about doctors? Find ratings and reviews on RateMDs and Vitals. Employers? Try Glassdoor, Comparably and Indeed. Local businesses? There are plenty of options: Google, Facebook, Yelp, Angie's List, HomeAdvisor, Manta and OpenTable.

Staying at an Airbnb? Reviews are essential when deciding which house to stay at for your next trip. Not only can guests rate their host on Airbnb, but hosts can also rate guests. This can help the hosting community avoid difficult customers. The same relationship exists between drivers and passengers on Uber and Lyft as well as buyers and sellers on Facebook Marketplace. Don't forget about movie ratings on IMDb, Metacritic and Rotten Tomatoes. Reviews continue to fill every market and product category. You can even find reviews for obscure products, such as disc golf equipment at InfiniteDiscs.com.

The bottom line: Using reviews for online and offline purchases is mainstream. Having good reviews has become a non-negotiable component for any type of business. Organizations with good reviews have a distinct competitive advantage. Companies with poor ratings are forced to compromise on one or more fronts to stay relevant to consumers.

Is the widespread impact of reviews a modern marketing phenomenon? Or have consumers always used recommendations to validate their purchasing decisions? I would say the answer is the latter. No, not the ladder, that wasn't an option. Although, now that you mention it, the progression from traditional marketing to contemporary marketing could be compared to a ladder. Let's take a look at the key eras of consumer influence that have led us to our current state.

Figure 1.7: The progression from traditional to contemporary marketing is like a ladder

Traditional OGC marketing

In 1835, Jared Bell began printing the first modern American billboards in New York. These billboards measured 9x6 feet and typically advertised circus shows. By 1850, billboards were used along roadways. Billboards started being leased in 1867.[14] By 1922, the first paid radio ad in America was broadcast. The New York-based radio station WEAF aired a commercial for the Hawthorne Court Apartments in Jackson Heights.[15] Also in New

York, about 4,000 viewers saw the world's first television commercial in 1941. It was a 10-second ad for the Bulova watch company, telling New Yorkers that America runs on "Bulova Time."[16]

Throughout these technological innovations, company-customer messages were one-directional. Companies were telling consumers what to think about their products. Organizations believed they either knew the minds of their customers, or they could shape opinions through advertising. Such content can be classified as organizational-generated content (OGC).

OGC is defined as content or media derived from the ideas and concepts of an organization. At its root, OGC is one-way messaging dictated by an organization and delivered to consumers.

The era of traditional OGC influence began as a dictatorship. Brands used their own reasoning to create consumer-facing messages. As radios became the primary medium for home entertainment in the 1930s, market research was conceptualized.[17] Advertisers slowly became more armed with demographic and preferential data. This increased the influence of OGC as content became more tailored toward target audiences.

Internet search

Technologies and market research mechanisms continued to advance through the later half of the 20th century. However, up to this point, consumers played a passive role on the influence of other consumers. A consumer could have an indirect influence on OGC advertising through a national phone or mail-in survey. This certainly wasn't an equal opportunity for sharing feedback with brands, let alone other consumers. Individual influence on others' purchases was also limited to word of mouth by means of in-person conversations, phone calls and snail mail.

Then Al Gore invented the internet—or maybe not? To this day, people debate about who invented the internet and when it first launched. The truth is, the development of the internet happened over several decades, and many individuals and organizations contributed key developments.

The largest breakthrough was the invention of the Transmission Control Protocol and the Internet Protocol (also known as TCP/IP). These protocols remain the primary components of transferred data across the modern internet[18] and specify how data should be transmitted and received between devices.[19]

Vinton Cerf and Robert Kahn developed the TCP/IP, which was a project funded by the U.S. Department of Defense from 1973 to 1974. This was preceded by the development of the Advanced Research Projects Agency Network (ARPANET). Created in the late 1960s, the ARPANET was another project funded by the U.S. Department of Defense. It proved the viability of grouping data transmission or packet switching.[20]

By 1993, only 1% of information passed through two-way telecommunication networks.[21] A total of 130 websites were live at the time. By 1996, over 100,000 websites were up and running.[22] The percentage of information transferred grew to 51% in 2000 and surpassed 97% in 2007.[21]

Access to the internet opened a door for consumers. They could now actively search for information, instead of relying on one-directional OGC messages. You could say it was the beginning of the end of marketing dependency. As information became more accessible, consumers no longer had to drive around town; they could compare products and prices at home on the internet.

Internet sales

While the information revolution was underway with the internet, commerce as we knew it was also changing. The early days of online shopping could be described as a novelty. Phil Brandenberger of Philadelphia made history when he became the first person to make a purchase on the internet. On August 11, 1994, he ordered a CD of the Sting album, "Ten Summoner's Tales." The CD was purchased from the Net Market Company based in Nashua, New Hampshire. This company pioneered encryption privacy software, making internet transactions viable. The New York Times described this venture as "the equivalent of a shopping mall in cyberspace".[23]

Over the next several years, Americans slowly warmed up to the idea of paying for something you could only see on a computer screen. Amazon was founded the month before Brandenberger's landmark purchase. The company started selling books online within months. By 1999, ecommerce sales accounted for approximately 0.6% of all retail sales in the U.S.[24]

To buy something online and wait for it to be shipped to you, seemed less convenient than driving to the store. Yet, adoption rates continued climbing as Americans frequently added things to their virtual shopping carts. By 2002, ecommerce volumes had tripled since 1999. Besides searching for the best shopping places in town, consumers could simply pay online and be done.

Customer reviews

It wasn't too long before online ordering had its own pain points. What if you ordered something and it wasn't what you expected? Mailing it back was not only inconvenient, but costly. How did you know which vacuum was best without going to the store? Retailers still had the upper hand in the mid-1990s and early 2000s as people could experience products in-store before making a purchase.

This advantage gradually began to diminish as online shopping became more sophisticated. Online retailers became more knowledgeable about what type of information was relevant to consumers. For example, a clothing size chart helps a consumer order the right size, therefore preventing customer returns and dissatisfaction. This type of OGC content was dictated by the seller. Ultimately, it was the inclusion of reviews that made online shopping mainstream.

Some believe online reviews became a part of ecommerce in 1999. This was the same year Epinions.com, RateItAll.com and Deja.com hit the internet. All three sites collected consumer opinions on everything from product purchases to doctor recommendations. However, there are multiple examples of Amazon reviews dating back to 1995. In fact, according to Amazon's 1997 year-end report, the company announced to investors that customers could "read and post reviews," which was sufficiently tested by that time.[25]

The use of customer voice (aka online reviews) marked a paradigm shift in marketing. It was the departure of OGC control. It was a decision to embrace market opinions. This change felt risky to most businesses. After all, what would happen if customers didn't like a company's product and that opinion was posted online? This could cause a product to fail or a company to go out of business (and it did). Yet, Amazon had made the decision to let their customers rate products and share their opinions. Writing reviews was no longer reserved for professional critics. Amazon gave the power to the people. They had created the first-ever online community: reviewers and shoppers.

During the early 2000s, this new online community grew as more people began shopping online, reading reviews and posting them. Consumers were more confident in their purchases with trusted community ratings, and they felt empowered to share their opinions after making a purchase. Ultimately, reviews have made Amazon the online hub for product research, and they've grown respectively. In 2016, Amazon surpassed Google for the first time with a 55% market share of initial online product searches.[26] By 2018, 50% of all online purchases in the U.S. were made on Amazon.[27] Amazon's reviews have become a competition barrier for ecommerce.

Reviews have permeated almost every facet of shopping since then, including brick-and-mortar retailers. The data is now indisputable. Reviews influence purchasing decisions. Yes, there are questions of trust and authenticity due to manipulation, but these concerns have not affected the role reviews play in the purchasing journey. Online reviews are the second most trusted source of information, after personal recommendations.[28] The reach of reviews extends beyond any personal network exponentially, making them the most impactful form of influence on consumer buying behavior.

The conventional adaptation of online customer reviews has created a community decision model. The voice of the shopping community, manifested in average ratings, dictates which products the market will buy the most and least.

UGC and influencers

Going beyond the normalization of online shopping and customer reviews came the evolution of User-Generated Content (UGC). UGC can be defined as any content produced by a user or customer. Today, UGC has many forms, including customer reviews, blog articles and social media posts. This content can be in the form of text, pictures and videos. Reviews and ratings are a form of UGC, but the term UGC didn't become mainstream until these other forms of UGC developed and were categorized together.

UGC rose to prominence with social media. SixDegrees.com was the first of many social media sites. It launched in 1997 but shut down in 2000.[29] Myspace came out in 2003, followed by Facebook in 2004. During this time, people started building relationships online and interacting with each other's content on social media. Several new social media platforms emerged in the late 2000s and early 2010s and by 2011, more than half of the American population was using social media.[30]

As social media continued to evolve, consumers started communicating with one another about their purchases. The power of word-of-mouth began to reach entire personal networks across social media.

Businesses started using social media not too long after consumers did. Successful brands have learned to be a part of the consumer conversation rather than controlling it. Rather than telling a customer what to buy, they prompt consumers to share their marketing message with other consumers. For example, consider a hashtag contest. Sharing a customer's rating in an advertisement is another example of capitalizing on UGC. This type of ad is likely to have four times the click-through rates and cost half as much as a traditional OGC ad.[31] People believe other people more than companies.

Going a step further, brands have leveraged social media influencers to be their ambassadors. An influencer is a social media user with a large following. Influencers' following size rank from small to celebrity status. Micro-influencers tend to be defined as those with 2,000 to 50,000 followers. Macro-influencers—today's self-made celebrities—have more than 50,000 followers.

Celebrity marketing is the grandfather of influencer marketing. Celebrity endorsements were historically OGC fueled and lacked authenticity. As of 2016, Google reported 70% of teenagers relate more to YouTube creators, or influencers, than traditional celebrities.[32] These new-age celebrities are online themselves. They attract followers who relate to them as people. Effective influencers typically only endorse goods or services that align with their personal brand. When promoting a product or company, smart marketers give influencers more creative freedom to incorporate their own marketing objectives. In 2015, the influencer marketing industry had an estimated market cap of $500 million. By 2018, the industry had $4 billion.[33] Incorporation of UGC and leveraging non-celebrity influencer endorsements is becoming a norm.

Technological influence will continue to evolve. Effective marketers must adapt to current trends. However, customer reviews will always remain the most influential form of UGC.

Consider the graphs above. A product with more reviews and a healthy star rating will have higher sales potential. Fundamental efforts of review management should be prioritized over other forms of UGC optimization.

In today's omnichannel-shopping environment, consumers reference an average of 10.4 information sources prior to making a purchase.[34] As many as 51% of consumers begin their research by looking at reviews and prices on Amazon.[35]

Regardless of where you market to your audience, the majority of consumers will find your reviews. These reviews will confirm their decision to buy or not to buy. First and foremost, focus on your reviews, then create a proactive marketing strategy.

Section 1.2: Natural Review Bias
Not all reviews are equal

You should care how consumers engage with reviews because it helps you see your product or company through your customers' eyes. Through this perspective, you can know what's shaping potential buyers' opinions with greater accuracy.

Keep this in mind as you consider the following story. Sit back and relax. This is going to be fun!

It's Friday night. You're visiting a new city. You hear a growling noise. It wasn't the hotel's TV, nor was it Chewbacca. It's your stomach pleading with you to "chew back" a big piece of meat at the barbecue joint across the street. What keeps you from racing to the elevator and indulging in that saucy goodness? Oh, just that little computer guy that lives in your pocket. He has a good vibe, unless you put him on silent. What's its name again? Apple? Android? Let's call him Johnny, to protect his privacy. Johnny tells you everything. You know that. So, what do you do now? You ask him, "Hey, Johnny, I know you've never been to that random hole-in-the-wall BBQ joint. How do you like it?

Without thinking of himself, what he had for breakfast, or if he's even hungry, Johnny aggregates 443 experiences from people who have visited Chewbacc-at-cha's BBQ as found on Google. He's such a machine. The place has a 4.3-star rating. You click the listing and then skim the top six reviews. The most recent reviews are positive as well. One of them had a picture of a skeleton riding a horse. Odd, but ok. You notice another restaurant, Millennial's Falcon sandwich shop next door. It also has a 4.3-star rating but only 187 total reviews. A few other restaurants pop up in your search, but the ratings aren't quite as good.

Chewbacc-at-cha's BBQ it is! You think to yourself, "I'm an informed customer who's headed to this restaurant with the inside scoop." In fact, you order the Chicken Good Licken, recommended by Cowboy Dingleberry in the most recent review on the listing. Little did you know that the owner's signature recipe is the smothered sweet pork, which is a local favorite. Other reviews talked about this dish, but you didn't know because the reviews you read didn't mention it.

After leaving the restaurant, you agree with the reviews you "studied" and give the restaurant a 4-star rating. They were right. The food was delicious, but the environment was lacking. What you didn't know was that the restaurant had been closed due to a major rat infestation one year ago. We're talking conversation-disturbing sounds from the attic. Also unknown to you, the new management team did their best to clean everything, but the locals still questioned if there were rats in the building. At least management got one thing right. They hired a talented chef, worthy of the title Pit Master, who reworked the menu. Chef Organa represented the restaurant at the annual state Bachelor's and Bums BBQ competition, winning the best-of-sauce award. It was spicy, but hey, he's a bit of a rebel.

Your eloquent 4-star review may have been different knowing the full story behind the restaurant. It all comes down to perception. We see things through our own unique lens. Perceptions are based on information we gain and experiences we have with our senses. Whatever we perceive becomes our reality. For example, it doesn't matter that Chewbacc-at-cha's had a rodent infestation. Why? Because you didn't know that, and it didn't impact your experience or your review. If you would've known this before making your decision, your perception might've changed, and you may have gone to Millennial's Falcon instead.

You can predict a shopper's perspective by understanding what information they're exposed to. As illustrated in Section 1.1, most consumers use reviews, but that doesn't mean they're using all reviews equally. The unbalanced use of reviews is the source of naturally occurring review biases. Let's see what these biases are.

Minimum rating standards

While searching reviews for Chewbacc-at-cha's BBQ, several other restaurant listings appeared on Google. Only Millennial's Falcon was considered as an alternative. The other options were not even considered because they either had a low star rating or not enough reviews.

As of 2018, 57% of consumers will only visit a business with a 4-star rating or higher. That's up from 49% in 2017.[3] According to research by KTH Royal Institute of Technology referenced in Section 1.1, the majority of all online purchases occur for products with ratings between 3.8 and 4.7 stars.[8] Most consumers have a general rating tolerance. If your product doesn't meet this standard, consumers won't consider it an option.

The minimum rating standard is the bottom level threshold a customer expects in order to click on a product listing. For example, I may have a personal rating standard of 10 reviews and 4-stars. In this case, I will only consider products that meet these two requirements, as a minimum. Most consumers likely won't voice an explicit limit for themselves, but we know from trend data that better ratings and higher review counts result in more clicks.

The effect of minimum rating standards is observed while consumers browse search results. Comparing all options, your star rating and review count are likely the biggest draw or deterrence from your product offering. Recognize that this bias doesn't consider review content at all. It is completely dictated by numbers. Chewbacc-at-cha's negative reviews citing rats can't impact the consumer unless their minimum rating standard is meet and the listing is clicked on. Once on the listing, a viewer could be exposed to the nightmare reviews and not choose Chewbacc-at-cha's. Note that some consumers skip reading reviews and make a decision solely based on ratings. Those are easy wins if you have better ratings and more reviews than the alternative. Even if someone goes to your reviews, the nightmare review may not kill your business unless it's a very recent review or one that has been voted as a top helpful review.

Generally speaking, a listing can overcome the negative effects of minimum rating standards bias by having 100 or more reviews and a star rating between 4.3 and 4.7 stars. A 4.8-star rating is acceptable on certain review platforms, depending how the stars are displayed visually. For example, on Amazon and Google, 4.8 stars is visually displayed as 5 stars. This is bad, as it's perceived as too good to be true. On other sites, a 4.8 rating doesn't fill the 5th star all the way, which helps consumers perceive authenticity.

The beginning goal of 100 reviews and 4.3 to 4.7 stars is superseded by comparison selection. This means if your biggest competition has over

2,000 reviews, then 100 reviews is comparably worse. If your competitor only has 18 reviews, then 50 reviews is a comparative triumph.

To overcome the minimum rating standard of most consumers, you must have 100 or more reviews and a star rating between 4.3 and 4.7 stars. Only offers that meet the minimum rating standards will be considered by the majority of shoppers.

Badge Bias

The restaurant example didn't mention badges, but they're impactful nonetheless. Have you ever seen a "best-seller" badge on a product listing? How did it change your perception? For many consumers, this definitive claim eliminates comparison altogether. According to Jungle Scout, an ecommerce sales analytics tool, an Amazon best-seller can earn twice as much as the second-best listing.

Many badges exist across review sites. For product review sites, common badges include best-seller, new arrival and on sale. Some sites even have badges for better shipping, extra perk points, and other benefits. Amazon even has an "Amazon Choice" badge, which is awarded based on the term searched for by the shopper. On Airbnb, new listings get a temporary badge. On Glassdoor, top employers get a "Best Place to Work" badge. CEOs can also earn badges.

Keep in mind that the badge bias is most influential while browsing, although some badges aren't viewable until after clicking on a listing. Once a consumer clicks on your listing or profile, they're usually looking for additional confirmation in your reviews. Also, note that the badge bias is typically secondary to the minimum rating standards.

Top review bias

Remember, after seeing a 4.3-star rating with 443 reviews in the search results, you leaned toward Chewbacc-at-cha's BBQ. Your minimum rating standards were met, so you decided to dig deeper and read a few reviews. The reviews voted most helpful were at the top of the list and most visible to you. The top reviews you read are all good enough, so you moved forward with your decision to eat at Chewbacc-at-cha's BBQ.

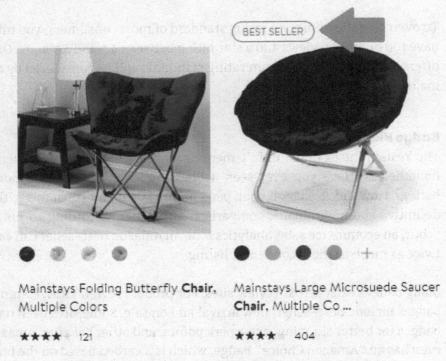

BEST SELLER

Mainstays Folding Butterfly **Chair,**
Multiple Colors

★★★★ 121

Mainstays Large Microsuede Saucer
Chair, Multiple Co ...

★★★★ 404

Figure 1.8: Walmart displays a "Best-Seller" badge
highlighting a popular chair[36]

However, let's say a 1-star review about the rats was voted as the most
helpful review. This could influence your decision whether or not to eat at
Chewbacc-at-cha's, even though your minimum rating standards were
met.

How much more do your top reviews get viewed than the rest? Most review
sites don't provide data on view per review, but Glassdoor does. Through
personal observation, I discovered that the first page of 10 reviews matter
the most. For every 100 views on page 1, page 2 reviews average only 2.9
views. Page 3 reviews average 0.7 views. Additionally, individual views per
review indicate that consumers typically don't read more than the top six
reviews.

Content display algorithms vary by website, so the amount of time reviews live at the top is different from site to site. For example, Amazon uses an algorithm that considers the age of a review as it ranks top reviews. A review with 20 helpful votes may be displayed above another review with 100 helpful votes because it's more recent. Regardless, top reviews are read more often than other reviews, making them the most influential.

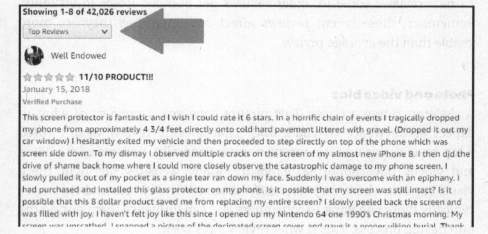

Figure 1.9: This review on an Amazon screen protector listing has over 1,100 helpful votes. It's likely to stay at the top of the 42,000 reviews for some time[37]

Recent review bias

In the restaurant example, you followed the advice of Cowboy Dingleberry and ordered the Chicken Good Licken. Their review was posted two days before yours and was the most recent review. Similar to top-voted reviews, recent reviews are also more visible to consumers. This type of bias is secondary to minimum rating standards because the bias typically occurs after a shopper has clicked on a listing or profile.

According to Glassdoor review stats, the most recent reviews are viewed almost as much as top-voted reviews. Page 1 of the most recent reviews are viewed only 2% less frequently than top-voted reviews on page 1. A similar drop-off happens with pages 2 and 3 of recent reviews compared to the top-voted reviews.

Recent reviews usually have a shorter lifespan in the spotlight than top-voted reviews, but it depends on how frequently reviews are posted for a particular product or profile. A new review on a top-selling product on Amazon may stay on the most recent page for under 24 hours due to high review volumes. Some profiles and listings get so few reviews that a review could stay on page 1 for a year or more.

As new reviews come in, older reviews get bumped lower in visibility. Remember, these recent reviews affect consumers, as they are more visible than the average review.

Photo and video bias

A skeleton riding a horse. This picture gave you a preview of what to expect at Chewbacc-at-cha's BBQ. That specific review wasn't voted a top review, nor was it a recent review. Generally, reviews with photos and videos have abnormal exposure. Many websites highlight these visual reviews where they can easily be seen. Why? Photos and videos are typically more engaging to consumers and can influence them during the purchasing process. This is what review sites want.

Remember, any review with pictures or videos will be viewed more than other reviews and will have greater influence. Again, this bias is secondary to minimum rating standards because it doesn't usually occur until after a viewer has clicked on your listing or profile.

Figure 1.10: This Overstock listing features picture and video reviews in the top-right corner of the review section. Consumers can easily see these visual reviews[38]

Search bias

Many review sites let you search for keywords within the reviews of a listing or profile. In this case, the bias can be as specific as the shopper's search. Some review sites have themed tags that appear within a review. These tags are generally words or phrases repeated in reviews. Amazon does list these phrases, allowing shoppers to easily filter reviews with recurring themes. Glassdoor segments frequent mentions in positive reviews as "pros" and frequent mentions in negative reviews as "cons." Any type of search feature increases exposure to specific review content. For that reason, it is another type of bias.

Self-fulfilling prophecies

This final bias is similar to the bandwagon effect. In the restaurant example, two of the top four reviews had a 4-star rating, stating the atmosphere was a little dull. One review even showed a picture of a skeleton riding a horse. For this reason, you were slightly pessimistic about eating at the restaurant. You ultimately agreed with the review and gave the same 4-star rating.

Read reviews that mention

put together	easy to assemble	lumbar support	gaming chair
great chair	arm rest	easy to put	get what you pay	son loves

Figure 1.11: Frequently mentioned phrases are highlighted in the review section of an Amazon listing with clickable tagged search terms.[39]

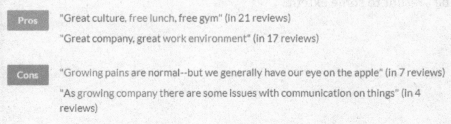

Pros
"Great culture, free lunch, free gym" (in 21 reviews)

"Great company, great work environment" (in 17 reviews)

Cons
"Growing pains are normal--but we generally have our eye on the apple" (in 7 reviews)

"As growing company there are some issues with communication on things" (in 4 reviews)

Figure 1.12: Pros and cons about a company are listed on Glassdoor[40]

The acknowledgement of specific praises or concerns in a review encourages future buyers to look for a similar outcome. This often perpetuates the same mentions in future reviews. The impact goes beyond just perpetuating similar review content. It's also likely to be a primary motive for awarding a star rating—positive or negative.

This is one of the most interesting biases I have observed. As I've managed reviews on certain foam-based pillows, I've noticed a recurring theme of "smell." An early review would sometimes state, "I love this pillow, but it has a weird smell when you open it." The next thing you know, you're seeing other reviews saying, "Like the other reviews stated, the pillow has an interesting aroma. I wouldn't describe it as a new sneaker smell; it's more like a rustic boot smell." In Chapter 4, we'll discuss how to avoid negative perpetuation as you strategically respond to reviews.

I've highlighted the most prominent biases, but many other types of biases can occur as a result of referencing reviews. The takeaway is that consumers will never be exposed to all reviews equally. For this reason, most reviews do not impact your business beyond the star rating. The review content itself will have minimal exposure over time as new reviews are posted.

Be aware that these bias trends vary. For example, would you spend more or less time reading reviews when shopping for a dishwasher or paper plates? Generally speaking, the more expensive a product is, the more likely consumers are to thoroughly research. An avid tennis player is more likely to spend more time researching tennis racket reviews compared to a grandma buying one as a gift for her granddaughter. These changes can alter review-impacted biases, but naturally occurring biases will always be present to some extent.

Section 1.3: Review DNA

Every review is posted with a motive, method and stimulus

Approximately 97% of consumers use reviews in today's marketplace.[1] In Section 1.2, we evaluated biases that affect people using reviews to make buying decisions. Practically, everyone is likely to fall victim to these filtered realities.

Now, let's consider how many people post reviews. According to PowerReviews, a review monitoring site, only 3-10% of shoppers will write a post-purchase review, even after being asked by the company.[41] On Amazon, I've witnessed review rates as low as 1.5%, and that's across millions of orders. Review rates will vary by product category, website and other variables. Regardless, it's safe to say that the minority of people actually post reviews. You will learn how to improve reviews rates in Chapter 3: Asking for Reviews.

What motivates reviewers to share their opinions on the internet? If only reviewers knew how much cosmic power they wield with those five stars. One negative Yelp review can cost a business 30 paying customers.[42] On the other hand, the first positive review can improve conversion rates by 10% indefinitely. Most of the time, a customer's motive to review is not to reward or punish a company. Understanding how, when and why people post ratings and reviews will help you interact with consumers to influence your reviews for good.

Although every online review is different, I have identified three common components that all reviews share. These three qualities are discovered by answering the following questions:

· What **motive** did the reviewer have for sharing?

· What **method** did the reviewer use for rating?

· What **stimulus** convinced the reviewer to post?

We'll explore the most common motives for sharing reviews, methods of rating and stimulus for posting. The unique combination of answers to these three questions is review DNA. It is possible for two reviews posted by the same reviewer to have different DNA. It's the same relationship parents have with their children. Children from the same set of parents have different DNA, although they share characteristics. Reviewers may tend to write reviews with the same DNA motive, method and stimulus blend. This isn't uncommon. It's just not a hard-fast rule. While you're reading, see if you can identify the review DNA traits your reviews are made of.

Component 1: Motive for writing reviews

Why do you work? To provide for yourself? Your family? To further your career? Elevate your quality of life? Do you genuinely care about what you do? Want to make a difference in the world? We all have our reasons. Similarly, every reviewer has a reason they write online reviews. This first component of review DNA addresses why.

To study this topic, I examined 11 different online articles published over a 13-year period. Review management companies like Bazaarvoice and Trustpilot have content on the topic. Specialized news sites like Social Media Today also address this question. There are also forum-based discussions around this question on TripAdvisor and Quora. Three of the articles are summaries of independent survey studies, each involving hundreds of respondents. On average, each article outlines an average of five and a half motives for people's reviews.

Each motive is ranked in the table below by frequency of mention. Only motives mentioned two or more times have been labeled specifically. The "other reasons" listed below include a few odd motives for writing reviews like learning English or finding a date. Yes, people write reviews in an attempt to meet up with someone of romantic interest. Odd, I know.

Without further ado, here are the results:

Review Motive	Frequency of Mention	Description of Motive
Give Back to the Community	90.9% (10 of 11)	A feeling of gratitude and compulsory need to repay the review community for the benefit reviews have afforded them.
Obtain Measurable Community Status	63.6% (7 of 11)	A desire to be formally recognized as a valuable contributor within an online community. Examples: a high review rank on Amazon and an advanced Google local guide tag.
Express One's Opinion	54.5% (6 of 11)	Sharing one's opinions with the world.
Reward a Company	54.5% (6 of 11)	Wanting to help a company succeed.
Other Reasons	45.4% (5 of 11)	A personal motive, such as learning a new language, writing for a blog or finding dates.
Punish a Company	36.3% (4 of 11)	A desire to damage a company.
Obtain Perceived Community Status	36.3% (4 of 11)	Receiving recognition, such as likes, votes comments and shares from peers in an online community.
Gain an Allowable Incentive	36.3% (4 of 11)	Obtaining incentives formally provided by a review site. For example, Wayfair has offered giveaway entries in exchange for reviews. Rakuten has given 25 points (25 cents) per review and G2 Crowd has given gift cards up to $10 for reviews of software solutions.
Give Feedback	36.3% (4 of 11)	Providing feedback on how a company can improve.
Gain an Illegal Advantage	27.3% (3 of 11)	Receiving compensation to post reviews, both positive and negative. Review sites and lawmakers are fighting this problem, but it still persists.
Personal Enjoyment	18.2% (2 of 11)	Analyzing and reviewing products, services and experiences for enjoyment.
Engage in Social Interactions	18.2% (2 of 11)	Positive interactions between reviewers as a bi-product of participating in a reviewer community.

As you can see, there are a lot of different reasons why people post reviews. It's completely reasonable for more than one of these factors to motivate someone to post a review, but I'd argue there's always a primary motivator. Additionally, two primary themes exist across these motives. Each motive is rooted in a desire to give something or receive something. The desire to give is a slightly stronger motivator than to receive.

	Review Motive	Frequency of Mention
Givers 52.6%	Give Back to the Community	90.9% (10 of 11)
	Express One's Opinion	54.5% (6 of 11)
	Reward a Company	54.5% (6 of 11)
	Punish a Company	36.3% (4 of 11)
	Provide Feedback	36.3% (4 of 11)
Takers 47.4%	Obtain Measurable Community Status	63.6% (7 of 11)
	Other Reasons (learning English and finding dates)	45.4% (5 of 11)
	Obtain Perceived Community Status	36.3% (4 of 11)
	Gain an Allowable Incentive	36.3% (4 of 11)
	Gain an Illegal Advantage	27.3% (3 of 11)
	Personal Enjoyment	18.2% (2 of 11)
	Engage in Social Interactions	18.2% (2 of 11)

In most cases, you can't read a review and understand the motive behind it. If you could ask the reviewer why they posted it, then it would be easier to identify the motive. Although you can't always label motives for other's reviews, understanding the emotional drive behind a review will do the following:

· *Optimize your response strategy.*

　　· *Empathy is a powerful tool for communication and conflict resolution. We'll explore this topic in Chapter 4: Responding to Reviews.*

· *Improve your request strategy.*

　　· *This knowledge empowers you to connect to consumers on a subconscious level by appealing to their motives in a review request which can drive more people to post reviews. You will learn more about this strategy in Chapter 3: Soliciting Reviews.*

Component 2: Method of assigning a rating

Now that we know why reviewers write reviews, let's evaluate how reviewers rate a product or service. This second component of review DNA evaluates a person's decision-making style when assigning a rating.

People reason differently, including when they post ratings online. Even though the end result of this decision is typically limited within the standard 5-star scale, there are many ways to arrive at a final star rating. The method of rating is the second component of review DNA; it is the predominant philosophy a reviewer uses to award a star rating.

Through years of observation, reading and responding to thousands of reviews, I've observed five common methods for assigning a star rating. Here, we're going to study these rating philosophies supported by real-life examples.

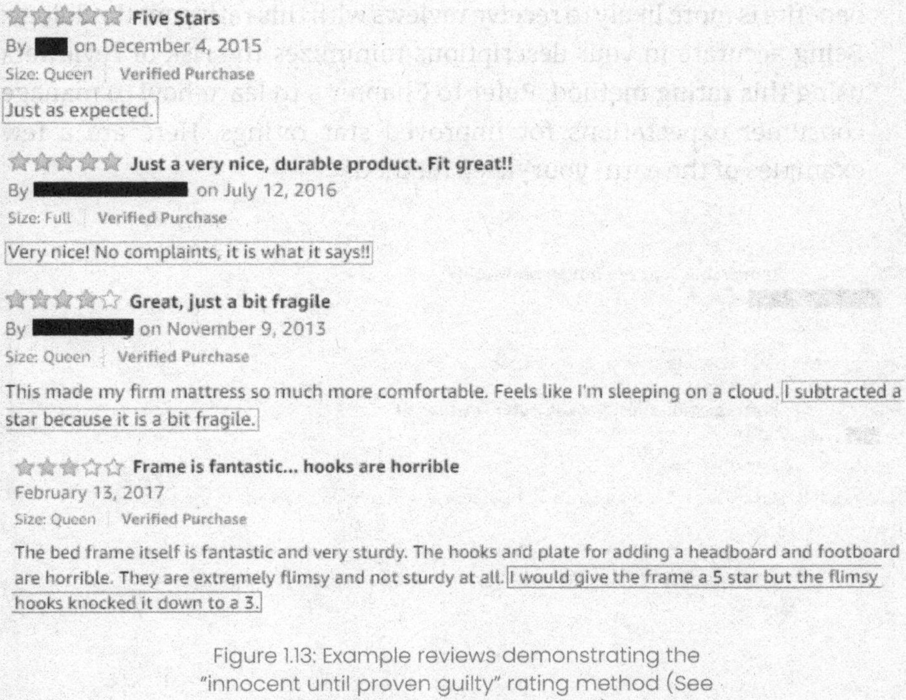

★★★★★ **Five Stars**
By ▇ on December 4, 2015
Size: Queen   Verified Purchase

Just as expected.

★★★★★ **Just a very nice, durable product. Fit great!!**
By ▇▇▇▇ on July 12, 2016
Size: Full   Verified Purchase

Very nice! No complaints, it is what it says!!

★★★★☆ **Great, just a bit fragile**
By ▇▇▇▇ on November 9, 2013
Size: Queen   Verified Purchase

This made my firm mattress so much more comfortable. Feels like I'm sleeping on a cloud. I subtracted a star because it is a bit fragile.

★★★☆☆ **Frame is fantastic... hooks are horrible**
February 13, 2017
Size: Queen   Verified Purchase

The bed frame itself is fantastic and very sturdy. The hooks and plate for adding a headboard and footboard are horrible. They are extremely flimsy and not sturdy at all. I would give the frame a 5 star but the flimsy hooks knocked it down to a 3.

Figure 1.13: Example reviews demonstrating the "innocent until proven guilty" rating method (See references 45, 46, 47 and 48)

Method 1: Innocent until proven guilty

This first philosophy is by far the most common. It is the belief that a product should be given a 5-star rating unless there is a reason to reduce the rating. Stars are removed as features underperform or the experience underwhelms. Amazon's high sitewide 4.27-star average illustrates that this is the most common rating method.[44]

If your product is priced fairly, adds value for the user and is advertised accurately, it's likely to acquire positive organic reviews. Here are some examples showcasing this rating method.

Method 2: Earn your keep

This second, less common, rating method is the opposite of the innocent-until-proven-guilty mentality. It's the belief that a product inherently starts with a 1-star rating and earns additional stars as the features impress the consumer, or the experience is positive. Usually, reviewers who use this rating method are more negative and sometimes neutral. A product listing that oversells the features and benefits is more likely to receive reviews with this rating methodology. Being accurate in your descriptions minimizes the risk of reviewers using this rating method. Refer to Chapter 5 to learn how to manage consumer expectations for improved star ratings. Here are a few examples of the earn-your-keep method.

Figure 1.14: Example reviews demonstrating the "earn your keep" rating method (See references 49 and 50)

Method 3: Don't offend

The third rating method is focused on not offending the product's company or others who might read the review. A reviewer using this method wants to share their opinion, but they don't want to be extreme. Someone using this method tends to rate products between 2 and 4 stars and isn't passionately positive or negative. Oftentimes, they're completely satisfied with their experience but feel a 5-star rating is too generous.

These don't-offend reviewers aren't common, and there isn't much that can be done to avoid them. By nature, someone using this rating method usually isn't passionate enough to even post a review. However, when asked, these more timid reviewers will step up to the plate. Here are two examples of this rating method.

Figure 1.15: Example reviews demonstrating the "don't offend" rating method (See references 51 and 52)

Method 4: Light switch

The light switch method is the belief that ratings should be either good or bad. Reviewers who use this method tend to award only polarized ratings fueled with emotion. This means they usually give a 1-star rating or a 5-star rating. There's no shame in confrontation, praise or transparency here.

GatherUp, a location-based review management company, surveyed 600 consumers on when and why they write reviews. According to the study, 33% of respondents said only when their experience was either really good or really bad. About 25% of respondents said they write a review only when their experience was really good.[53]

Those who rate with a light switch mentality can't be avoided. They go out of their way to share their opinions. We'll discuss how to ask for review updates after providing customer solutions to reviewers in Chapter 3: Soliciting Reviews. Such actions can result in negative ratings being changed to positive ones. Here are some examples.

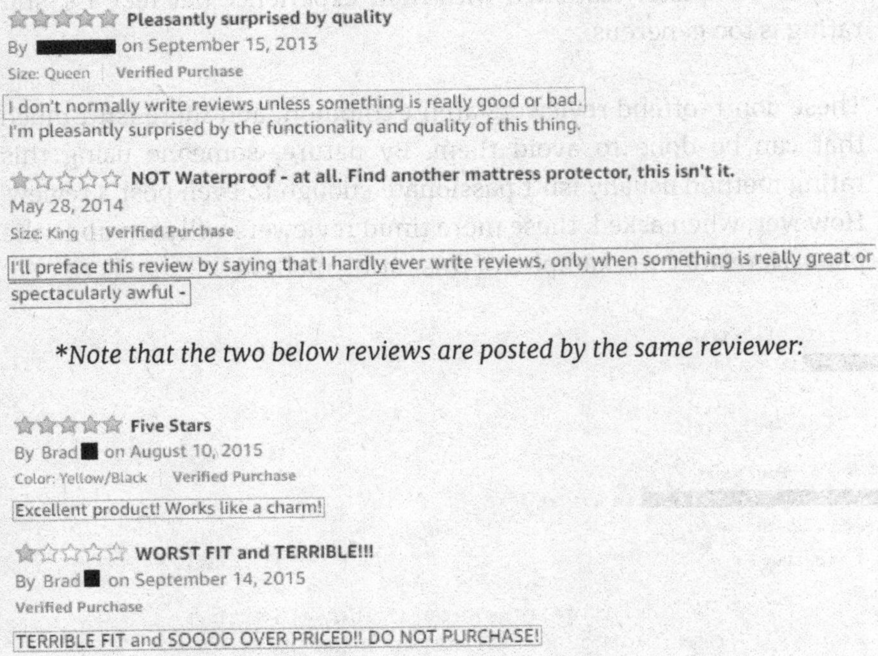

☆☆☆☆☆ **Pleasantly surprised by quality**
By ██████ on September 15, 2013
Size: Queen   Verified Purchase

I don't normally write reviews unless something is really good or bad.
I'm pleasantly surprised by the functionality and quality of this thing.

☆☆☆☆☆ **NOT Waterproof - at all. Find another mattress protector, this isn't it.**
May 28, 2014
Size: King   Verified Purchase

I'll preface this review by saying that I hardly ever write reviews, only when something is really great or spectacularly awful -

Note that the two below reviews are posted by the same reviewer:

☆☆☆☆☆ **Five Stars**
By Brad ■ on August 10, 2015
Color: Yellow/Black   Verified Purchase

Excellent product! Works like a charm!

☆☆☆☆☆ **WORST FIT and TERRIBLE!!!**
By Brad ■ on September 14, 2015
Verified Purchase

TERRIBLE FIT and SOOOO OVER PRICED!! DO NOT PURCHASE!

Figure 1.16: Example reviews demonstrating the "light switch" rating method (See references 54, 55, 56 and 57)

Method 5: Enthusiast

The final rating method states that some products and services cannot earn a 5-star rating. Reviewers who use this method believe uninteresting or mundane products and services don't deserve a high rating. Household goods fall victim to this reasoning.

On the other hand, products and services that are interesting to the reviewer are capable of earning a 5-star rating. This would be demonstrated by a detailed positive review of a new Google device written by a Google fan.

This philosophy is further illustrated by what these reviewers will take the time to review at all. A more extreme enthusiast reviewer will not review items in their purchase history outside of their personal interests. Say a reviewer loves tech gadgets. Even though tech products only account for 15% of their online purchases, that's the only subset of items they choose to review.

An enthusiast reviewer also tends to only post reviews on websites of personal interest. An example would be an avid moviegoer who often posts reviews on Rotten Tomatoes but rarely reviews other products or services elsewhere. Additionally, reviews written with the enthusiast mindset tend to be more detailed, extreme and emotionally charged. If an enthusiast happens to review utilitarian products or other things outside their spectrum of interest, their reviews will be more straightforward, without emotion and often neutral at best.

Below are three reviews posted by the same enthusiastic reviewer. The first review is for a white noise machine, which this person obviously loves. The second review is for a house robe, which didn't have anything wrong with it, but it received a 3-star rating. The third review is for a Halloween mask, which also fell victim to a neutral rating for as-advertised quality.

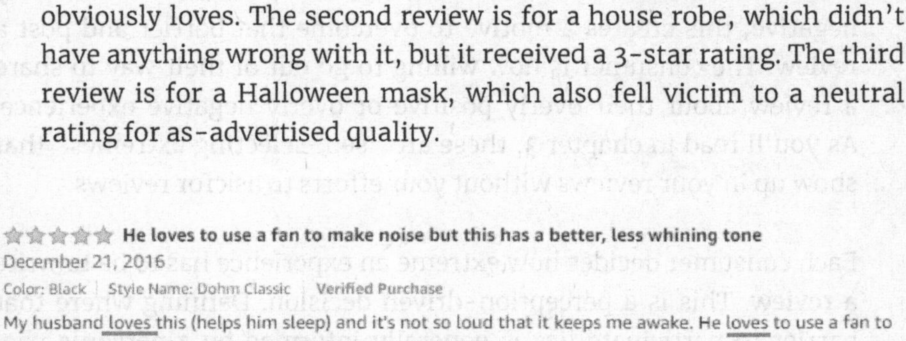

☆☆☆☆☆ **He loves to use a fan to make noise but this has a better, less whining tone**
December 21, 2016
Color: Black | Style Name: Dohm Classic | Verified Purchase
My husband loves this (helps him sleep) and it's not so loud that it keeps me awake. He loves to use a fan to make noise but this has a better, less whining tone. GREAT

☆☆☆☆☆ **Three Stars**
December 21, 2016
Size: Large / X-Large | Color: Beige | Verified Purchase
good value for the money and comfortable

☆☆☆☆☆ **Three Stars**
October 26, 2015
Size: One Size | Color: Multicolor | Verified Purchase
for the price this will work fine.

Figure 1.17: Example reviews demonstrating the "enthusiast" rating method (See references 58, 59 and 60)

These five methods for assigning a star rating make it easier to understand why customers sometimes leave ratings that don't make sense to us. Why would a consumer leave a 4-star review for a product they absolutely loved? Why would they leave a 1-star review when they said it was decent? After all, that's not how you would rate your product, or any product for that matter. The point here is to consciously acknowledge the various ways others approach a rating decision to help you have greater empathy for the customer.

Component 3: Stimulus to act

The third and final component of review DNA is the stimulus that leads to posting a review. There are two primary motivators for posting reviews: experiences and requests.

Experiences

Every consumer has a barrier blocking them from leaving a review. After all, why spend time going out of your way to share feedback online? When an experience is extremely positive or extremely negative, this creates a motive to overcome that barrier and post a review. The consumer is now willing to go out of their way to share a review about their overly positive or overly negative experience. As you'll read in chapter 3, these are "self-selecting extremes" that show up in your reviews without your efforts to ask for reviews.

Each consumer decides how extreme an experience has to be to write a review. This is a perception-driven decision. Defining where that barrier to participate lies is generally informed by a person's past experiences and comfort navigating technology.

For example, if you've only ever stayed at low-end motels for travel, staying at a middle-class hotel might be so positive that you go out of your way to write a glowing 5-star review. But if you're used to spending hundreds of dollars on hotels, that same middle-class hotel might pass your negative barrier and motivate you to write a 1-star review.

Comfort-navigating technology also influences how tight or loose a consumer's barriers to share a review are. For example, a college freshman may be tech-savvy and familiar with reviews. They may have tighter expectations. It doesn't take much to impress or offend this student. They review most of their experiences and cite the smallest disappointments and pleasures.

Compare that to a baby boomer who purchased their first smartphone recently. They could have either a very positive experience or a very negative one, and still not post a review. Why? The barrier to share a review is too high. It's too difficult to figure out how to post a review. Let's say the server spilled a cup of coffee on that same baby boomer and the incident caused a trip to the emergency room. Now, do you think they're more likely to post a review? Definitely. This experience created a strong enough motive to figure out how to post a negative review. Even if it means asking their tech-savvy nephew in college.

Extreme experiences, both positive and negative, motivate consumers to go out of their way to share reviews without being asked. Defining how extremely negative or positive an experience must be to stimulate a review is perception-driven by each consumer.

Review requests
Barriers to post a review online become less extreme when a consumer is directly asked to share. Say a consumer has an arbitrary barrier of +10 and -10 for their self-selecting extremes. They will go out of their way to share a review if they determine an experience is that positive or negative. If the server at a restaurant directly asks for a review, those barriers to share may drop to +6 and -6. By asking for a review, the restaurant increased its odds of this consumer sharing one.

A business can invite consumers to post a review in many ways from post-purchase texts and emails to product inserts, handouts and in-person solicitations. Regardless of the method, review requests increase the number of people who post reviews.

When an incentive is attached to a review request, the likelihood of a consumer posting a review increases even more. If that same restaurant customer was offered a free appetizer for posting a review, the consumer's barriers to share may drop to a +1 on the positive side and stay at a -6 on the negative side. Incentives can skew feedback to be more positive. Even if the restaurant experience was marginally negative at a -2, the consumer may still write a mostly positive review after receiving a free appetizer.

Entire review platforms have harnessed and mastered the positive effects of incentivizing reviews. For example, Wayfair offers a giveaway entry for each posted review. This small incentive results in more habitual reviewing and higher ratings. As a comparison, I evaluated the difference in review rates and star ratings between Wayfair and Amazon. Wayfair offers a giveaway entry with its post-purchase review requests. Amazon also sends a post-purchase review request but doesn't offer an incentive. Looking at nearly 10,000 reviews for the same products on both sites, the difference was significant. Wayfair's average rating was 0.4 stars higher than Amazon's rating. Additionally, they secured 2.7 reviews for every one Amazon review.

Asking for reviews is almost always guaranteed to improve ratings when done correctly. We'll discuss laws and best practices for incentivizing reviews in Chapter 3.

Review DNA in summary

Review DNA is the unique blend of a reviewer's motive for writing, method of rating, and trigger for posting a review. Now that we've looked at the three components of review DNA, we can see how they come together in the table on the next page.

Every review has a primary element from each of these three components. Pull out your mobile device and look at a review you've written. Can you identify your motive for writing the review, the method for your rating, and the stimulus for posting the review? If you have never written a review before, consider writing one now. What's the DNA of your review?

	Motive	Method	Stimulus
Givers 52.6%	Give Back to the Community	Innocent Until Proven Guilty	Extreme Positive Experience
	Express One's Opinion	Earn Your Keep	Extreme Negative Experience
	Reward a Company	Don't Offend	Review Request
	Punish a Company	Light Switch	
	Provide Feedback	Enthusiast	
Takers 47.4%	Obtain Measurable Community Status		
	Other Reasons		
	Obtain Perceived Community Status		
	Gain an Allowable Incentive		
	Gain an Illegal Advantage		
	Personal Enjoyment		
	Engage in Social Interactions		

There are 120 possible review DNA combinations. They can all be found online, but some combinations are more prevalent than others. The most common positive and negative review DNAs are listed below:

Most common positive review DNA:

- *Motive: give back to the community*

- *Method: innocent until proven guilty*

· *Stimulus: extreme positive experience*

From research and personally responding to over 5,000 reviews, I can confirm this DNA combination is the most common. Most online reviews are positive. Believe it or not, most people still use reviews as a tool to help others. Now, take a look at the most common negative review DNA:

Most common negative review DNA:

· *Motive: give back to the community*

· *Method: innocent until proven guilty*

· *Stimulus: extreme negative experience*

The strongest motive for writing a review is to give back to the community. The innocent-until-proven-guilty method is the most forgiving but can still result in 1-star reviews. The majority of people don't jump to extremely negative reviews, nor do they post negative reviews without merit. This undesired accolade is typically earned at least from the reviewer's perspective. Lastly, experiences remain the primary driver for posting negative and positive reviews.

The components of review DNA can sometimes be difficult to identify in reviews. Conversely, these components are much easier to identify introspectively. It's not always necessary to label every review. However, understanding the biology of reviews allows you to think more like a reviewer and enhance your review management strategy.

Chapter 1 Summary
Section 1.1: Dollar Signs in Disguise
Why reviews precede profits

How does the current review-focused marketplace compare to the past?

In today's marketplace, consumers are empowered to influence other consumers' purchase decisions via technology. Compared to the traditionally one-directional marketing methods of the past, organizations today can leverage the consumer voice in marketing as a strong form of influence.

What consumer decisions are impacted by reviews?

As many as 97% of consumers use reviews for everyday purchasing decisions. This includes decisions like what products to buy, where to eat, where to visit and where to work.

How influential are reviews in today's marketplace?

Doctors, the most trusted professionals, are trusted by 49% of consumers. Compare that to 85% of consumers who trust online reviews. Using reviews for everyday decisions is mainstream.

Why are reviews trusted so much?

Consumers are exposed to two types of information when making a purchasing decision: organizational-generated content (OGC) and user-generated content (UGC). For many consumers, OGC content (e.g. an advertisement) is believed to be inherently biased because the information source is coming from the seller. UGC content (e.g. social media posts and reviews) is believed to be impartial and trustworthy due to lack of incentive and diversity of opinions.

Section 1.2: Natural Review Bias
Not all reviews are equal

How do consumers engage with reviews while shopping?
First, consumers evaluate star ratings and review counts. Next, they typically read about six top filtered reviews before making a purchasing decision.

What types of review biases affect the purchase journey?
Review biases occur when a purchasing decision is based on a subset of information. This occurs regularly due to search result patterns, and filtering of review content by review popularity, time-stamp and inclusion of photos and videos.

Section 1.3: Review DNA
Every review has a motive, method and stimulus

What motivates people to write reviews?
There are 12 identified motives for posting reviews. All of them are under the umbrella of giving or receiving something. The most common motive is to give back to the community.

How do people assign a star rating?
There are five primary methods of assigning a star rating. Each method is influenced by personal experience and preferences. The most common method is to remove stars as a product underwhelms the reviewer.

What prompts the posting of a review?
Positive and negative experiences are the primary triggers for posting reviews. An invitation to review a product or service is also a stimulus to post.

Why do these insights matter?

When you understand the influence of reviews, how they're used, and why they're written, you can relate to more reviewers and design a stronger review management program for your organization.

CHAPTER TWO

THE REVIEW CYCLE

Understand the review–driven decision–making process

QUESTIONS TO CONSIDER:

What is a purchase funnel?

What is The Review Cycle?

What are the four stages consumers follow in The Review Cycle?

What are the four decision points consumers pass through in The Review Cycle?

What are the four components of owner influence in The Review Cycle?

Why would an organization address stages of The Review Cycle from last to first?

Section 2.1: The Cyclical Consumer Experience

It's more than just a path to purchase in today's digital era

Have you ever heard of a purchase funnel? No, it's not one of those coin funnels you see charities using at the mall. Those are called donation funnels, but they are fun! A purchase funnel is a marketing model that illustrates the progress a consumer goes through towards buying something. This marketing model was first developed in 1898 by the American advertising advocate Elias St. Elmo Lewis.[1] In his theory, Elias proposed that consumers advance toward the purchase of a product or service with increased focus.

First, a consumer must become **aware** of the existence of the product or service. Then, they gain **interest** in that product group. A **desire** to purchase a particular model or brand comes next. At the bottom of the funnel, the **action** of purchasing the desired product or service occurs. This model is generally called the AIDA-model[2] and is illustrated in figure 2.1 below.

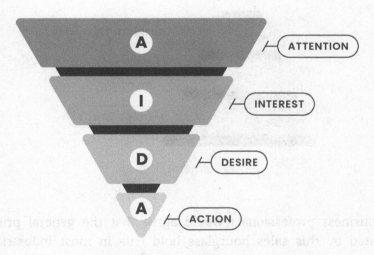

Figure 2.1: AIDA Model Sales Funnel

It's difficult to argue with the soundness of the AIDA-model. However, it paints truth in very wide, general brushes. Since this revelation from St. Elmo, the concepts of the purchase journey and post-purchase consumer behavior have been further developed and refined. Take the sales hourglass in figure 2.2 as an example. It highlights a similar narrowing of interest as the AIDA-model with the pinnacle action being the purchase. From there, a relationship between the consumer and the company continues to develop and strengthen as post-purchase interactions take place. The consumer receives support from the company, which in turn translates to customer loyalty and eventually brand advocacy.

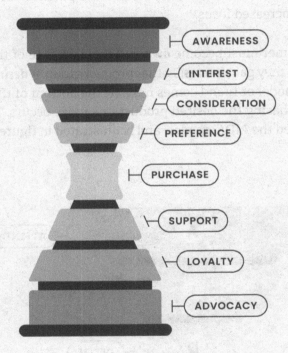

Figure 2.2: Sales Hourglass

Most business professionals would agree that the general principles illustrated by this sales hourglass hold true in most industries and sales paths. However, many variations of these two models have been established with greater detail in specific applications.

Another common variation of the purchase funnel is the conversion funnel. This model is very similar to the AIDA-model except it has been uniquely adapted to ecommerce. The model follows the same general path from awareness to purchase but tracks the progression toward purchase with specific traceable actions. Here's one example in figure 2.3. The consumer first starts with a viewing session of a website. Then, they click into one specific product page among several available options. From there, the product is added to cart and then purchased.

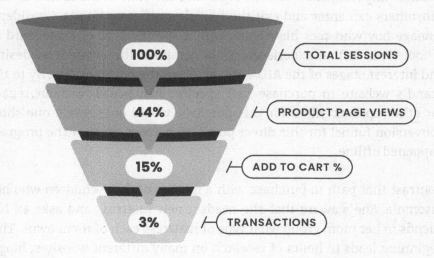

100% — TOTAL SESSIONS

44% — PRODUCT PAGE VIEWS

15% — ADD TO CART %

3% — TRANSACTIONS

Figure 2.3: Conversion Funnel

There are a couple important things to note about conversion funnels. First, success metrics (often referred to as key performance indicators, or KPI's) can be tracked. Steps in the AIDA-model cannot usually be measured as easily or accurately. Here are a few of the important KPI's for ecommerce:

· **Click-Through Rate (CTR):** *Ratio of consumers exposed to your product in search results or in an ad to the number of consumers who click-through to the offering. This metric tells you what percentage of consumers you are pushing to enter the top of your conversion funnel.*

- **Conversion Rate (CR):** *Ratio of page views to purchases. This metric tells you what percentage of potential customers start at the top of the funnel and actually purchase.*

- **Shopping Cart Abandonment Rate (CAR):** *Ratio of digital shopping carts used to number of completed purchases. This metric tells you what percentage of customers progress from the second to last step to the final purchase.*

Another important observation regarding the conversion funnel is that consumers can enter and exit the funnel at different points. Consider a teenage boy who sees his friends with a specific type of skateboard at school. This offline experience could comprise the awareness, desire, and interest stages of the AIDA-model. Then the boy goes directly to the brand's website to purchase that specific skateboard, without regard for other options. KPI's for this purchase would only reveal one short conversion funnel for this direct purchase because most of the progress happened offline.

Contrast that path to purchase with a mother of three children who has insomnia. She's aware that she needs a new mattress and asks all her friends in her mom group what type of mattress each of them owns. This beginning leads to hours of research on many different websites, blogs, and other online content sources before she finally purchases a mattress. Come to find out, the one she purchased was not that great for her, so she returns it and goes through three other mattresses before finally finding the perfect one. In this case, every mattress this mom looked at online contributed to the conversion funnel KPI's of the respective products. Only the product listing with the final mattress she kept was impacted favorably, while all others experienced a decrease in their success metrics.

Here's a final point regarding conversion funnels. The average consumer consults 10.4 information sources prior to purchase.[3] Today's consumers take an omnichannel approach to purchase research. They aren't exclusively visiting a single website, browsing options, then selecting one of them. They are searching many websites that sell and talk about the product or service. They are watching unboxing videos on YouTube. They are seeing what friends and influencers say about it on social media. They are also reading reviews. All these online content sources can influence consumers to progress towards a purchase, evaluate another option, or abandon the purchase path altogether. Keep in mind that there isn't a single path that all consumers follow to purchase, nor do consumers have the same post-purchase experiences.

If we look back to chapter one, we established that online reviews are incredibly influential. As many as 97% of consumers are influenced by reviews while 85% of consumers trust reviews as much as personal recommendations[4] We know that not all paths to purchase are exactly the same, but reviews and ratings are likely the most commonly referenced and most influential content consumers are exposed to on their individual paths to purchase.

Keeping these numbers in mind, let's proceed to discuss a purchase funnel that incorporates the very real impact of online reviews. The principles here have been developed over many years of observation and research through dozens of ecommerce sites, employer review sites and brand review sites.

What you're about to read below is not an exclusive substitute for the AIDA-model, conversion funnels, or other consumer behavior frameworks; rather, it is a new specialized model designed to demonstrate review usage patterns and methods of influencing those consumer behaviors for your benefit. The high amount of influence reviews have in today's digital era justifies this model.

I call this model **The Review Cycle**. Typically, the cycle begins when someone decides to consider a decision such as what to purchase, where to visit, or where to work. A web browsing session is started on mobile or desktop. The consumer is now *considering* a decision and evaluates surface-level data such as price, brand name and star-rating found in the search results. The layout of all primary data exposed to the consumer at this stage is predominantly controlled by the search platform, such as Google, Amazon, or Glassdoor. As you can see in figure 2.4, each of the search results displayed for the search term "Laptop" shows a picture, brand name, price, star-rating, review count, and several other standardized pieces of info considered essential for filtering results of that product category.

Figure 2.4: A Google search result for "laptop" returns filterable results[5]

The second stage occurs as soon as a consumer *engages with organizational-generated content (OGC)*. At this point, the consumer shifts from browsing surface-level search results to evaluating a single option by clicking into a website, product listing or company profile. Now the consumer is viewing images, reading content, and watching videos produced by the organization seeking to sell something to the consumer. The "purchase" action could be an actual transaction, visiting a location, or applying for a job online. Continuing our example, figure 2.5 shows Microsoft's product listing for this laptop seen in the search results. You can see that the banner image at the top is produced by the organization, Microsoft. Scrolling down you'd also see much more OGC content.

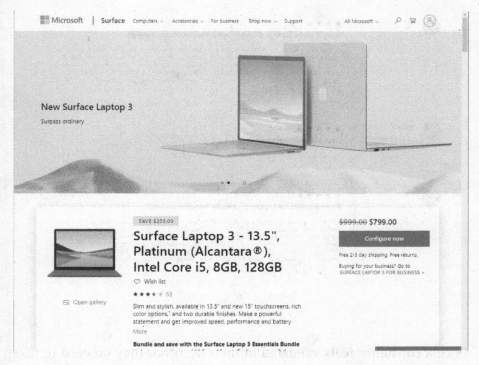

Figure 2.5: A view of a single product page clicked on from Google results[6]

The third stage begins after the consumer feels satisfied with the OGC they engaged with and turns to online communities for confirmation of their decision. This is called **engaging with user-generated content (UGC)**. Although a star-rating may have been enough to get a consumer to click into a listing in the consideration phase, now the consumer scrolls down to the reviews to actually read what other customers are saying. They may view photo and video reviews on the listing, read Q&As, view a social media feed that's integrated on the product page and/or open another web tab to consult other UGC found on social media, blogs, YouTube etc.

In figure 2.6, the review section of the product page is now viewed. Consulting reviews generate validation to buy or not to buy. From my research, I've seen that consumers typically read an average of six reviews before they decide to purchase or not.

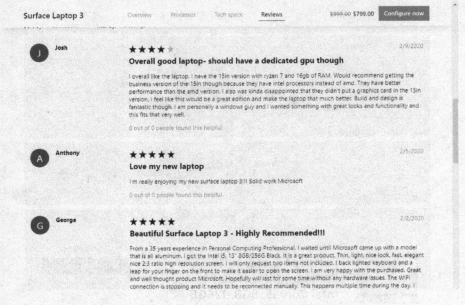

Figure 2.6: A view of the review section on the same product listing page[7]

Once a consumer feels validated in their decision, they proceed to take action. The purchase is made, the restaurant is visited or the job application is sent. Conversely, if the consumer is not validated, they go back to the consideration stage to find an alternative offering. Figure 2.7 shows the checkout page on Microsoft's website.

Figure 2.7: The laptop is now purchased on the checkout page on Microsoft's website[8]

After action is taken and the laptop is purchased, the fourth stage begins as the consumer has their **post-decision experience**. Does the product do what is promised? Did the restaurant really have amazing guacamole dip? What's it actually like working for the company? In our example, did the Microsoft laptop function as expected?

Just like we saw with the conversion funnel, consumers can enter The Review Cycle at various stages. Someone may know they want a vacuum and already love Dyson. For these reasons, they may skip the consideration and engage with OGC stages altogether and just read reviews of varying Dyson vacuum models before buying one. Conversely, someone may know they need a new job and browse company profiles (engage with OGC) and employee reviews (engage with UGC) on Glassdoor and Comparably for weeks before they finally apply. In essence, that person is passing through stages 1 through 3 many times before proceeding to stage 4.

Figure 2.8 shows the four stages of consumer behavior in The Review Cycle. Note that there is an arrow from the final stage (number 4) to the first stage (number 1). You may wonder why that is. Have you ever browsed a product category online after you've already purchased one of the options? Why? Perhaps it was to make another purchase. Perhaps you weren't fully satisfied with your purchase and you now want to compare your purchase to alternatives. Maybe you're curious if the model you purchased is now on sale for less than you paid. Or maybe you posted a review of your unit then saw what else was on the site and started browsing casually. There are many reasons a person might start the cycle again. It is important to note that even after a decision is made, online content is always available and accessible by past customers. Consumers may pass from post-decision to consideration and begin The Review Cycle again and again. In these cases, past experience impacts a consumer's behavior the next time they begin The Review Cycle.

Now that we've looked at the four stages of The Review Cycle, let's discuss the associated decisions for each stage. Consider figure 2.9. Each of the four stages begins with a decision.

A consumer must first **decide to consider potential purchase options** in order to **start The Review Cycle and enter stage 1: consideration.**

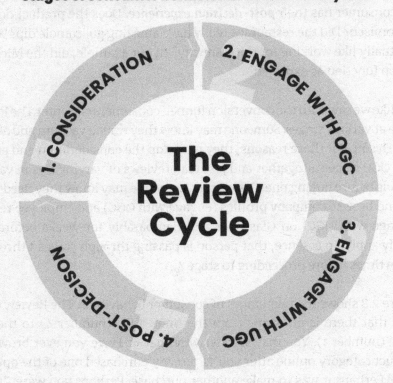

Figure 2.8: Stages of consumer behavior in
The Review Cycle

After browsing many options at the search view level, a consumer *decides to narrow their consideration by clicking into one available search result.* This leads to *stage 2: engaging with OGC.*

When the consumer feels positive about this particular option, they *decide to validate the selection by reading reviews.* This is *stage 3: engaging with UGC.*

If the reviews and other UGC positively reinforce the selection, the consumer *decides to make the purchase.* This moves the consumer to *stage 4: the post-decision stage.* Stage 4 is the only stage with two decisions connected to it. The purchase decision moves a consumer into this stage and the *decision to post a review comes later.*

Posting a review is the final decision within The Review Cycle and reflects the highest possible impact a consumer could have on your organization

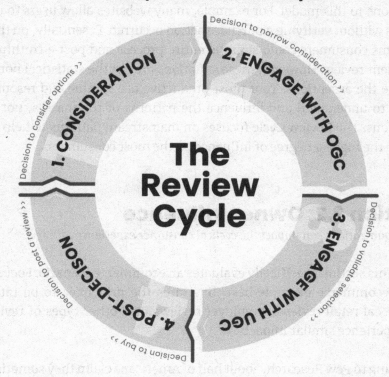

Figure 2.9: Decision points in The Review Cycle

and other consumers. A purchase is, for the most part, a one-to-one impact. One consumer may choose to make, or not to make, a singular purchase. However, when one consumer decides to post a review, their impact multiplies exponentially as they affect The Review Cycle for the rest of the online community. This new piece of content then alters the information other consumers are exposed to when they progress through the four stages of The Review Cycle.

Also note that your average consumer may view stages 1 through 3 as broadly as "shopping". Going back and forth through these stages may be inconsequential to the consumer. Yet, if you are seeking to influence consumers towards your offering, acknowledging each stage of The Review Cycle independently is critical. Higher sales rates are achieved when you have higher quantities of consumers progressing through each stage of The Review Cycle towards your offering.

One final caveat is helpful when considering The Review Cycle. There are exceptions to this model. For example, many websites allow users to post reviews without verifying a purchase action occurred. Essentially, on these platforms consumers could skip the entire process and post a truthful or fraudulent review. However, these situations are not the statistical norms; they are the exceptions. Your most productive use of time and resources will be to understand and influence the patterns of the masses, not the exceptions. The Review Cycle focuses on mainstream patterns to help you achieve the highest degree of influence on the most consumers.

Section 2.2: Owner Influence
How organizations can impact the cyclical consumer experience

Note: This section specifically evaluates an ecommerce scenario. Focusing on an ecommerce example best illustrates the principles to be taught here. Local retail reviews, employer reviews, and other types of reviews will experience similar impacts.

According to Pew Research, about half of Americans claim they sometimes post reviews online.[9] The true frequency of what "sometimes" means, is likely much lower than you'd think.

Let's begin by overlaying commonly trackable ecommerce KPI's with The Review Cycle. The amount of people exposed to your offer in search results would coincide with the consideration stage (stage 1) and would be traceable by impression/view count. The amount of people who engage with OGC and UGC (stages 2 and 3) coincides with your page view count. The number of purchases represents the number of people who enter the post-decision stage (stage 4). And finally, the number of people who post an online review while in the post-decision stage (stage 4) is also trackable. View figure 2.10 below to see these associated KPI's.

Now that we've established which metrics are associated with which stage of The Review Cycle we can calculate how many people typically make it through the complete cycle using the below KPI's. Some of these will look familiar from section 2.1:

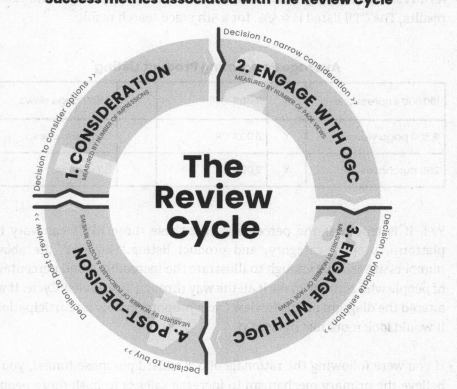

Figure 2.10: KPI's associated with The Review Cycle

- **Click-Through Rate (CTR):** *Ratio of consumers exposed to your product in search results or ads [IMPRESSIONS] to the number of consumers who click through to the offering [PAGE VIEWS]. For organic search results, click-through rates vary from about 31.7% for the number one search result down to 3.1% for the number ten result on a page (Dean, 2019).*[10]

- **Conversion Rate (CR):** *Ratio of people who click on your offering [PAGE VIEWS] to the number who buy the item [PURCHASES]. According to Invesp, ecommerce conversion rates in the U.S. averaged around 3% through the 2010's.*[11]

- **Review Rate (RR):** *Ratio of people who buy the item [PURCHASE] to the number of people who post a review [REVIEWS]. I've observed review rates ranging from 0.5% to 5% on ecommerce platforms, with an average of around 2%.*

As an example, average ecommerce circumstances may lead to the below results. The CTR listed is 9.5%, for a 5th place search result.

Average Performing Product Listing

100,000 impressions	X	9.50% CTR	=	9,500 page views
9,500 page views	X	3.00% CR	=	285 purchases
285 purchases	X	2.00% RR	=	5.7 reviews

Yes, it is true that the percentages for these three KPI's can vary by platform, product category, and product listing. However, the above numbers are reliable enough to illustrate the incredibly small percentage of people who actually make it all the way through The Review Cycle. If we altered the diagram of The Review Cycle proportionately by participation, it would look more like figure 2.11.

If you were following the rationale of a standard purchase funnel, you'd believe the primary mechanism to increase sales is to push more people to the top of your funnel. That would get you more impressions, more page views, more purchases and more reviews. This is a linear way of thinking and is only fractionally true. Yes, if you push more people to enter the consideration stage of The Review Cycle, you will have higher participation at each subsequent stage.

However, there are greater forces at play that impact the percentages of people who advance through The Review Cycle. First you must acknowledge the disparity of clicks based on search rank. As referenced above, the average CTR of the number one search result is 31.7% while the tenth is 3.1%. The change in CTR from your number one search result to number ten is not linear. It's exponential and looks more like what you see in figure 2.12.

Proportionate perspective of The Review Cycle

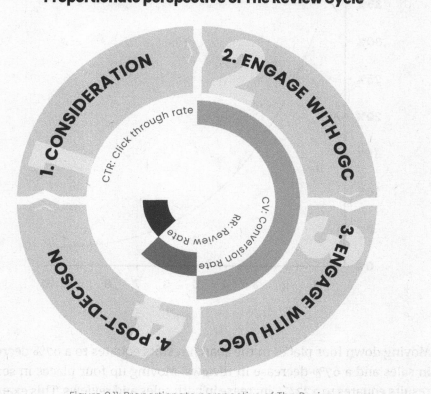

Figure 2.11: Proportionate perspective of The Review Cycle shows exponentially decreasing participation at each stage consumer can go through

In our example equation above, we used an average CTR of 9.5% for the 5th place search result. Increasing or decreasing your search result performance would cause an exponentially significant impact on your downstream KPI's: both your conversion rate (CR) and review rate (RR). If we consider no other variable changes except movement of your search result up or down by four places, your listing would experience the following impact:

% of clicks by search result placement

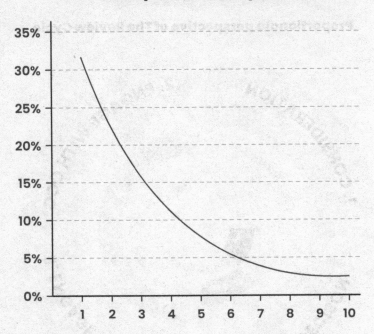

Figure 2.13: Graph of the price elasticity of demand

Moving down four places in the search results equates to a 67% decrease in sales and a 67% decrease in reviews. Moving up four places in search results equates to a 334% increase in both sales and reviews. This example shows how changes in inputs create disproportionate outputs.

In a similar way, changes in star ratings and review counts impact conversion rates exponentially. First, consider the economic principle of price elasticity of demand. Price elasticity is the responsiveness of consumers (demand change) to a price change. Think back to your Econ 101 class. In figure 2.13 below, you see price (P) on the y-axis and quantity (Q) in the x-axis. The intersection between the supply curve (S) and demand curves 1 and 2 (D1 and D2) are the points of market equilibrium at the respective levels of demand. You can see that a shift in demand from D1 to D2 affects both price and quantity. Price goes up from P1 to P2 and quantity goes up from Q1 to Q2.

POOR 9th place search result

100,000 impressions	X	**3.10% CTR**	=	**3,100 page views**
3,100 page views	X	3.00% CR	=	**93 purchases**
93 purchases	X	2.00% RR	=	**1.86 reviews**

AVERAGE 5th place search result

100,000 impressions	X	**9.50% CTR**	=	**9,500 page views**
9,500 page views	X	3.00% CR	=	**285 purchases**
285 purchases	X	2.00% RR	=	**5.70 reviews**

EXCELLENT 1st place search result

100,000 impressions	X	**31.70% CTR**	=	**31,700 page views**
31,700 page views	X	3.00% CR	=	**951 purchases**
951 purchases	X	2.00% RR	=	**19.02 reviews**

Because both the demand curves and the supply curve are not linear, the rate of change for both price and quantity demanded by the market changes exponentially. Moving the demand curve one unit up would result in a larger change in price than moving one unit down Additionally, moving the demand curve one unit up would result in a smaller change in quantity demanded than moving one unit down.

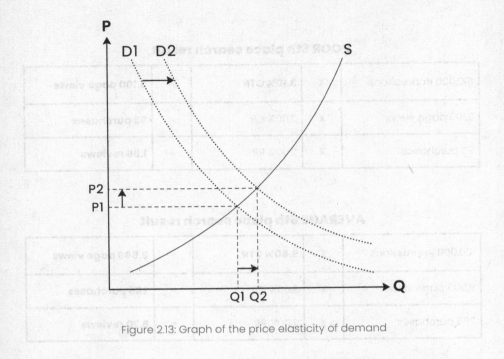

Figure 2.13: Graph of the price elasticity of demand

A final principle to note about price elasticity of demand is the unequal effect this principle has on various goods and services. If a product has very little change in demand as price goes up, it is said to be inelastic. An example of this would be electricity. Electricity is relied upon so heavily that if price doubled, demand may dip a little, but not much. The opposite is a product that is very elastic. For example, a hair dryer. If the price of a specific hair dryer doubled, the demand would likely drop dramatically for that model. Generally speaking, products that do not have a viable substitute, such as electricity, food or prescription drugs are inelastic.[12]

Just as price can change demand, I have observed an overwhelming number of instances when reviews induced changes in both demand and price. If we take a look back at figure 1.3 in section 1.1, it shows the results of an ecommerce sales study conducted by the KTH Royal Institute of Technology in Sweden.[13] The graph highlights the drastic increase of sales as star ratings increase, along with the sudden drop of sales as a product is rated close to a perfect 5-star average.

Let's expand this principle further. If we take the basic sales pattern portrayed from figure 1.3 and put it on a graph with star ratings on the y-axis and demand on the x-axis, we can see what's happening more clearly. Reference figure 2.14 below. If we look at this from the peak of demand downward, we observe:

- *Whatever the demand is at around 4.5 to 4.7-stars is considered maximum demand.*

- *From there, every half-star rating drop results in demand cutting in half:*

  - *So, around the 4-star mark demand is half what it is at 4.5-stars. 3.5-stars is half the demand of 4-stars and so on.*

- *1-star average rating has almost zero demand because it is the lowest rating possible to give on the standard 5-star metric.*

- *From 4.8-stars to 5.0-stars we see a dramatic drop in demand to as low as the 2.5-star demand threshold. This is because consumers will generally believe the ratings to be too good to be true, faked, manipulated or otherwise not trustworthy.*

The graph in figure 2.14 depicts what we will call a **smooth star rating elasticity curve**. A smooth star rating elasticity curve is expected to exist on product listings and review profiles where the 5-star image reflects each and every 0.1-star change. Smaller incremental changes in that displayed image result in a smoother elasticity curve. Figure 2.15 depicts two employer ratings on Indeed. Look how the filled line on the star rating images changes ever so gradually with each 0.1-star change. This coincides with a smooth star rating elasticity curve.

Now look at figure 2.16. This graph depicts a *stepped star rating elasticity curve.* This type of demand curve is found on review platforms that round displayed star ratings by half stars. By introducing half-star rounded search results, a review platform introduces artificial concentration of demand at each half-star "step". Here are the key observations for demand impact of a stepped star rating elasticity curve:

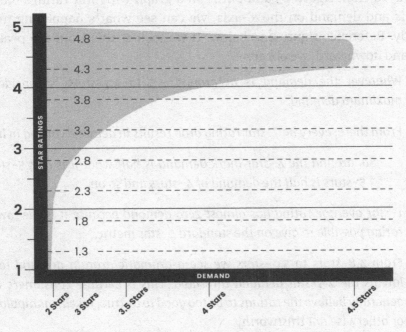

Smooth Star Rating Elasticity Curve

Figure 2.14: Standard star rating elasticity of demand graph

- From 4.3 to 4.7-stars is the peak pocket of demand. This is where a 4 ½-star image is displayed.

- As is true for the smooth standard star rating elasticity graph in figure 14, demand cuts in half with each half-star drop in a product's average rating.

Figure 2.15: A smooth star-rating elasticity curve coincides with incremental 0.1-star changes to the 5-star graphic on two employer profiles on Indeed[14]

- *The difference is, there is much less of a curve. The half-life demand change is concentrated at the 0.1-star change where the star rating rounding occurs. Figure 15 shows the rounding star rating brackets where this happens.*

- *In the middle of a rounded rating, only marginal demand occurs with each 0.1-star rating change. For example, changing from 4.4-stars to 4.5-stars will only lift demand a little because no change to the displayed star rating is made with that shift. Either way, the site displays an image of 4 ½ stars.*

- *It is also true here that a 1-star average rating has almost zero demand.*

- *Below 1-star is still not possible as the lowest rating possible to give on the standard 5-star metric is 1 star.*

- *Unlike the smooth standard star rating elasticity model, the half-star rating model displays ratings for 4.8, 4.9, and 5 stars with an image of 5 filled stars. What this does is effectively drop sales as low as that 2.5-star demand at the 4.8-star mark and higher.*

See this example comparison between two products on Amazon in Figure 2.17. Although the two products are rated differently by 0.4-stars, they share the same 4 ½-star image. Demand for these two products will be much more similar on a stepped star rating demand curve than on a smooth star rating demand curve.

As is true of price elasticity, keep in mind that some products and services will be **review inelastic.** That means even if a product has bad reviews, it will still sell because there are not viable substitutes. In many cases, products and services that are inelastic may not be exposed to the effect of reviews at all. Consider the electricity example again. You may only have one electricity service provider where you live. With no other options even possible, the entire review cycle simply doesn't apply. You can't consider options. With no options to consider, there is no need to engage with the company (OGC) or community (UGC) regarding a purchase decision. Google still lists reviews for your electricity provider, but will you stop using electricity if they are rated poorly? Likely not.

Stepped Star Rating Elasticity Curve

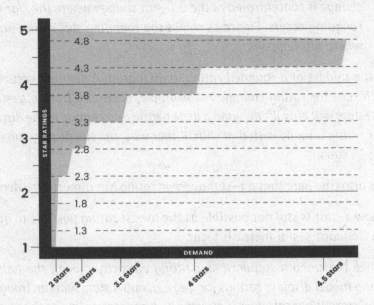

Figure 2.16: A stepped star rating elasticity curve
concentrates demand at half-star intervals

Figure 2.17: Two products on Amazon both display 4 ½
stars while one is rated 4.3 and the other is rated 4.7

On the other hand, most consumer products, services, and employers would be considered **review elastic**. If ratings drop too low, sales and job application rates will also drop. If ratings go up, sales and applications go up. The star rating directly affects conversions. So now let's evaluate the exponential impact on our second KPI, the conversion rate (CV) caused by changes in star ratings. For this example, we're assuming an average conversion rate of 3% for an average 4-star rating. Under the review elasticity model, dropping to 3 ½ stars would cut that conversion rate in half to 1.5%. Moving up from 4 stars to 4 ½ stars would double conversions from 3% to 6%.

POOR 3 ½-star rating

100,000 impressions	X	9.50% CTR	=	9,500 page views
9,500 page views	X	**1.50% CV**	=	**142.5 purchases**
142.5 purchases	X	2.00% RR	=	**2.85 reviews**

AVERAGE 4-star rating

100,000 impressions	X	9.50% CTR	=	9,500 page views
9,500 page views	X	**3.00% CV**	=	**285 purchases**
285 purchases	X	2.00% RR	=	**5.70 reviews**

EXCELLENT 4 ½-star rating

100,000 impressions	X	9.50% CTR	=	9,500 page views
9,500 page views	X	**6.00% CV**	=	**570 purchases**
570 purchases	X	2.00% RR	=	**11.4 reviews**

Dropping from 4-stars to 3 ½-stars equates to a 50% decrease in sales and a 50% decrease in reviews. Moving up from 4-stars to 4 ½-stars equates to a 100% increase in both sales and reviews. We see that the second KPI, is also exponential, not linear in nature.

The last KPI you want to increase is your review rate (RR). Looking at the chart above, it may seem that increasing reviews isn't critical because it takes place after the primary KPI: conversion rate. Why should you do anything that doesn't increase sales? Remember, these KPIs are associated with a cycle, not a funnel. Cycles repeat. Downstream KPIs affected by your review rate include your click-through rate (CTR) and your conversion rate (CV) for the next shopper or job seeker.

So yes, you do want to increase your review rate (RR). Both the absolute quantity of reviews on your listing today and the rate at which you acquire new reviews matters. Take a look back to figure 1.2 in chapter 1. It shows the conversion rate impact created by review quantity. Going from zero to one review lifts conversions by 10%. Getting to 10 total reviews increases conversions by a total of 20%. By the time you reach 50 reviews, conversions have lifted 30%. At 200 reviews, the conversion rate impact starts to level mostly around a 40% lift. The law of diminished returns takes effect with each additional review increasing conversions at a smaller rate than the previous review.

In one aspect, getting a listing started from ground zero is a one-time effort. You want to get that lift of 40% or more on your listing by getting your first 200 reviews. From there, the game is all about comparisons. If your listing gets to 200 reviews, but all your competitors have 2,000+ reviews, you may not get that average 40% lift you would expect. Comparatively, your listing still looks new and less trust-worthy.

The opposite would be true if your competitors' listings have very few reviews. If most of your competitors don't have more than 100 reviews, you look like the most obvious choice to consumers with 200 reviews.

To beat out the competition, it is good to be aware of your absolute review count compared to competitors. However, the way that I view sustainable success is by rate of change. If you are improving at a faster rate, you are winning the long game. Basically, if you are gaining more reviews faster than your competition, it doesn't matter if they have more than you right now. You will eventually surpass them and build an increasingly larger gap of reviews they won't be able to match.

As a side note, you can easily calculate your review rate and the review rate of a competitor by dividing the number of reviews received in a set time frame. I'd recommend counting at least 30 days back. For example, if you have 72 reviews received in the past 30 days, then 72 / 30 = 2.4 reviews per day. Chapter 3 will cover how to increase your review rate (RR) by asking for reviews.

POOR 0.5% RR rate

100,000 impressions	X	9.50% CTR	=	9,500 page views
9,500 page views	X	3.00% CV	=	285 purchases
285 purchases	X	**0.50% RR**	=	**1.43 reviews**

AVERAGE 2.0% RR rate

100,000 impressions	X	9.50% CTR	=	9,500 page views
9,500 page views	X	3.00% CV	=	285 purchases
285 purchases	X	**2.00% RR**	=	**5.70 reviews**

EXCELLENT 5.0% RR rate

100,000 impressions	X	9.50% CTR	=	9,500 page views
9,500 page views	X	3.00% CV	=	285 purchases
285 purchases	X	**5.00% RR**	=	**14.25 reviews**

As we look at our 3rd KPI below, the listed poor, average, and excellent review rates are based off personal observation of hundreds of product listings. Although rate of change for review rates (RR) have not been formally studied to the extent of CTRs and CVs, I can confirm that exponential growth does occur just the same.

Now that we've seen how changes in CTR, CV, and RR have exponential affects, see how they work together to truly accelerate or hinder your success. Consider the below graph, which includes poor, average and excellent KPI's across all three categories.

POOR: search result (9th place), star rating (3 ½-star rating), and RR (0.5%)

100,000 impressions	X	3.10% CTR	=	3,100 page views
3,100 page views	X	1.50% CV	=	46.5 purchases
46.5 purchases	X	0.50% RR	=	0.23 reviews

AVERAGE: search result (5th place), star rating (4-star rating), and RR (2.0%)

100,000 impressions	X	9.50% CTR	=	9,500 page views
9,500 page views	X	3.00% CV	=	285 purchases
285 purchases	X	2.00% RR	=	5.70 reviews

EXCELLENT: search result (1st place), star rating (4 ½-star rating), and RR (7.0%)

100,000 impressions	X	31.70% CTR	=	31,700 page views
31,700 page views	X	6.00% CV	=	1,902 purchases
1,902 purchases	X	5.00% RR	=	95.1 reviews

The sales difference between a poor performing listing and an excellent performing listing is astronomical. In this example with average estimates, the difference in sales between a fully de-optimized and a fully optimized listing is just over 4,000%. Yes. 4,000%.

Where to start

Up to this point, we've focused on consumer behavior. In chapter one, we evaluated why reviews are used to make decisions and we broke down the components of the decision process. This is great info to have, but how do you influence the consumer experience for your gain? That is where we are headed next.

The Review Cycle has been designed to highlight the impact you can have on consumers. Your impact is referred to as *elements of owner influence.* The "owner" is you, the person or organization attempting to affect the consumer. These elements live within the center of The Review Cycle and are outlined as follows:

Consumer Review Cycle Stage	Associated Consumer Decision	Associated Owner Influence	Associated KPI to Improve
Consideration	Consider options & narrow consideration	Market with reviews	CTR (Click-Through Rate)
Engage w/ OGC	Validate selection	Harvest insights	CV (Conversion Rate) & Star Rating
Engage w/ UGC	Buy	Respond to reviews	CV (Conversion Rate)
Post-decision experience	Post a review	Ask for reviews	RR (Review Rate) & Star Rating

At the consideration stage, a consumer decides to evaluate purchase options. Good reviews help the consumer narrow consideration to a single product. As the owner, you can market with reviews by incorporating review text and ratings into your ads. This action pushes more consumers to narrow their selection to consider your product. In other words, your click-through rate (CTR) will improve.

Once on your listing, a consumer engages with your content (OGC). Enhancing your product and product listing with harvested insights you've found in your review data helps more customers validate their purchase selection and buy from you. In other words, OGC designed with user feedback from reviews is more helpful to your shoppers and directly increases your conversion rate (CV). Accurate and informed listing content also helps increase your star rating by ensuring customers have aligned expectations of the product or service experience.

After a consumer has engaged with your OGC content and found it to be agreeable, they move to engage with (UGC)– they read your reviews. As you write responses to your reviews, you increase consumer trust, and more people will buy from you. More purchases mean an increased conversion rate (CV).

Finally, after a purchase has been made, the consumer enjoys their post-decision experience. Here is where consumers can choose to post a review. By asking for a review, you stand to increase your review rate (RR) and your star rating. Both things increase sales for the next person starting The Review Cycle.

See the four elements of owner influence in The Review Cycle as listed in figure 2.18. Visually, you see how each of the four elements are connected to a specific consumer behavior and decision you want to influence.

On the surface, these four elements of owner influence are straightforward and simple. You could say the same thing about shooting a free throw in basketball, yet how many differing opinions are there on how to increase your free throw percentage? A lot. In the end, a player's free throw percentage is the best reflection of their performance. Results tell the most important story.

The same goes for managing reviews with the four elements of owner influence. Results tell the story of your performance. In this chapter, we've discussed which results matter, namely your CTR, CV, RR and star rating. These are the metrics you want to maximize. These are the baskets you're shooting for.

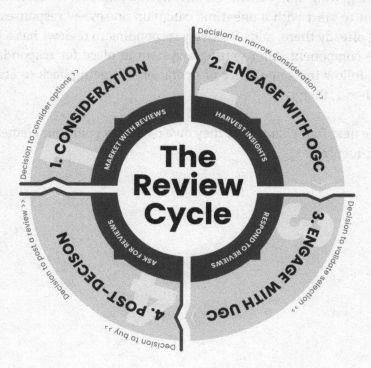

Figure 2.18: The four elements of owner influence within The Review Cycle

To help you effectively address each of these important items, we will work through the elements of owner influence backwards from stage 4 to stage 1. If you are starting from ground zero with no reviews, the first thing you need to do is start asking for reviews (stage 4). Next, when you have reviews, you can respond to them (stage 3). After building up a decent set of reviews, you can perform an analysis of all your feedback and harvest insights to improve your product and listing content (stage 2). Now that you have done all these things, your listing is optimized, and you can start pushing people to it by marketing with your best reviews (stage 1). This is the most effective order of operations for your influence, even though it's the exact opposite order consumers go through the stages of The Review Cycle.

If you are getting started with an already existing base of reviews, you may want to start with a one-time catch-up on review responses first. They are already there, and effectively responding to reviews has a time-sensitive component. After getting a system in place for responding to reviews, follow the same order of operations by going back to stage 4, then 3, then 2, then 1.

Enjoy the next four chapters as they dive deep into your four elements of owner influence.

Chapter 2 Summary
Section 2.1: The Cyclical Consumer Experience
It's more than just a path to purchase in today's digital era

What is a purchase funnel?

A purchase funnel is a consumer behavior model representing the progression a consumer passes through from awareness to purchase of a product or service. The original purchase funnel, the AIDA model, was established in 1898 and has the following stages: attention (awareness), interest, desire, and action.

What is The Review Cycle?

The Review Cycle is a new specialized consumer behavior model designed to bring awareness to review usage patterns consumers follow when making decisions in today's world of online information. Methods of influencing these behaviors within The Review Cycle are called elements of owner influence.

What are the four stages consumers follow in The Review Cycle?

Stage 1: Consideration. A consumer **decides to consider** a decision such as what to purchase, where to visit or where to work. A mobile or web browsing session begins, and search results are evaluated.

Stage 2: Engage with OGC. A consumer **narrows consideration** from browsing options in search results to evaluating a single option on a website, product listing or company profile. The consumer now views images, reads content, and/or watches videos produced by the organization seeking to influence the consumer. This content is called OGC, organizational-generated content.

S*tage 3: Engage with UGC.* A consumer continuing to progress towards a decision now seeks to validate and/or inform a potential choice by reading reviews, viewing social media, blogs, and other forms of user-generated content (UGC).

Stage 4: Post-decision experience. After the consumer has made a decision (such as buying a specific product, visiting a specific place or applying to a certain job) the consumer has a firsthand experience with their choice. This stage can last as long as the decision influences the life of the consumer.

Section 2.2: Owner Influence
How organizations can impact the cyclical consumer experience

What are the four decision points consumers pass through in The Review Cycle?

1. *Decision to consider options.* This is the first decision a consumer makes. It is the conscious or unconscious chose to evaluate multiple possible options for a choice, such a what to buy, where to visit or where to apply for a job. This choice puts an individual in stage one: Consideration.

2. *Decision to narrow consideration.* After considering several options in search results, a consumer chooses to consider a single option among many. This choice is marked by clicking into a single product listing or company profile. Upon completing this decision, a consumer enters stage two: engage with OGC.

3. *Decision to validate selection.* If a consumer likes the organizational-generated content (OGC) on a single product listing or company profile they will choose to validate their selection by engaging with UGC. This moves the consumer to stage 3: engage with UGC.

4a. *Decision to buy.* If a consumer feels validated in their selection by both OGC and UGC, they will proceed to the decision of purchasing the product/service, visiting the location or applying for the job. This decision puts the consumer in stage four: post-decision experience.

4b. *Decision to post a review.* After a space of time in stage four, a consumer may decide to post a review about the product, service, company location, etc.

What are the four components of owner influence in The Review Cycle?

1. Market with reviews. Affecting how many people consider your product among many, reviews can be used in marketing materials to super-charge your advertising.

2.Harvest insights. Analyzing consumer feedback shared in reviews is the cheat sheet to know what your customers want, and don't want. Using this data, you can improve products, services and experiences as well as engineer your OGC content to increase sales and ratings.

3. Respond to reviews. You can showcase your care for customers by publicly responding to reviews on your product listing or profile. This increases consumer trust and purchase intent.

4. Ask for reviews. The most effective way to increase the number of reviews you have and your star rating is to ask for more reviews. The collection of new reviews strengthens your impact on stages 1 through 3 for the next consumer.

Why would an organization address stages of The Review Cycle from last to first?

Consumers tend to follow the stages of The Review Cycle from 1 to 4 in sequence. However, it makes the most sense for the organization to address the respective stages in reverse order. First you must ask for reviews (stage 4 influence) before it's even possible to respond to reviews (stage 3 influence) or harvest insights from reviews (stage 2 influence). Once your listing or profile is optimized with plenty of reviews with strategic responses and informed OGC content based on your review research, you're ready to attract people to visit it. That is done through marketing with reviews (stage 1 influence).

## CHAPTER THREE

ASKING FOR REVIEWS

Fuel all stages of the review cycle by collecting more reviews

QUESTIONS TO CONSIDER:

What is the law of self-selecting extremes?

What are primary and secondary reviews?

What variables should be considered when asking for reviews?

How can you improve your review request efforts over time?

What is review syndication?

What is a vendor feedback program?

Can you incentivize reviews legally?

What components of building an in-house feedback program should be considered?

How do you get employees to share reviews?

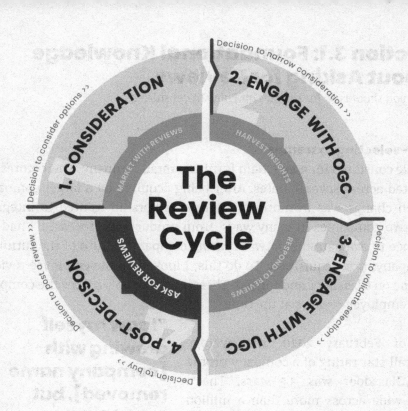

Figure 3.1: Asking for reviews is the element of owner influence associated with stage 4 of The Review Cycle: post-decision experience.

Asking for reviews is the element of owner influence associated with stage 4 of The Review Cycle. After a decision to purchase a product or service, visit a location, or apply for a job, most consumers will not share an online review. By strategically asking for reviews, you stand to:

- *Increase your ratings and review totals*

- *Unlock the opportunity to showcase customer care in public review responses*

- *Inform product and experience design and OGC content*

- *Gain UGC content that can improve marketing effectiveness*

Section 3.1: Foundational Knowledge about Asking for Reviews

Why you should ask for reviews and how to get started

Self-selecting extremes

I once consulted for a 40-chain furniture retail company. Their stores are located across several states. After being acquired by a larger company, much change was in motion. The new ownership wanted to integrate the two companies in many ways, from products to processes. I had the chance to evaluate the outward facing company culture of the furniture company, pre-acquisition. To do this, I looked up the employee reviews online on Glassdoor and Indeed. These were the only places the company had employee reviews at the time.

As of February 2020, the average overall star rating of a company profile on Glassdoor was 3.5-stars. That's site-wide across more than a million company profiles.

Well, this company had an impressive star rating of 2.6-stars. To say the reviews were below average is being generous. They were horrible. Reviews spoke of a poor work environment with long hours, low psychological safety, low pay and a demeaning executive team. Just read this anonymous employee review to get a feel for what I'm talking about.

> **"I saw myself growing with [company name removed], but I would rather chop a finger off than work for a bunch of corporate snakes that can not sufficiently run a business."**
> – *Anonymous Glassdoor Review of the 40-chain furniture company*

"*I saw myself growing with [company name removed], but I would rather chop a finger off than work for a bunch of corporate snakes that can not sufficiently run a business.*"
– *Anonymous Glassdoor Review of the 40-chain furniture company*

Working there may not cost you an arm or a leg, but really, who wants to lose a finger for a job? Fast forward a few months. The acquisition had now taken place and a new executive team had been appointed. I had sent the full company culture report to the new executive team and was about to make my first visit to their headquarters. What would I find? A group of over-worked and highly dissatisfied people? Some real jerks? Someone missing a finger when they shook my hand? I wasn't sure.

To my surprise, everyone I met was very nice. I saw lots of smiling faces and happy people. You might think that some people were just putting on a front, and that could have been true in some cases. You could also say some people were now happier because the acquisition brought a fresh outlook, and you might be right about that as well. But still, the feel around the office was not a 2.6-star company culture. In fact, it felt much better than an average 3.5-star culture. You could tell that some people were genuinely passionate about what they did there and enjoyed their coworkers.

If so many people were actually happy here, why were the reviews so awful? The answer is what I call the *law of self-selecting extremes.* When you don't ask for reviews, the only reviews you get are the extremes, both positive and negative. Only the people who had an overwhelmingly positive or negative experience are motivated to go out of their way to share their experience online.

Look at figure 3.1. In the case of this furniture company, they had never asked employees for reviews, so the only reviews they received were the end extremes. Their 65 total reviews went back 11 years on their Glassdoor profile. Considering the company employed over 600 people, that's about 1% of the employee base sharing feedback per year. This statistically insignificant minority doesn't tell a fair or complete story of what the culture is actually like. From personal observation of similar scenarios, I can confirm things skew very negatively when a review site is exposed to the law of self-selecting extremes.

A few months after the acquisition, we were able to launch an internal-only employee engagement survey. 55% of the 600 plus employees

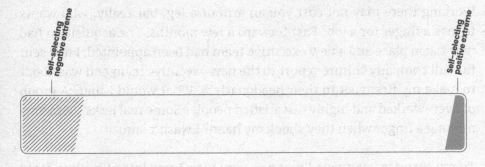

Figure 3.2: Diagram of the law of self-selecting extremes. Only the most extremely positive and negative experiences are shared in online reviews when you do not ask for reviews. Self-selecting extremes tend to skew negative

participated. With a more significant rate of participation, the feedback from this survey told a different story than the Glassdoor profile. The overall average employee engagement score was 65%. That translates to about a 4-star rating on Glassdoor.

Not only were employees at this company happier than Glassdoor portrayed, but some of the topics mentioned were very misrepresented. For example, the third most mentioned negative topic on Glassdoor about this company was work scheduling and work-life balance. However, on their engagement survey, work-life balance was the number one top-mentioned positive topic for the company. This is a critical observation about self-selecting extremes. Because this small set of feedback was the only set of feedback publicly accessible, it was dramatically shaping perceptions both inside and outside the company. And those perceptions were mostly false.

About six months after that initial visit to this company, their Glassdoor rating was up to 3.3-stars. By ten months, it was up to 4.0-stars. What made the difference? They started asking employees for reviews. The act of asking for feedback lowers the barrier to share. Asking for reviews consistently overcomes the bias of self-selecting extremes simply because you're getting a more representative sample of your user group, whether that's customers or, in this case, employees.

As you can see in figure 3.2, there is much more positive feedback to gain by asking for it. I've seen this time and time again on product listings, employee ratings, Google ratings and elsewhere. A 2016 study of seven million Amazon reviews found the average star rating across the site was 4.36 stars.[1] Having seen averages much lower on other ecommerce sites, I can tell you this is not by chance. Amazon actively solicits reviews from customers post-purchase. This helps them overcome the law of self-selecting extremes, display better ratings and sell more.

The positive and negative majorities simply need to be prompted to share. Their experiences have not been extreme enough for them to go out of their way to share. It's up to you to ask them. Later in this chapter, we'll discuss strategies on how to do this.

Figure 3.3: Diagram of the law of self-selecting extremes. Simply by asking for reviews, you are likely to get better ratings as the majority of users are more willing to share

In business and life, I believe there is always a degree of good, better, and best. That holds true in the quest for good reviews. It's **good** to have a place online where people can review your product or service. That transparency builds trust. Yet, we've seen this situation expose businesses to self-selecting extremes, which often paints an overly negative picture.

It's **better** to ask for reviews. Simply by asking, you get better representation in your sample, which is likely to be more positive.

And still, it is **best** to ask for reviews in a *strategic manner*. By thinking critically about the user experience and finding the best timing and method to ask for reviews, you stand to gain even more reviews and better ratings.

Take a look at figure 3.3. The additional *positive* and *negative* feedback (aka, reviews) can be obtained by asking for feedback in a strategic manner. This graphic represents not 100% of your customers, but 100% of your potential reviewer participation. For ecommerce, this entire graph may represent only 0.5% to 5% of total customers. For employer sites like Glassdoor, the entire graph may represent 10-50%+.

Ask for reviews. You will benefit. Optimize how you ask for reviews and you will benefit even more.

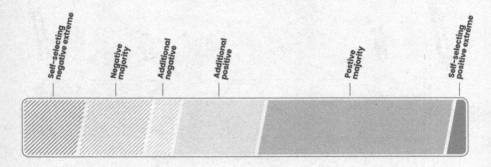

Figure 3.4: Diagram of self-selecting extremes. Beyond just asking for reviews, using strategy to optimize the timing and method of your review request will help you maximize the volume of reviews you receive. It can also help you maximize your star rating

Diversifying your reputation

Let's pretend for a moment that you're a portfolio manager for a hedge fund. How would you minimize risks? One answer is diversification. By placing money in a variety of investments, your risk is better controlled. In the case of one investment failing, the other investments prevent your portfolio from failing.

Managing your reputation is very similar. You want to diversify your reputation across many review sites. This is done by asking for reviews across all the various places where consumers can review you online. There are two primary types of reviews you should be aware of:

A *primary review* is written on the site where a transaction occurs. For products and services, that will be on the ecommerce site(s). For employer profiles, the equivalent "transaction" would be applying for a job. For local retail that only does transactions in person, the primary review may be on Google, with the "transaction" being the act of getting map directions to the store location. Essentially, primary reviews have the highest, most direct impact on purchases.

Secondary reviews are not tied to a transaction. On secondary review sites, consumers read reviews for validation. Examples of secondary review sites for a consumer buying a product would include Google, Facebook, BBB, and even employer sites like Glassdoor and Comparably. Consumers want to know how you treat your employees.

In some scenarios the label of primary and secondary can be switched. For example, when building your employee review cycle strategy, Glassdoor and Comparably become your primary sites. Here, candidates apply for jobs, which is the equivalent action to consumers making a purchase. Product and company reviews then become secondary review sites for job seekers who want to see what the consumer experience is like prior to applying.

Each individual product listing or company profile you have online is exposed to the law of self-selecting extremes. As you build your review request strategy, ensure there is a plan to ask for reviews on all known locations online. This level of care for each review site creates a protective layer of reviews across all your profiles, effectively insulating you from the damaging effects of occasional negative reviews.

Your initial reputation audit
If starting your review management program from scratch, you need to

begin by conducting a reputation audit. Depending on the size of your business, this could be a large project. For example, When I started at iFIT in 2020, I spent about a full week doing nothing but searching for online profiles connected to iFIT and its brands NordicTrack, ProForm and several others. I found over 100 profiles, more than half of which were unclaimed. Unclaimed profiles come into existence when consumers rate your business on a review site prior to you starting a profile on the website. The review sites don't ask permission to do this. They simply start a page for your business because consumers are reviewing you.

In addition to the many unclaimed profiles, I found duplicate profiles. On Indeed, I found eight duplicate profiles. This happens when consumers enter your name incorrectly in a search and create another profile instead of contributing to an existing page. Review sites don't have a vested interest in your success as a single business on their platform. If you partner with a review site for advertising and branding, then they will start dedicating resources to help you.

To conduct a thorough reputation audit, do the following:

1. Start a spreadsheet for documenting findings:

   · *Use these as headers: Website, Profile Name, Star Rating, # of Reviews, Claimed? (Y/N), URL to profile, Notes*

2. Search the internet:

   · *Search various search engines for your company name, brand and other prominent things someone might search about your company.*

   · *Go through at least the first two pages of search results, adding all info you find to your spreadsheet.*

3. Save screenshots:

   · *This initial reputation audit is your baseline.*

   · *You want screenshots of each and every profile you find to document your progress over time. Be sure to include the URL and the time stamp (date and time) in your screen shot.*

4. Claim and complete profiles:

- *Contact each platform as needed to claim your business profiles.*

- *Do a cleanup of all info and ensure it's accurate.*

- *If profiles are already claimed, you'll need to find who in your company already has access and coordinate with them.*

If you sell products online, you will likely want to do this same process for all your products. For me at iFIT, this included hundreds of products sold across about a dozen websites. Rather than searching for hundreds of products, the sales department was able to give me several lists of product page URLs for many of the websites, which drastically sped up the auditing process.

Monitoring your reviews

If you're getting antsy to hear advice on how to collect more reviews, just keep reading. Like a math equation, we have an order of operations to follow. Before going out and getting more reviews you want to ensure your program is properly built with sustainable tracking of your efforts. One of the most important personal credos I've adopted in my career is: "Process over project". Defining and building your process will always trump the value of any single completed project. Build your process first, then work on the individual projects that follow your process.

Conducting your initial reputation audit is the very beginning of building your review management processes. It is the initial recording of where you're starting from or drawing your benchmark. Next, you want to build your progress tracking resources so you can measure review performance over time.

Thinking back to section 2.2, there are two primary KPI's (key performance indicators) you should value and track:

- *Review Rate (RR): Ratio of people who buy the item [PURCHASE] to the number of people who post a review [REVIEWS].*

- *Star Rating: The number between 1 and 5 displayed on your review profile or product page.*

The most efficient way to track these two KPI's is by recording the new total # of reviews and the displayed star rating on your review profile or product page. If being done manually, I'd recommend noting these two numbers for each of your review pages once a week. Figure 3.5 features a generic template of what your tracking sheet could look like. You'd simply add a new column with the date as the header each time you record your numbers.

	Platform	Profile	Listing Link	Star Ratings & Total Reviews	3-Sept-21	10-Sept-21	20-Sept-21
	A	B	C	D	E	F	G
2	Facebook		cebook.com/ifi t/reviews	Star Rating	3.2	3.3	3.3
3		Brand 1		# of Reviews	102	110	119
4			rdictrack/revie ws	Star Rating	4.1	4.1	4.3
5		Brand 2		# of Reviews	13	17	26
6			cebook.com/pr oform/reviews	Star Rating	3.9	3.9	4
7		Brand 3		# of Reviews	57	60	65
9	Google My Business		15:0x3058b65a dac56502.1...	Star Rating	4.1	4.1	4.1
10		Brand 1		# of Reviews	994	996	1003
11			74859e5713c9 db9c.1...	Star Rating	2.9	3	3.4
12		Brand 2		# of Reviews	31	32	48
13			e69:0xc5eea02 a363573e9.1...	Star Rating	3.4	3.4	3.4
14		Brand 3		# of Reviews	81	81	81
16	Consumer Affairs		om/health/nor dic-track.html	Star Rating	3.9	3.9	3.9
17		Brand 1		# of Reviews	654	654	857
18			bs/proform_fit ness.html	Star Rating	3.6	3.6	3.5
19		Brand 2		# of Reviews	49	49	50
20			html?#sort=old est&filter=none	Star Rating	3.9	3.9	3.9
21		Brand 3		# of Reviews	173	172	193

Figure 3.5: A sample review KPI tracking sheet allowing you to record the star rating and number of reviews weekly for your review profiles

Yes, manually tracking your reviews may be tedious, but it is worth it. In some cases, you may not need to manually track your reviews in this way. Here are a few other scenarios:

Employer reviews: All the primary employer sites like Glassdoor, Comparably and InHerSight have some tracking abilities from the admin portal. As the admin of your company page on one of these sites, you can see star ratings and review total data over time.

Scraper & Monitoring Services: If you go to Capterra.com and G2Crowd.com, you can read reviews of many SaaS companies in the review management space. Some of these companies provide monitoring services. I've used Reviews.ai (formerly known as ReviewMonitoring.com) for years. Their service allows you to list URLs to all product listings on dozens of ecommerce sites within their portal. The tool then monitors review and Q&A data on your product listings, allowing you to track trends over time, export your reviews for analysis, and other valuable functions.

Direct to Consumer Review Collection and Display Services (DTC): Another type of review management SaaS company specializes in supporting DTC websites. DTC websites are sites that provide direct-from-brand purchases. For example, Levi.com is a DTC website where you can buy Levi jeans. DTC review management companies facilitate the collection and display on your website from customers that buy from you. If this is your business model, your product reviews will be monitored through their admin portal.

At the end of the day, your review monitoring needs will vary based on your business needs. Find where your reviews are online and track them regularly.

Section 3.2: Maximizing Your Review Acquisition Efforts
How to get more reviews for your product or service online

After conducting your initial reputation audit and building your review monitoring processes, you're now ready to begin actively asking for reviews. The mere act of asking for reviews will curb the damaging effects of the *law of self-selecting extremes.* But you don't want to only do the bare minimum. You want to maximize the quantity of reviews you collect and get the best star rating you can.

I'll now share the several variables you want to optimize when asking for reviews. It's best to think of these principles generally, then adapt and apply them specifically to your unique business needs.

Timing of request

The best time to ask for a review is after the customer has sufficiently experienced the product or service. If you're selling a product and can directly contact your customer by email or text, send your review request at least two days after the delivery. If you sell a more complex product, you may want to wait a week or two before sending the review request. Complex products would be items that require substantial assembly prior to use, and/or a learning curve before full utility.

If a primary method of requesting reviews is via email, text or other digital communication, you may want to track your success by day of week and time of day. In 2021, ReviewTrackers conducted a study of 150,000 Google reviews. They found that most reviews are written between 12:00 p.m. and 7:00 p.m.[2]

I conducted a similar study to see how review volumes and star ratings varied by day of week on a sample of 20,000 reviews. On Mondays we received fewer reviews with lower star ratings. Thursday was the best day for both the star rating and quantity of reviews collected. Perhaps people are in a slightly more irritated mood on Monday and by Thursday it's practically the weekend, so people are more positive. Use information like this on your own data set to alter the timing of your review requests for improved outcomes.

If you own a physical retail store or a restaurant, the best time to ask for a review is likely when the transaction is happening or when the customer is leaving the building. Hotels could deliver a review request a few hours after checkout. A pest control or yard maintenance company could leave a review request card with a receipt on a door hanger. There are lots of ways you could deliver a review request; just be sure the timing is after the purchase and after a service or experience has been provided.

Reminder requests

When possible, it's very common for companies to send review request reminders. You may wonder if this is a good idea. Will customers get annoyed? Undoubtedly, a small number of customers will be annoyed. Is it worth it? Yes, to an extent. Sending a reminder request will get you more reviews. This is a numbers game, after all, so this is a positive thing. Just don't send too many requests. I'd recommend only asking for reviews twice—an initial request and one reminder.

If your business model is subscription based, you interact with customers again and again over time. In this environment, you could skip the reminder and simply ask for reviews on an ongoing basis. You could first ask for a review of the item or service purchased. Months later, ask for a company or brand review on Google, Consumer Affairs or elsewhere. Continue asking for reviews across your several locations that need reviews over a long-term period of time.

Reduce barriers to share
The more time or steps required to leave a review, the less reviews you'll collect. You want to make it as obvious and easy as humanly possible to leave a review.

If you are emailing or texting a review request, always have a clickable link that goes directly to the review submission page of the product listing or review profile. If you have the opportunity to make an image of a product a clickable link, do that as well. Multiple links going to the same review submission page will increase the number of people who share.

If you are collecting reviews in-person, say at a store front, create a QR code customers can scan easily with a mobile device that will take them straight to your review submission page. There are plenty of free QR code generators available online if you search for it. You simply input the URL, and it generates a custom QR code image you can download and print on a flier, poster or elsewhere.

A review submission page is where you click your star rating and type the text of your review. Many review sites have unique review collection URLs designed for sharing and navigating users to your review submission page. Google does this. If you open your Google My Business admin portal, you can copy your "review form". You can use this URL to make a hyperlink on some custom text or put it in a QR code that will navigate users to your review submission page.

Leverage motives for sharing

Remember back in section 1.3 we learned about review DNA. Every review is posted with a motive, method and stimulus. You can get more people to write reviews by knowing what motivates them to share and incorporating those motives in your request. Let's look again at the primary consumer motives for sharing reviews.

	Review Motive	Frequency of Mention
Givers 52.6%	Give Back to the Community	90.9% (10 of 11)
	Express One's Opinion	54.5% (6 of 11)
	Reward a Company	54.5% (6 of 11)
	Punish a Company	36.3% (4 of 11)
	Provide Feedback	36.3% (4 of 11)
Takers 47.4%	Obtain Measurable Community Status	63.6% (7 of 11)
	Other Reasons (learning English and finding dates)	45.4% (5 of 11)
	Obtain Perceived Community Status	36.3% (4 of 11)
	Gain an Allowable Incentive	36.3% (4 of 11)
	Gain an Illegal Advantage	27.3% (3 of 11)

Here are some examples of how you could incorporate these motives into written review requests. Keep in mind that these suggestions are not meant for you to copy exactly, but more as guidelines to prompt your own creative juices to construct review requests of your own.

Give back to the community

· *Pay it forward by sharing your feedback with other shoppers. Rate us on Tripadvisor.*

· *Do you read reviews before buying? Help the next shopper by rating us online.*

Express one's opinion

- *Your opinion matters. Let it be heard. [Add clickable review link]*

- *Others want to know what you think. Share your review now. [Add clickable review link]*

Reward a company

- *We're a small family business. Your review helps us grow. Review us on Google.*

- *Did we earn your satisfaction? Share your review. [Add clickable review link]*

Punish a company

- *NOTE: this is a negative motivator. Don't write your review request with this focus.*

Provide feedback

- *Your feedback helps us improve. Share your experience in a Google review.*

- *Loved your experience? Share your feedback in a review to help us be even better.*

Obtain measurable community status

- *Level-up your Google local guide status by reviewing us. [Add review QR code]*

Other reasons (get creative and funny)

- *Good karma comes to reviewers. The stars will align in your favor. [Add review QR code]*

- *Leave us a review and see how awesome it makes you feel.*

Obtain perceived community status

- *Looking for your next perfect post? How about a review? Your friends will love it.*

- *Tell your friends on Facebook about your dining experience today. [Add review QR code]*

Gain an allowable incentive

- *Leave your review before [Add date] to be entered to win [Add prize]. [Add review QR code]

    - *Note that this would be considered an incentive. You'd have to ask reviewers to add a disclaimer to their reviews for this request to be FTC compliant.

Gain an illegal advantage

- NOTE: this is a negative motivator. Don't write your review request with this focus.

Offer customer support

Would you serve tortilla chips without salsa? What about cake without ice cream? Like these classic pairings, asking for a review and offering customer support should always go together.

When you ask for a review, don't forget the possibly unhappy customers. Offering customer support in this critical moment pushes the majority of those needing help to a private line of communication. This protects your ratings from unnecessary negative reviews.

What does this look like in application? Here is a boring, but effective layout of a review request message featuring customer support.

Thank you for shopping with us!
Review your experience [Text made into a hyperlink to the review submission page]

Need some help?
Contact our support team by emailing [add email address]

Never "gate" reviews

In 2017 Birdeye, a review management SaaS company experienced an unfortunate hardship. An attempt to help clients get ahead ended up in thousands and thousands of Google reviews being deleted.

What happened? Birdeye developed a clever review request process flow. The first step included a message being sent to a client's end customer. This message asked if the customer was happy with their experience with the business or not. If the customer indicated yes, they were happy, Birdeye would send them to the Google review submission page. If they indicated no, they were not happy, the customer would be provided with customer support information.

This action "gated", or blocked, those most likely to leave a negative review from ever reaching the Google review page. It artificially inflated the ratings, which broke Google's terms of service and many reviews were deleted. Many clients using this service lost extreme amounts of reviews.

There is a less egregious way that many companies attempt to gate reviews and only collect positives. Consider this example:

I visited a doctor's office that had an 8" by 10" framed document on the receptionist desk featuring a review request that read: "If you've had a good experience at our office, we'd love you to write a Google review." A Google logo and a picture of five stars accompanied this statement.

To some, this may seem like a great effort to collect reviews. To me, this is horrible foul play. Why? What do you think when you see a sign like that? If you were to go read all their reviews, would you completely believe them? After all, they only encourage reviews from people who had a "good experience." They also insinuate that only 5-star reviews are acceptable with the accompanying image of five stars.

This well-intended note has a poisonous byproduct—customers may be more skeptical about the true authenticity of your reviews and ratings. There is no need to be afraid of negative reviews. You will get them. But if you consistently ask for reviews, you will overcome the negative effect of self-selecting extremes. Let the number game develop and simply ask for reviews with no caveats of what type of review you want or expect. This will reinforce the authenticity of your reviews.

Be creative

When I was 19, I served a Christian mission for my church. I lived in Amarillo, Texas, where I saw homeless individuals every day. Almost all of them had some type of sign asking for money. Many signs communicated intense needs and sad circumstances. Most of them received few tips.

There was one day I saw a homeless person on the side of a busy road by a stop light with a large jar full of money. Not only was his jar full, but he was frantically picking up coins out of the grass where he was sitting.

Can you guess what his sign said? It was a large piece of cardboard with a hole in the middle. Around the hole several large circles were drawn, like a target. Above the target, read the text: "I bet you can't hit me with a quarter!" He would wave his sign and give people funny looks, inviting them to pelt him with their change.

This guy won the beggar challenge. He skipped over the reason why he needed the money and went straight for delivering something of value to his contributors—a fun and simple game.

I've made my fair share of review requests for various products, companies and brands. Figure 3.6 features one of my favorites. This product review insert was included with the packaging of most Linenspa bedding products.

This insert was designed after a test-buy research project. My team ordered 20 products from various product categories and evaluated what could be learned from the approach of others.

Rather than cutting straight to the chase with a Happy? Review us!, we led with a game. It was an invitation to play truth or dare. Upon opening the insert, the reader likely wants to know what the truth or dare includes. Lucky for us, both options are self-benefiting. The "Truth" action is to write a review. The dare action is to write a review and incorporate the name of your favorite TV show or movie. This fun twist turned the action of writing a review into a little game.

Figure 3.6: A creative review request starts with a
game of truth or dare—to leave a plain simple review
or a silly review

As the customer continues reading, they are given support information that properly manages availability and response time expectations.

Stay on brand

However you decide to ask for reviews, make sure you deliver a request your customers will recognize. Evaluate the voice and look of your brand. If you're working for a large organization, you likely will benefit from involving your marketing team and copywriters in the creation of your review requests.

New launches

If you're launching a new product, retail location or business for the first time, you may wonder how to get reviews. Ultimately, asking for reviews requires you to first have customers. That means you need to do whatever it takes to stimulate some sales. Run any type of promo and advertising you can. Get people to buy from you, visit your location, or sample your services. This is the beginning of the numbers game. The more customers you have, the more opportunities you have to ask for reviews.

A/B test

Good marketers are familiar with split testing, otherwise known as A/B testing. In practice, a marketer would create two ads with different variables. Performance would be measured and the lower performing ad would be discontinued. Over time, other variables would be tested and each time the higher performing ad would be used in comparison to a new test.

This same principle can be applied to asking for reviews. If you're wondering where to start, do something basic and simply ask customers for reviews. Using your tracking sheet to monitor your displayed star rating and total number of reviews, you can measure performance of your V1 review request. Next, test a V2 review request, noting the date it was launched. You can then measure how effective V2 was compared to V1. This will inform your V3, and so on.

Section 3.3: Using Paid Review Collection and Display Programs
When and how to collect and syndicate reviews using 3rd party services

Syndication of reviews

We talked about the need to get more reviews to overcome the negative impact of the law of self-selecting extremes. What if you could share or duplicate your reviews across many locations online? That would certainly speed up the process.

There is a way to do this for some reviews and it's called review syndication. Syndication is the sale or licensing of materials for publication or broadcasting. There are several review management companies that offer syndication, the biggest currently being Bazaarvoice.

Founded in 2005, Bazaarvoice is one of the oldest review management SaaS companies. At its root, their syndication services work like this:

- *You share your order details with them from your Direct to Customer (DTC) ecommerce website.*

- *They email your customers on your behalf and collect reviews.*

- *These collected reviews are displayed on your DTC website.*

- *These same reviews can then be syndicated to marketplace sites like Walmart.com, BestBuy.com and others in the Bazaarvoice network.*

- *Reviews shared through syndication appear on the product listing of marketplace websites for the matching product sold on your website. These reviews are tagged as shared reviews coming from your website.*

Figure 3.7 shows a review written by "Ham Radio" on BlackAndDecker.com. This exact review also appears on Walmart.com for the same hand-held vacuum. Notice how the review on Walmart is tagged: "Written by a blackanddecker.com customer", noting it is syndicated content.

Figure 3.7: An example of review syndication. The review written by "Ham Radio" on blackanddecker.com is syndicated to the same product listing on Walmart.com[3]

At the time of the publication of this book, syndication is only available for products sold on ecommerce sites. If you sell products online, you may think this is the no-brainer option for scaling your reviews. After all, for every review you collect on your DTC website, you can push that review to most marketplace sites.

Like all investments, you should consider the return on investment. Syndication is not cheap. Most contracts are annual or multi-year and can cost tens of thousands of dollars. I like to break down the contract price all the way down to an estimated cost-per review.

Let's say the possible syndication contract is $10,000 for up to 5,000 reviews (typically, prices are given based on the quantity of reviews to be syndicated). If you have 5,000 reviews across all your products on your own DTC site, they can all be syndicated to your marketplace product listings if they are in the service provider's network. Here's how your price per review syndicated would change based on the number of marketplaces that also sell your products:

# of Reviews Available for Syndication	Total Price Paid Annually	# of Marketplace Sites	Price per review syndicated
5,000	$10,000	1	$2.00
5,000	$10,000	2	$1.00
5,000	$10,000	3	$0.67
5,000	$10,000	4	$0.50
5,000	$10,000	5	$0.40

This may seem quite appealing. The cost per review drops to an impressive $0.40 if you have 5,000 reviews to syndicate across 5 marketplace websites. But what if you aren't using the full 5,000 capacity? If you only have 1,000 reviews available to syndicate, your price per review would look like this:

# of Reviews Available for Syndication	Total Price Paid Annually	# of Marketplace Sites	Price per review syndicated
1,000	$10,000	1	$10.00
1,000	$10,000	2	$5.00
1,000	$10,000	3	$3.33
1,000	$10,000	4	$2.50
1,000	$10,000	5	$2.00

These syndicated reviews carry the same weight and impact on the receiving marketplace sites as organically-collected reviews. That means your syndicated reviews will have an impact on the star rating and number of reviews across all receiving product listings. This is a huge benefit, assuming you are able to collect mostly positive reviews via your own DTC website.

Whether you're able to use the entire syndication capacity or not, it's critically important to know that syndicated reviews are only displayed while you're a paying customer. The day your contract ends, all syndicated reviews are removed from all receiving marketplace listings. That also means they are no longer impacting your star rating or total number of reviews on the marketplace sites.

In the end, paying for review syndication is like renting your reviews. You benefit only as long as you are paying for the service. Keep in mind that the cost will continue year after year. This may still be a good option for you based on the size and complexity of your business and your availability to actively ask for reviews.

Vendor feedback programs

Some marketplace sites have programs to help you collect reviews for your products. This is especially important when launching a product for the first time. Amazon has the Vine Voice Program. A participating seller pays a fee to submit a product to the program. The seller ships units to Amazon as instructed and covers all product and shipping costs out of pocket. Amazon ships the units to individual "Vine Voices" participating in their feedback program. These individuals are pre-existing Amazon customers selected by invite only based on the helpfulness of previously written reviews on Amazon.com.

This program is important for Amazon sellers to effectively launch new products. Soliciting reviews has become so restricted in recent years in response to review manipulation that Amazon has battled on their platform.

Other retailers have similar programs. Home Depot has the Seed Program and Walmart has the Spark Program. These operate similarly to Amazon's Vine Voice Program, coordinating delivery and review collection from a vetted list of product testers.

All feedback programs run by marketplace sites have a couple limiting factors. First, they don't guarantee that every unit you submit to the program will result in a review. They'll generally say that 80-90% of the units will give you a review. Second, participants in these programs are asked to only write a review on the single marketplace website. That's a fairly small amount of content provided for the cost of your unit, the shipping and the participation fee.

Bazaarvoice and some other 3rd party syndication companies also run their own feedback programs. They operate in a similar way: Pay a fee to enroll products, provide the unit for free and pay to ship it to them. Then the unit is assigned to a participant who is asked to write a review. The leveraged advantage is syndicating those collected reviews. If only 80% of the units you enroll end in a review, but those reviews are posted on 5 sites, you end up averaging four posted reviews per unit enrolled. Keep in mind that syndication would be a separate expense, but if you're already doing it, there's added value for using your syndication partner for additional review collection.

Section 3.4: Running an In-House Feedback Program

When and how to legally run an incentivized feedback program

For businesses with large product catalogs, it can be cost effective to build your own in-house feedback program. Rather than paying to participate in vendor feedback programs, you can build your own network of product testers and solicit honest reviews. Rather than renting syndicated reviews, this would be like buying reviews. It's a one-time cost resulting in permanent native reviews posted directly to your various product listings across the web.

Don't be alarmed by the terminology "buying reviews." I'm not about to teach you anything illegal or unethical. In reality, even your organic reviews are "bought" with a price. For example, let's say you run a restaurant. Some bad reviews previously posted to your Google profile mentioned long wait times. You then decided to hire a couple more servers and another cook to address the issue. The bad reviews mentioning wait times decreased and your star rating went up. What was the cost of getting better reviews? The extra payroll expense, time spent training, and establishing new team norms with added personnel.

In the product review space, the cost of collecting more reviews with a feedback program is simply more direct. You know the price of a unit, the cost of shipping and the locations you'll ask for reviews. It's simply easier to assign a cost per review than the restaurant example, even though both have underlying costs and benefits. And truthfully, using vendor feedback programs and syndication services are forms of legally allowable purchases of reviews. Running your own in-house program is a way to be more cost efficient, assuming you have a justified economy of scale.

In the past seven years, I've built two large and sophisticated in-house feedback programs covering over 3,000 product listings on 50 marketplace sites for over a dozen brands. The approach that I'm going to share with you in this section works and is, for the most part, future proof. Like any business function, things can change, but the core principles and order of operations I'll share here will cut a lot of wasted time, trial and error, and frustration out of your journey.

Next up, you need to understand the legal considerations of asking for reviews. Then I'll give you my secret recipe for building a powerful in-house feedback program.

Legal considerations of asking for reviews

Alright, folks. I'm going to be honest about this section. It is not as entertaining as some of the others. I've been told that my humor is pretty dry, unless it's a rainy day. Well, this section is not a rainy day. It's dry.

But don't skip it! The stakes are too high. After learning about the law of self-selecting extremes and building your own feedback program I'd expect your creative juices have started flowing. You've begun thinking of all the creative ways you could ask for reviews and increase your ratings.

Without cramping your style, you might want to make an important note as part of your brainstorm. Being legally compliant is crucial. It could be the difference between wild success and closing your business.

All laws relating to review collection and use of reviews in marketing are established by the Federal Trade Commission (FTC). The FTC exists to protect consumers and competition in the marketplace by preventing deceptive and unfair practices.[4] You can consider it the U.S. government's business regulation division. They prescribe a few very specific regulations concerning reviews, all of which are based in the following overarching principle:

"Material connections between an endorser (aka, a reviewer) and an advertiser (aka the business) must be disclosed" (Federal Trade Commission, 2009).

"Material connections between an endorser (aka, a reviewer) and an advertiser (aka the business) must be disclosed".[5]

If you are asking customers for reviews with nothing in return, there is no material connection to disclose. You can consider this scenario 100% allowable, expected and encouraged. An email or text to regular paying customers would not require a disclosure of connection in the review. They aren't connected to you. They're regular paying customers. The same would be true if you have a sign in your retail business with a QR code to your review page. As long as they are not getting something in return, no disclosure is required for your customers to write a review.

But what if you want to give something away to encourage reviews? I get this question a lot: Can you legally incentivize reviews? The short answer is: Sometimes.

First, understand very clearly what incentivizing a review means. Incentivizing a review is any action that results in a benefit for the reviewer in exchange for their action of posting a review. This would include giving away free or discounted products or services, payment of any kind or entry into a drawing or sweepstakes. Even if the reviewer is not required to leave a review after receiving a benefit, this action still counts as incentivizing a review.

So when can you incentivize reviews? According to the FTC, it is allowable to incentivize reviews if this fact is clearly and conspicuously disclosed in the review itself. If a review is incentivized in any way, you as the company must instruct the reviewer to openly state that fact in their review. This could be as simple as them writing: "The company gave me a discount on this product in exchange for my honest feedback in this review."

Getting a freebie isn't the only type of "material connection" you must openly disclose. If someone is an employee, family member, investor or otherwise connected to the company in some way, that fact could also affect consumers' opinion of a claim in a review. For this reason, these connections must also be disclosed. For example, if an employee wants to write a review of their company's product, they could say: "I work for _____ company name_____ and here's what I like about the new product...."

The FTC also requires that you as the organization make reasonable efforts to ensure reviewers are complying with this law. Within reason, you must periodically look for the reviews your incentivized reviewers and/or employees/friends/family have posted and re-instruct them on the disclosure requirement if it is not occurring.[5]

Why does the FTC require a stated disclosure of connection? Put yourself in the shoes of a customer reading the reviews. You're frantically shopping Black Friday deals online. You find the perfect fuzzy house shoes for your partner. It even has a picture of their favorite laughing emoji on the front! The adrenaline of seeing this lightning deal about to expire in two hours and 17 minutes makes you feel rushed. You quickly glance at the reviews. 4.5-stars. The several reviews you read sound good. Purchased.

Fast forward to Christmas morning. Your partner unwraps the house shoes. Although they love the ultra-fuzzy pattern and memory foam feel, the seam on the side is already busted and the emoji face was sewn on crooked! The nerve! If you found out that the seller incentivized 87 glowing and undisclosed reviews to that listing the month before, how would you feel? Probably like a frowny face emoji. If you would have read review after review that said: "Best slippers ever! 5-stars! Got these for free from the company!" You may have first looked at the negative reviews to balance out your opinion prior to purchase. Thank the FTC. Thank them for being the regulating body in this space and demanding transparency for consumers, which includes you.

So you're telling me I can always incentivize reviews if the disclosure is included? Remember I said it's legally allowable to incentivize reviews, sometimes.

There are websites that have made incentivized reviews against their terms of use and/or community guidelines. In these cases, even an FTC-compliant incentivized review would be illegal. Take Amazon for example. On October 3, 2016 they updated their community guidelines by prohibiting all forms of incentivized reviews.[6] Amazon has the right to press charges against both sellers and reviewers when their community guidelines are breached. Oddly enough, Amazon kept one exception to the rule. They still allow incentivized reviews of books with proper disclosure. That means it's still legal and Amazon compliant to give away copies of a book in exchange for reviews if those reviews have the proper disclosure of material connection.[6]

Although Amazon has the right to prosecute, the most likely outcome is they police the issue themselves by deleting the reviews and/or banishing sellers from their platform. Glassdoor is the same way. They prohibit incentivized reviews of any kind. If a company incentivizes employees to write reviews, they reserve the right to remove the company profile from their site.

Keep in mind that this info is current as of the time of this book printing. Always check the FTC website for updated info. I'd also recommend checking for the most up-to-date terms of service for the platform you hope to collect reviews on. If they allow incentivized reviews, then you simply have to follow what the FTC requires to be legally compliant. If they do not allow incentivized reviews, don't do it. Typically, companies breaking platform terms of service risk losing their ability to sell on that platform and additional legal action.

The trend I've seen over the years is platforms becoming increasingly more sophisticated in identifying fraudulent review behaviors. In Amazon's case, their policing evolved to include:

- *Limiting the number of reviews that can be posted on a product per day.*

- *Blocking reviews from Amazon accounts with unusual purchasing and reviewing patterns.*

- *Removing the ability to write reviews from Amazon accounts with irregular activity.*

I would fully expect to see more review platforms follow in Amazon's footsteps by algorithmically policing review fraud. The best strategy today is one that protects you tomorrow. Although some companies and individuals may break the law and get away with it, who's to say they won't get caught in the future. Besides, is it worth your integrity and honor? I'd say no. Stay compliant with both FTC regulations and the terms of use for all platforms you participate on.

For some additional light reading from the FTC, check out these resources online:

1. Guides Concerning the Use of Endorsements and Testimonials in Advertising

    - *https://www.ftc.gov/sites/default/files/attachments/press-releases/ftc-publishes-final-guides-governing-endorsements-testimonials/091005revisedendorsementguides.pdf*

2. The FTC's Endorsement Guides: What People Are Asking

    - *https://www.ftc.gov/tips-advice/business-center/guidance/ftcs-endorsement-guides-what-people-are-asking#soliciting*

3. The Consumer Review Fairness Act: What Businesses Need to Know

    - *https://www.ftc.gov/tips-advice/business-center/guidance/consumer-review-fairness-act-what-businesses-need-know*

Lastly, Section 6.1 expounds upon legal considerations that extend to the use of reviews in advertising. That section is a good one to cross reference with what you just read. You'll learn about the legality of using reviews in advertising. This is incredibly effective, but permission to use the review must be acquired. Section 6.1 outlines the proper steps to make this possible.

Building an in-house feedback program

Some people and companies may tell you to absolutely never incentivize reviews. As we read in the previous section, there's a way to do it and be completely legal and ethical. An in-house feedback program is built on incentivized reviews, so following the FTC law is critical. The objective of this program is to collect authentic and honest reviews from real users across your product listings.

Growing a participant list

In order to send out products for review, you need to have a list of people you can work with. You could start by reaching out to some actual customers with an invite to test some product in exchange for honest feedback. Legally, you can ask employees, family and friends, but these individuals would have to disclose their material connection to the company and state the item was received at a discount or for free. I'd discourage allowing employees to participate in your program as the conflicting interest may be too high. Friends and family of employees could be a good starting point though, when starting to build your group.

Realize that your group will best reflect the feedback of your actual customers if they are as diverse as your customer base. For this reason, you'll want to specifically build a diverse pool of participants based on geography, demographics and other identifiers that may be specific to your business. For example, maybe you sell car accessories and you want to purposefully diversify your participants by car ownership: those who own their car outright, those making payments and those who lease a vehicle.

When reaching out to potential participants, you'll need two things:

1. *A program overview document:* This outlines expectations of participants and what they can expect from you. Let them know a little about your company, what types of products they could be testing, how much time they will have to complete assignments, and what type of sharing commitments they may have.

2. **An application form:** This, preferably digital, form allows you to collect all information about a potential participant that may be important to know. Here are some things you'll want to collect:

- *Contact info: Name, phone number, email, shipping address*

- *Demographic info: Optional, but helpful when applicable, including age, gender, height, weight, ethnicity.*

- *Product relevant info: Think of participant preferences or circumstances that relate to your business or product that could be helpful to know. This data can help you make more informed assignments that are more likely to end in higher satisfaction.*

When reaching out to potential participants, ensure that your messaging is communicating this as an opportunity to apply, not guaranteed admittance. I've seen participants build entitlement mindsets, so you want to make everything sound like a privilege. They may be selected for admittance rather than reserving a spot. See the difference?

Tracking group participation

As your group starts to grow, you'll need to keep accurate records of participants, their info, their history of items received and current status if they have items assigned/pending/completed. I'd recommend building an excel or google sheet that includes the following:

- *All participant info from the application form*

- *Current status:*

  - *Are they available? (Meaning they have no product right now)*

  - *Are they pending? (Meaning they have a product being tested now)*

  - *Are they overdue? (Meaning their time limit for an assignment is past)*

- **History of assignments:**

  - *An ongoing list of what items they received and where they reviewed. This data could be helpful in the future. For example, let's say you give out 10 units of product A. If that product is launched on a new website next month, you could try contacting the 10 people who previously received the unit for reviews before you give away additional units.*

Making feedback assignments to approved group members

Every time you have a product you'd like to collect reviews for, you'll first reference your tracking list of participants. Highlight the several individuals you'd like to offer the product to. Put one email together with all the details for the assignment, then BCC all participants. Ask them to email you back, confirming they accept the assignment within 24 hours.

Every time you make an assignment, you should reiterate what you expect of them including the time frame for completion, links to the websites you'd like them to share on, delivery time frame, etc.

If you'd like to be on the safe side, each assignment can have a legally binding contract. The contract would in essence say the following:

- *The participant agrees to provide honest feedback in the time frame agreed to on the websites indicated.*

- *The participant agrees to include a FTC-compliant disclosure.*

- *The company agrees to give the unit to the participant free of charge.*

- *If the participant does not complete the requirements, the participant will be required to purchase the item at regular price.*

Contracts of this nature are generally needed only for high ticket products where significant financial burden would be placed on the company in the case of participants' neglect. However, such a document would provide strong evidence of your FTC compliance if your company was investigated for some reason. I've never dealt with that firsthand, but these contracts would be a powerful paper trail showing you've done what is legally required.

Logic for identifying product listings for assignments
A feedback program is not your entire review management strategy. The purpose of the program is to give stability to new launches and boost listings in need of a small lift. Being reliant on a feedback program for the collection of most or all or of your product reviews will be damaging. After all, what would you think of a product that has only reviews with a legal disclaimer? It doesn't look as good as regular reviews from regular customers.

So when would a product listing qualify for a feedback program assignment? There are two kinds of ideal candidates: new launches and products "on the bubble".

> **New launches:** A newly launched product will struggle to sell and rank well in search results until it has a good batch of reviews. Assign 10 to 20 reviews for a brand new listing. This starts to build sales momentum which will help it continue ranking well and selling. You'll then start to get organic reviews from your review request made to regular customers.

> **Existing products "on the bubble":** Over the years, my team adopted this terminology to indicate a listing close to popping up a half star. If you have a listing at 4.2-stars, that rounds down to a displayed 4-star image in search results on many platforms. Assigning a few reviews through your program to get it to a 4.3-star, rounds up (pops up) to a 4 ½ star image in search results.

Before assigning reviews for a product on the bubble, calculate the cost of the investment. You'll need to calculate the raw star average and how many new 5-stars it would take to pop up from a 4.2-star to a 4.3-star. Look at figure 3.8. This is a basic star-rating calculator made in excel.

STAR RATING CALCULATOR	Current RAW Star Rating	
	4.233	Point totals:
# of 5's	37	185
# of 4's	10	40
# of 3's	7	21
# of 2's	2	4
# of 1's	4	4
TOTALS:	60	254

Figure 3.8: A basic star rating calculator built in excel allows you to estimate the number of new reviews needed to round up a rating

Cell B8 is a sum of B3:B7, which is the number of reviews for each rating. Cell C8 is a sum of C3:C7, which is a point total for properly weighing the rating. Cells C3:C7 are calculated by multiplying the number of reviews in the adjacent cell on column B by the star rating indicated in column A. For example, cell C3 is calculated by multiplying 37 5-star reviews by 5. 37 X 5 = 185. 10 4-stars X 4 = 40 points, and so on.

Cell B2 is your calculated raw star rating. Total points / total # of reviews = raw star rating. (C8/B8 = B2). With your star rating calculator now built, you can estimate how many new reviews would be needed to round up to a 4.3-star rating. In the example scenario from figure 3.8, six additional 5-star ratings would put the raw average at 4.303.

You now know it would take six new reviews to get this listing to a 4.3-star rating. If your product costs $30 and shipping is $10, you're looking at an investment of $240 to get this listing bumped up to 4.3-stars. With our knowledge from chapter one, we know that a 4 ½-star product typically sells double what a 4-star product does. Using your sales data, you can calculate how many days it will take you to recoup your investment of $240 dollars. This information helps you make an informed decision if a listing deserves an assignment in your feedback program.

Here's a few additional considerations. Realize that many review platforms now use algorithms to calculate the displayed star rating. It's not always a raw average. Most algorithmic star ratings weigh newer reviews more and other traits more such as the helpfulness of a review and if the review is from a verified purchaser. Amazon was the first to introduce an algorithmic star rating in 2015. This means that your calculations will be estimates. For that reason, I'd always recommend assigning a few more reviews above an exact 4.3-star, in the case of this example.

The rule of 20: Pace and volume considerations

Since the goal of your feedback program is to supplement, not replace, your larger review management strategy, you need to be mindful of how many reviews you assign and how fast they are assigned. For example, would you find it odd if 80 of 100 reviews were all posted on a product within the last two weeks and the remaining 20 stretch back two years? To make it more suspect, those new 80 reviews are all glowing 5-stars with a disclaimer saying the product was given for free. You may end up passing on that product.

To keep things simple, follow the rule of 20:

- *New launches should get no more than 20 reviews.*

- *Existing listings should get no more than 20% of the existing number of reviews.*

- *Reviews should be scheduled at a pace no more than 20% of the organic review rate.*

We already discussed why a new launch needs new reviews, but you don't want to do too many. 20 is a good limit. For an existing listing with exactly 100 reviews, you would not want to assign more than 20 new reviews to supplement the organic reviews. If that same listing with 100 reviews gained five new reviews a week, 20% that rate would be one review assignment per week. You don't want a huge batch of assigned reviews to post to the listing all at once. It is too unnatural.

You may be thinking you need more than 20% quantity to bump the listing to 4.3. Sure, you could assign more than 20% and yes you could assign them faster than 20% of the organic review rate. If a significant number of reviews beyond 20% is required, the listing may be too far gone. From my experience, anything 3.2-stars or lower should be discontinued, improved and relaunched as a new product. Some other listings may simply not be cost effective to bump up due to the large volume of reviews required to affect change.

If you need just a little bit more than 20% volume to get your listing bumped up, use your best judgment on how to proceed. The rule of 20 is a safe space. It will help you avoid some of the negatives I've seen from "swinging too hard" to fix listings. Consumer trust can be lowered with an overwhelming representation of assigned reviews.

Additional tips and tricks for your in-house feedback program

- *Only admit adults 18 or older to your program. This is a legal precaution and will help you get better written reviews.*

- *Right from the first outreach to prospective participants, set the expectation that they will get up to a certain limit of items for review. Also set the expectation that they will have the opportunity to refer others to join the group before "graduating" from the program. Referrals could be rewarded with a bonus feedback assignment, or some other incentive.*

- *Try to maintain a healthy sized group that keeps participants engaged. If you have so many participants that they are waiting for six months for a new assignment, they will likely lose interest and not be helpful to you. On the other side, don't try to get too many assignments done in a condensed time frame from your participants. Giving out assignments every three to six weeks is a good pace to avoid overwhelming participants while keeping their interest. This is obviously flexible based on your unique situation and the responsiveness of your group.*

- When making an assignment, be sure to ask participants to share a review on all product listings for that product across the web. You can also ask participants to share a review of you as a business on company profiles on Google, BBB, Consumer Affairs and many others. Asking for more reviews per assignment lowers the cost per review. Keep in mind the time commitment though, compared to the value of the item you're offering. If you're giving away a $10 product, you will likely have poor luck getting people to sign up for writing 10 reviews. If your product costs $100 or $1,000, it becomes easier to ask more of your participants as part of the assignment.

- If your products are a little more expensive, you could consider making assignments by household and requiring two participating adults complete all reviews. This doubles the number of reviews you collect while still getting unique feedback from all participants.

- Don't require 5-star reviews. It will look inauthentic to shoppers, even more so than the FTC disclaimer. Just accept what comes in. This is a numbers game. Like the law of self-selecting extremes, the more reviews you get, the better your average rating will be.

- Be sure to ask participants to share unique reviews for each location where they are asked to share. Copying and pasting the exact same review across multiple websites is not desirable.

- Only assign one product at a time. This creates some urgency for participants to complete the assignment in order to be eligible for the next opportunity.

- Give participants a reasonable time frame to complete each assignment. Two to four weeks is ideal. You may even consider requiring participants to use the product a certain number of times prior to posting reviews.

- Encourage, but don't require, visual reviews. Reviews with photos and videos are more visible and impactful on product listings. You don't need all of them to be visual reviews, so don't make it a requirement. By simply mentioning that visual reviews are welcome on your assignment, some participants will do them.

- You'll do a lot of communicating with your participants. To increase efficiency, build template resources and email text for the various types of communication you have.

- *Ask participants to provide you with screenshots of the reviews they submit. Sometimes different platforms may delete them or not post them at all. Record the submitted reviews for each participant and assignment after you've personally seen the reviews posted on the respective product listing. This pattern will help you identify if there are struggles getting reviews to post.*

- *Remember to track if participants are including their FTC disclosures of material connection. If they aren't, remind them to do so.*

Section 3.5: Soliciting Employee Reviews
How to get employee reviews for your employer

Product and company reviews impact sales. Employee reviews affect businesses as well.

Employee reviews impact recruiting efficiency:

- *92% of working Americans consider employee reviews to be important when deciding to apply for a job.[7]*

- *57% of job candidates avoid companies with negative employer reviews.[8]*

- *1 in 3 declined job offers in the U.S. are influenced by negative employer reviews.[9]*

Employee reviews impact profitability and operating costs:

- *7.8%–18.9% higher stock market valuations correlate with 1-star improvements in average Glassdoor company ratings.[9]*

- *A 1-star Glassdoor rating increase raises the odds that a typical employee will stay for their next role by 4%. That's 2.7 times the impact of a 10% pay increase.[10]*

- *Having a good culture is 6 times more likely to get candidates to move for a job than a $10,000 pay increase.[11]*

Collecting reviews from employees is a different, but similar, game compared to consumer reviews. You're working with the same audience over and over again. I'm going to break down how to approach the employee review side of things in this order:

- *Where employee reviews are collected*

- *Why collecting employee reviews across multiple locations is important*

- *How to ask employees for a review and at what frequency*

- *How to balance review requests across multiple employer websites*

- *Tips for crafting review request invites*

- *What to do with the reviews after they start coming in*

Where employee reviews are collected

At the time of this book's publication, the below employee review sites were active with the respective traffic estimates:

Employer Review Website	U.S. Alexa Web Traffic Ranking	Monthly Unique Visitors
Indeed	61	97 million
Glassdoor	313	26 million
Niche	4,531	2.7 million
Zippia	6,979	1.8 million
Comparably	7,927	1.2 million
Fairygodboss	23,291	700 thousand
CareerBliss	37,765	400 thousand
InHerSight	63,465	240 thousand

*Data collected from websiteiq.com, 9/25/2021[12]

My personal favorites to focus on include Comparably, Glassdoor, Indeed and InHerSight in that order. Comparably, although smaller, is growing rapidly and has a more employer-friendly methodology to their question set. Glassdoor is the gorilla in the space with the highest brand recognition for employee reviews. Indeed matters because it's a job board with high traffic that adopted employee reviews on the platform. InHerSight is great because you can collect reviews specific to female-friendliness in the workplace.

I have found great success focusing efforts on my four favorite platforms mentioned above. The game could change for you if your company is bigger or smaller. If your employer has 50 employees, you may only want to focus on your top two favorite sites for now. If you're working at a corporation with 10,000 or more employees, perhaps you decide to manage profiles on six of the sites. Commit to fully manage all profiles you open across all four stages of The Review Cycle.

If you happen to have pre-existing profiles on any other sites, you will likely have to embrace their existence and manage them as well. Keep in mind that the employer review landscape, like any industry, can evolve over time. Stay current with where your audience is talking about you and prioritize those online locations.

Why collecting employee reviews across multiple locations is important

The obvious answer to this question is job seekers. After all, they are "shopping" for a new employer. Of course they want to read reviews about working at your company. The principles we discussed about review elasticity impacting sales very directly relates to job seekers and the volume of applications your company receives.

However, job seekers aren't the only stakeholders you should care about. Current employees also look at your employer profile, read reviews from co-workers and make judgments about you as a company. If your reviews are really bad, it could negatively shape employees' perceptions. Increased turnover could be a result, as well as overall negative feelings about where they work.

Alternatively, if your ratings and employer profiles are positive and healthy, this impacts current employees for the better. Perceptions will be improved. Employees will be more proud of where they work and more likely to talk about it positively.

There are other stakeholders that will read your employee reviews as well. Consumers look at them. Someone considering doing business with you may factor how you treat your employees into their consideration. They can't just visit your office and interview your employees, but they can read what your employees have written in anonymous reviews online. Let's hope what they find reinforces the purchase instead of pushing them to your competitor.

Other stakeholders that care about your employee reviews could include financial institutions. Perhaps you're needing an investment, seeking angel funding or preparing to go public. You better believe the financial audience cares about how you treat your employees. Employee satisfaction and engagement are undeniably connected to profitability. That makes your employee reviews a financial consideration.

The general community, charity partners, past employees, and maybe even your mom could be looking at these reviews as well. Realize they are public and important. Do not neglect your employee review profiles.

How to ask employees for a review and at what frequency

Unlike most consumer review sites, employee review sites generally allow repeat reviewing over time. A review of a purchased item is mostly transactional and considered a one-time event. However, your employment experience with a company can evolve through the years.

At the time of this publication, Indeed, Glassdoor and Comparably all permitted repeat reviews from the same users every 12 months. InHerSight permits repeat reviews every three months. I personally feel a review annually is appropriate.

Mechanisms for asking for a review can vary as widely as your communication norms. If you're an email-heavy company, send an email. Are you on Slack or another messaging platform? Send the invites there. Are your employees not at computers all day? Hand out a flier with a QR code to scan that takes them to your profile on the respective website you're pushing. Just search for a free QR code generator online.

Regardless of the delivery method, I highly encourage giving the review request to batches of employees at a time and recording who you sent them to. This is NOT to track who could have posted a negative review. Don't do that. I'll explain in a bit. Keep reading. The reason for tracking who you've asked to review is so you don't ask the same employee twice in the same 12-month period.

Keep your invite records organized by date of invite and you'll be able to solicit a review from the same employees next year. Remember, consumers (and job seekers too) highly value recent reviews, so you need an ongoing flow of them on your profiles.

How to balance review requests across multiple employer websites

Following the same train of thought with your invite tracking, make a spreadsheet that has a column for each of your employer profiles. Make a template review request specific to each of your profiles with the proper links for writing a review. Now when you ask employee "A" to review on site "1" you mark the date. That starts the 12-month waiting period for that employee on that website. You are free to ask him or her to review your company on the other websites right away. When you do, follow the same pattern of marking the date of invite for that website.

If you want to get fancy, you could incorporate some conditional formatting on your spreadsheet so the date-of-invite cell is highlighted when 12 months have passed. You then know you can ask the employee for a review on that site again.

You will have to be the judge of how many invites you want to send out to your employees. Technically, each employee is eligible to review you once a year on all the profiles. It may make sense for your organization to do that if it's really small and you're starving for new reviews on these sites. If you're at a large corporation, dividing your employee count by four and sending 25% to each of your four profiles may be sufficient. No need to have all employees do reviews on all four websites.

Tips for crafting review request invites

However you divide your requests throughout the company, make sure your template request communicates the recurring nature of these invitations. Otherwise, when you go to ask a second time, employees may be annoyed, knowing they previously participated.

You will also want to include a direct team or individual to contact in your template request. This gives employees an additional way to share feedback with you if they would prefer not to write the review. From my experience, this acts as a defense against some negative reviews. Some employees may have a concern that they do not want to publicly shame you for. Rather, they just want to talk about it and have it addressed privately.

Here is an example employee review request template:

Hello [ADD EMPLOYEE NAME]!

Thank you for your contributions at [YOU COMPANY NAME]. Your individual efforts make a measurable impact on the success of the company and the development of our culture.

Today, you are invited to share your thoughts about working at [YOUR COMPANY NAME] on [EMPLOYEE REVIEW SITE]. This can be done once a year. Because things change over time, we want to hear what you have to say on a continued basis. Our HR team notes feedback on this page and shares it internally as applicable.

Note that your feedback is anonymous. If you have things you'd prefer to share confidentially with our employee experience team, email: employee. experience@[YOURCOMPANYNAME].com, or simply respond to this message.

Cheers!

What to do with the reviews after they start coming in

Remember that The Review Cycle applies to employee reviews as well. What you've read in this section is all about one of four elements of owner influence. You can get more reviews by asking. You also want to execute on the three other elements of influence you have on The Review Cycle: respond to reviews, manage expectations and market with reviews. You'll see how those three items come into play as you read the next three chapters.

Chapter 3 Summary

Section 3.1: Foundational Knowledge about Asking for Reviews

Why you should ask for reviews and how to get started

What is the law of self-selecting extremes?

It is a form of representation bias. When you don't ask for reviews, only those with extreme negative and positive experiences will go out of their way to share. In this environment, ratings tend to be more negative. As you ask for more reviews, you lower the barrier to share and typically get much more positive reviews.

What are primary and secondary reviews?

Primary reviews are written on sites where the transaction occurs. They have a higher, more direct impact on sales. Secondary reviews are written on review sites without a transaction tied to it. It is important to diversify your reputation by having a review management strategy that incorporates all reviews for your company and products across the internet.

Section 3.2: Maximizing Your Review Acquisition Efforts

How to get more reviews for your product or service online

What variables should be considered when asking for reviews?

The timing of your request should be after the purchase and after the consumer has experienced the product or service. How the reviewer gets to the submission page is also critically important. Make it easy for people to share with clickable links or QR codes.

How can you improve your review request efforts over time?

Split testing, or A/B testing, is a process where two approaches are measured against each other for effectiveness. The better performing approach then is compared to another idea and so on for continued improvement. This process can apply to your review request strategy.

Section 3.3: Using Paid Review Collection & Display Programs

When and how to collect and syndicate reviews using 3rd party services

What is review syndication?

It is a form of sharing reviews collected on one site with other sites selling the same product. Syndication is a paid service that can be cost effective with economies of scale for getting reviews posted across a large catalogue of products.

What is a vendor feedback program?

Some marketplace sites offer paid services to help you collect reviews from their curated group of product testers. Some 3rd party companies that offer syndication also have feedback programs. These services can be valuable, specifically for companies needing product reviews.

Section 3.4: Running an In-House Feedback Program

When and how to legally run an incentivized feedback program

Can you incentivize reviews legally?

Sometimes. As long as providing incentives in exchange for posted reviews is not against the terms of use of a review platform, then yes, incentivizing reviews is legal. However, the reviews must clearly and conspicuously disclose what incentive was offered to be legally compliant with FTC law.

What components of building an in-house feedback program should be considered?

· *Building a diversified group of participants*

· *Tracking participants and their assignments*

· *Identifying which listings are ideal for inclusion in the program*

· *Ensuring FTC compliant disclosures are included in all reviews*

Section 3.5: Soliciting Employee Reviews
How to get employee reviews for your employer

How do you get employees to share reviews?
Email or chat review requests to employees with clickable links to Comparably, Glassdoor, Indeed, InHerSight and others. Typically, you'll just want to ask for one of these at a time. Keep in mind that employees can submit up to one review per site per year, so ensure your messaging communicates the reoccurring nature of these invites.

RESPONDING TO REVIEWS

Increase purchase intent with showcased customer care and conversation moderation

QUESTIONS TO CONSIDER:

Why should you respond publicly to reviews and other UGC online?

Who is your target audience when responding to public reviews?

What is mirror messaging?

How many reviews should you respond to?

How should you respond to negative claims made in reviews?

What are Q&As and why should you care about them?

How is responding to employee reviews different from responding to customer reviews?

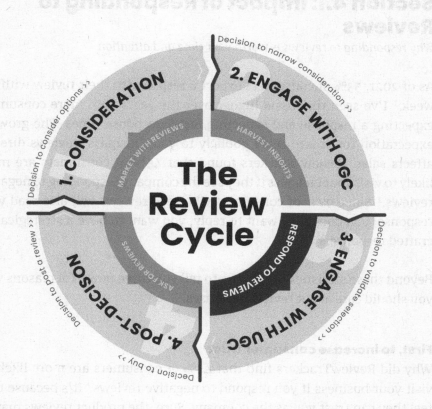

Section 4.1: Impact of Responding to Reviews

Figure 4.1: Responding to reviews is the element of owner influence associated with stage 3 of The Review Cycle: Engage with UGC

Responding to reviews is the element of owner influence associated with stage three of The Review Cycle. By the time a consumer has progressed to reading reviews, they are close to a purchase decision. Your public response can guide the conversation, discredit negative claims, and ultimately increase purchase intent.

Section 4.1: Impact of Responding to Reviews

Why responding to reviews is worth your time and attention

As of 2021, 53% of consumers expect a response to their review within a week.[1] I've seen this trend higher over the years with more consumers expecting a response and expecting faster response times. The growing expectation for you to reply publicly to your business' reviews directly affects sales. Review Trackers found that 45% of consumers are more likely to visit your business if they see the company responding to negative reviews.[1] Since 97% of consumers who read reviews will also read your response, you don't just want to reply, you want to have a strategically-crafted response.[2]

Beyond these statistics, I'm going to tell you three powerful reasons why you should care about review responses.

First, to increase consumer trust

Why did ReviewTrackers find that 45% of consumers are more likely to visit your business if you respond to negative reviews? It's because they feel they can trust you as the company. Sure, the product reviews may be great, but what if they happen to get a lemon unit? Your response increases their confidence that your company will make it right.

The screen shot in figure 4.2 shows a 1-star product review, a response from the company, and a response from another shopper. The product was horrible, but the company was right there offering support in a response. Another shopper then states: "The response to this review is what was helpful for me. The company seems very willing to back up their product, which gives me purchasing confidence. There have been multiple examples of this throughout the reviews."

Although you shouldn't expect to see a bunch of comments on your reviews like this, most consumers will share similar feelings about your care for customers. Consistency is key to unlock this primary benefit for your response program. Just like one parental teaching-moment is not likely to change your son or daughter's life, one review response won't give consumers sufficient trust. It's the consistent support that affects the greatest change over time.

Consumers are evaluating the most recent reviews more often and trusting them more than older reviews. For this reason, the timeliness of your responses also matters. Daily checking and responding to your reviews are the best practice.

Figure 4.2: A company response to a 1-star review.
Another shopper also comments on the review
stating they want to buy because of the company's
consistent care, demonstrated in review responses[3]

Second, to control the narrative

As you'll read in section 4.3, failing to respond to a negative review can be interpreted as passively agreeing with a negative claim. Directly confronting issues brought up in reviews can be your saving grace in response to an unfair consumer judgment.

Granted, publicly calling someone out for lying may end up damaging your reputation, even if it is true. There is an art to setting the record straight with the use of passive voice and other techniques you will read about in this chapter. When done correctly, you can come out of the courtroom cleared of all charges and in good standing with the media.

Third, to increase your ratings

Responding to reviews strategically and consistently improves your star ratings directly in two ways:

Avoid future negative experiences:
By providing helpful information in review responses, you better inform a product-to-consumer fit. This could be information that helps a customer know to order this model instead of that one. It could also be managing expectations of what a product does and does not do so consumers avoid unrealistic expectations that could end in a bad review.

Active customer support and review update requests:
As you include a customer contact in your responses, some customers will reach out to you directly for support. After dazzling your customer with kind and thorough support, you've earned the right to ask for something in return. Asking for an updated review that reflects their entire experience is likely to end in a more positive rating some of the time. This gives your listing or profile a boost.

As we move to tactical information on how to write the best responses, consider the following:

No single perfect response exists. I've personally written nearly 2,000 pages of review responses over the years. It took a lot of time and trial and error to develop and master the public response principles you'll read about in this chapter. Even still, I don't believe there is a single perfect response waiting to be uncovered for each review. There are a lot of ways to do it right and a lot of ways to do it wrong. Gain an understanding of the principles you're about to read, then practice, practice, practice. Take the time to get the right info needed for your best response. Ask colleagues for feedback when needed. Keep writing and stay motivated. You'll get better with time.

The strategies shared here also apply to public responses on the internet in general. If you are responding to a social media comment, a blog comment, or video comment, it is fundamentally the same as responding publicly to a review. The only difference is a review has a star rating associated with the comment.

Section 4.2: General Mechanics of Strategic Review Responses

Learn the fundamentals of crafting powerful public responses

Have a showcase mindset

When responding to reviews, who is your target audience? I'll give you a hint. It's not the person that posted the review. It is everyone else. The person that posted the review already went through every step of The Review Cycle. All the other people looking at your reviews have yet to confirm their purchase decision. You want to influence them. Here is the classic example story I use to teach this principle. It's quirky and hopefully memorable.

> *You're on the set of your favorite late night show. You're in one chair and your reviewer: "Purple_Fairy_Fart" is in the other. (Yes, I've actually seen that reviewer's pen name.) The studio is packed with a live audience of several thousand watching the broadcast, which is super emotional by the way. Purple_Fairy_Fart is telling the audience about the dramatic experience they had with your whale-shaped tea strainer.*

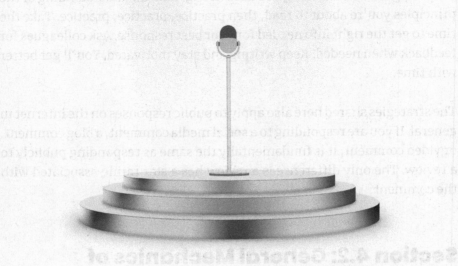

Figure 4.3: You and your reviewer are on stage,
having a public conversation with the whole internet
watching[4]

"His perforated tail is supposed to gingerly hang down from the side of my mug in the boiling water as the tea diffuses", she says, "but the whale fell into the mug. His fins are just too small and dainty. It just felt like he was drowning as he bobbed in the middle of my mug! I was sad."

"There, there." You reply. "Everything is going to be alright. Everyone slips once in a while, but with a good friend like you, the little guy is going to be ok. Just use your favorite eating utensil, and lovingly scoop him out of the cup. Resituate him on the side of the mug, but make sure both of his little fins are tightly grasping the mug. Everything should then be set to a "tea". If we can do anything else for you Purple_Fairy_Fart, anything at all, we are here for you. Just call."

The audience stands and applauds. Oddly enough, Purple_Fairy_Fart says absolutely nothing and just walks off the stage. Later that night, you see the re-run of the episode on TV along with millions of viewers. It's just as ridiculous as the live broadcast.

So, what do we learn from this touching TV interview? This story illustrates what is happening as you respond to reviews. You're engaging in a one-on-one dialogue with the reviewer, only you're not alone. The entire internet is watching.

Over the years I've personally led teams responsible for review management of over 3,000 unique product listings across 50 different ecommerce websites. I've seen single product listings get as many as 60,000 page views per day. Yes, you better believe that your message should be tailored to the 60,000 daily viewers you stand to influence more so than the single reviewer.

That doesn't mean you shouldn't care about the single customer that posted the review. It means you should have a showcase mindset. The way you interact with the one reviewer is visible to and judged by everyone else online. How well you respond can set potential customers at ease and give them purchasing confidence or alienate and dissuade them from buying.

Let's consider Purple_Fairy_Fart. As the single reviewer you were responding to, she didn't reply to your most sympathetic and strategic review response! Does that happen often? Yes. Is it a problem? Not necessarily.

Depending on the platform, not a lot of reviewers are alerted after their review has received a response. Some platforms only permit a single reply from the company and no one else. Although public reply rates from reviewers will vary by platform, there is no need to hope for a reply in most cases. Your public reply is the showcased service needed to positively influence customers.

Customize every message

In the world of responding to public UGC, never copy and paste responses. Just don't. Let's think about this for a sec. What does a copied and pasted response showcase to your target audience? The same "We're sorry, contact us here" message could leave your audience feeling like customers are just numbers to you.

Your responses to reviews or any UGC on the internet are publicly viewable responses. Future customers can scroll through the reviews and see how you've responded to others. You don't want them thinking your responses are automated, copied and pasted, or written by someone who doesn't care.

The caliber of your response showcases the level of service future customers can expect to receive if needed. You are setting expectations. For this reason, you must customize every single review response with a personal message. Even if you're responding to two reviews complaining about the exact same thing, you can change the wording choice to essentially deliver the same message in a personalized way. In one response you may say: "We're sorry for the inconvenience...". In the next review you may start with: "Your patience is appreciated as we work through this delay..." Doing so sends the subtle message that every customer matters individually and uniquely.

Address individuals by name

Dale Carnegie, an American business writer and lecturer wisely said, "A person's name is to him or her the sweetest and most important sound in any language." This principle applies to public review responses. Always start your response with the reviewer's name. Oftentimes, platforms only list a pen name. In those cases, use the pen name. This small action helps customize and personalize each response you write.

Where reviews, Q&As or other UGC has no username associated with it, this obviously won't apply. The good news is, in these cases you are not at a disadvantage. If all content you are replying to is nameless, there is no expectation of you using a name.

Take the discussion off stage

Remember that you're in public-showcasing mode when responding to reviews. Your target audience doesn't need to see the entire path to resolution for each customer complaint, nor do they want to. They are simply referencing reviews to validate a purchase decision. They want to see that you responded in a kind way and took care of the customer. That's it.

A critical function of review responses is to drive the individual discussion with the reviewer to a private communication channel. Once there, you can directly discuss the specific situation with that customer "behind the curtains" instead of on stage in your public conversation.

On some platforms, reviewers can publicly reply in a comment thread below the original review. In this environment, if a reviewer responds to your reply, use your best judgment on the need for a second response. I always avoid back-and-forth conversations and limit threaded replies to two total responses. The second response can openly set the expectation that you will not be responding with something like this: "Thanks for your reply. [Address specific needs mentioned.] Although we won't be replying again here, we're happy to continue the conversation by email or direct message. We look forward to helping you."

Reference the same contact

Consistency is key in your review responses. If each personalized reply listed a different email address or contact method, this dilutes the perceived strength and consistency of your customer service processes. Alternatively, responding with the same contact method in every customized review reply sends the subtle message of consistency. It confirms to customers that you have a well-defined process for helping customers they can trust if something goes wrong.

When you're writing your response and an invitation to take the discussion off platform is needed, use the same contact method each time. This could be a dedicated email address or phone number. It could also be an instruction to the reviewer to DM you on a specific social media platform. Just be consistent. Depending on the size and complexity of your business you may find it helpful to have different contact methods per platform (like direct messages for social media and an email address for ecommerce sites) or a singular contact method that is referenced across all platforms. Evaluate your needs with consistency in mind.

Standardize introduction and signature

In my time managing reviews, I've had as many as six team members on a team. Although you always want showcased consistency in your review responses, having an agreed upon format for your intro and signature becomes increasingly important when you have multiple team members writing public review responses. After all, your target audience knows you as one company, not six team members. It's your job to showcase a consistent brand voice in your public replies, regardless of how many team members are sharing the workload. Here are a couple examples of standardized introductions and signatures you could adopt. Ensure your formatting is on brand for your business.

> **Example #1:**
> *[Reviewer pen name], custom text responding to the review.*
>
> *Custom text responding to the review. Concluding invitation to contact the company.*
>
> *Thanks! – [Company name]*
>
> **Example #2:**
> *Hello [Reviewer pen name]!*
>
> *Custom text responding to the review.*
>
> *Concluding invitation to contact the company.*
>
> *[Company slogan]*
> *[Company name]*

Respond in 24 hours or less

Responding to reviews is not live-chat. There isn't a need to reply within minutes or hours. However, it is not snail mail either. A best practice approach is to clear out all reviews needing a reply once daily. Responding on weekends may be justified depending on the size of your business and the volume of reviews you tend to receive.

If you're wondering how to measure the size of your response workload, time how many responses you can do in an hour to get an average response time per-review. Then quantify how many reviews you get each day. Take that figure and multiply it by your average response time. You'll be left with the amount of time needed to be committed to your responses each day. Make sure to have enough team members contributing to your responses to appropriately maintain a 24-hour response standard.

Mirror messaging

In section 1.3 about Review DNA, there are several reasons why consumers write reviews, including expressing one's opinion and giving feedback. An effective review response will not just be well-structured; it will validate the reviewer's feelings and claims. One of the most effective ways to validate what a reviewer has said is to use what I call mirror messaging. The terminology is reflective of the principle. Pun intended.

By mirroring, aka reusing, some of the specific words, phrases or sentiments the reviewer has said in your response, you are showcasing good listening skills and a higher degree of care for the reviewer. This helps your target audience know that a competent human is on the other side reading and responding to reviews. No one likes to think it's just a bot or someone who doesn't care. Notice the matching color-coded highlights in the following example.

> *Review quote: (1-star) July 17th*
> "*...I hate this shirt. **The small size is too loose** and <u>the color is darker than it shows</u> in the picture...*"

Company response quote using mirror messaging: July 17th
*"...We apologize that **the small size is too loose** for you. <u>The colors may vary</u> only slightly in real life compared to what you see on the listing. This is due to the difference in screen color calibrations of various devices.*

*If **it's too dark** and <u>too loose</u> for your preference, we're happy to help you with a hassle-free return or exchange..."*

In this example, we see two types of mirror messaging. The first is the exact use of a word or phrase. In this example the phrase: "the small size is too loose" was exactly copied in the company's response. Copying an exact phrase in appropriate context showcases understanding of what has been said. Just be careful not to repeat entire sentences as that could be viewed as a lack of care and thought.

The second example of mirror messaging is referencing. In this example, the reviewer's phrase: "the color is darker than it shows," is not referenced with the mirrored mention: "The colors may vary". Mirroring by reference effectively shows understanding by application and good listening skills.

Passive and active voice

When a reviewer complains about a problem and you can see they are the cause, don't tell them they are at fault. It sounds unfair to you, but remember, you're performing on stage. Your target audience is very big compared to a single reviewer and they're watching how you react. You care more about impressing your audience than getting walked on by one bad actor.

You actually want to protect the negative reviewer from any form of public blame and avoid anything that could be viewed as aggressive or attacking. Your voice should be one of fact, not emotion. By taking this approach, your target audience will see that even with intense negative opposition, you have a level head and a kind demeanor. Using passive voice for mirroring negative mentions can accomplish this for you.

Dictionary.com explains passive voice as follows:

A verb is in the passive voice when the subject of the sentence is acted on by the verb. For example, in "The ball was thrown by the pitcher," the ball (the subject) receives the action of the verb, and was thrown is in the passive voice.[5]

Let's evaluate the use of passive voice in an example. You work for a camera manufacturer. A customer just posted a 1-star review of your camera saying it is low quality. The review says the camera was left in the car over a weekend and now it won't turn on. On your product listing and in the user's manual, it is clearly stated that the camera should not be exposed to temperatures above 100 degrees for more than a couple hours at a time. The camera was undoubtedly broken by the customer's neglect. Here are three ways you could respond to the situation:

Bad: *"You left your camera in the hot car all weekend and you melted your camera."*

Better: *"Leaving your camera in the hot car caused it to melt."*

Best: *"The camera may have been damaged due to prolonged exposure of excessive heat."*

Notice the use of the words: "You" and "your" in the bad example. When those words are connected to the problem, you are casting blame with an active voice. This is not a good thing for your target audience to see. In the best example above, notice how the camera is being acted upon. In a very passive way, you are mirroring a complaint about the camera melting, but stating what happened to the product, not what the user did to cause it. By using passive voice in reference to negative mentions in reviews, you maintain a more unbiased stance.

Taking this principle a step further, the best example uses the conditional phrase "may have been damaged" to indicate a lack of absolute outcome. This makes it clear that you are not blaming the reviewer for the damaged camera.

You can still explain that what happened to the camera is outside of the terms of the warranty. You don't have to guarantee a free replacement.

In many cases, a free replacement will buy you enough goodwill to sell many more cameras, but when that's not an option, you still want to offer something. In a case like this, it could be as simple as offering a discount on another unit. We'll learn more about negative review response strategies in section 4.3.

Active voice can be leveraged in an equally powerful, but opposite way. Dictionary.com defines *active voice* as follows:

> When the verb of a sentence is in the active voice, the subject is doing the acting, as in the sentence "Kevin hit the ball." Kevin (the subject of the sentence) acts in relation to the ball.[6]

When something positive is mentioned, you want to tie that mention to your business. You want to take ownership of the happy experience someone had or own a solution when it was provided. In the camera scenario described previously, here are some examples of how you could share information about a solution with the reviewer:

Bad: *"Your camera may have been defective. Call the retailer for assistance."*

Better: *"Your camera may be defective; you can email us for help."*

Best: *"We will address your concern and find an acceptable solution for you. Email us at: [Add email address]."*

In the bad example, no ownership is taken by the company. The better example is still offering help, but unwisely focuses on what the customer needs to do. The best example is very active and supportive. The company is claiming ownership of the solution. The target audience gains greater confidence and trust in you by seeing your showcased care for the customer. This leads to greater sales.

Plural vs singular voice

I've seen some businesses empower their team members to use singular voices in review responses. While it may seem more personal to receive a response signed from an individual team member, customers can gain a misplaced loyalty to the individual responding instead of the company.

Consider a couple scenarios. What happens when you have multiple team members responding to reviews by name and one of them is more proficient and generous than the others? In this case, customers develop a sense of comparison between the team members. One will always be better than the other. If the customer isn't able to work with the individual they perceive as being better, it is more likely the customer will be dissatisfied.

Here's another scenario. Let's say you have a rock star team member who handles your reviews. They sign each response with their name. One day they retire or get a different job. The new replacement team member starts signing review responses with their own name. You've now created a time comparison. Customers who received responses by the first team member are perceived as comparatively better or worse than the replacement.

In either of these situations, your target audience gives at least a measure of credit to the team member responding. The brand loses that measure of social good will. To concentrate all social good will on the brand, always use first person plural voice in review responses as follows:

Subject Pronoun	Object Pronoun	Possessive Pronoun	Possessive Adjective
we	us	ours	our

Using first person plural voice also provides consistency of brand voice across all UGC responses when multiple team members are tasked with responding publicly.

Once you've had a customer contact you directly via email, chat, DM or another private channel, your voice can then shift to first person singular. At that point, you are communicating with your customer "behind the curtain". It becomes advantageous here to increase the perceived level of personal attention by writing in first person singular voice and signing your name. Additionally, customer "A" doesn't know what you've said to customer "B". In this environment, using well-thought-out standardized templates for certain situations can increase speed and efficiency in helping customers. Use first person singular voice in private customer messages and templates as follows:

Subject Pronoun	Object Pronoun	Possessive Pronoun	Possessive Adjective
I	me	mine	my

Skimmable formatting

Understanding where the eyes of your target audience will go when reading your responses can help you optimize the structure of your reply. Think of word placement like search rankings. When you search for something on Google, you're most likely to click the top result. The second result has the second-most likelihood of being clicked on and so forth.

With your review responses, the first word in each sentence and the first sentence in each paragraph are most likely to be read. Many times, your full response will not be read. You can maximize the chance customers read key components of your reply by the way you format it. You also want your response to thoroughly address the review in appropriate detail.

You can accomplish both needs for the skimmer and the in-depth reader using strategic skimmable formatting in your responses.

Use mini paragraphs of no more than a few lines to separate and bring increased focus to each new thought or topic in your reply. Here's an example:

Review quote from Jessica James: (2-stars) April 20th
Although I've heard good things about this hair salon, my experience was not great. I just left the salon and am now running late for work. Their wait times are too long, and I even had a scheduled appointment. The pricing was more than I usually pay too. In the end, the haircut was still pretty good.

Company response: April 21st
Jessica, we're so glad you've heard good things about our salon and liked your haircut in the end. Because we care about our customers' feedback, we'd like to address your concerns:

Looking back at our work schedule, we were understaffed that day. One of our stylists had an unexpected emergency. We apologize for the consequent delay you experienced.

Although our pricing is a bit above average, so is our service. Every service is completed with a warm towel facial resting session, and only the highest quality products are used in our patrons' hair.

We hope you'll let us demonstrate our commitment to your satisfaction with a free service. Contact us at: WeCare@MyAwesomeHairdo.com to schedule your next appointment on the house.

Keep it real! ~My Awesome Hairdo

If the first sentence in each response is all you read, you'd get the point made by the company. For many consumers, that is all they need to have purchasing confidence. They just want to know you took care of the situation. For others, they'll want to read the whole reply before deciding to buy or not. They want to know how you took care of the situation. Either way, being aware of your response structure and making it easy to read will benefit you. Notice the mirror messaging in this example as well.

Writing your responses from the same file

Although you could write your review response directly in the text box below a review, this is not recommended. Rather, write your response in a Word or Google doc first. After it is written and you're feeling good with it, copy and paste your response into the submission text box and post. I'd recommend keeping one single Word or Google file for all your responses and working from the same document each time you are replying to reviews.

There are three specific benefits to doing this:

· *Preventing unintended typos and errors*

> · *Some review platforms do not let you edit your response once it has been posted. An accidental submission of a half-completed response will reflect negatively on your company. Additionally, using a Word or Google doc gives you spelling and grammar checks to help ensure a higher quality response.*

- *Training and collaboration on response quality*

  - *Working from your own personal response document on Word or Google docs online allows you to share your document live with a team member or manager. You are then able to work together on a response until all collaborators are ready to post. Granted, you likely don't need to do this often, but for a new team member in training or responding to an abnormally sensitive review, this can be valuable.*

- *Searchability of past responses*

  - *There are several times you may want to search your review response document. If you find yourself responding to a review that is similar to one you've done in the past, you can search for a key word or phrase to see how you previously responded. If you have a team of people responding to reviews and you happen to find a poorly written response posted, you can search individual team members' review documents to see who wrote it. This can be used for constructive training purposes.*

The 3QPD rule

In 2016, two Cornell University researchers, Chris K. Anderson and Saram Han performed a study of the revenue impact of review response rates on TripAdvisor. Using statistically significant data with millions of reviews, they found that businesses responding to their reviews had a positive and direct impact on the number of bookings, but only up to a certain point.

Assuming a hotel on TripAdvisor responded to none of their reviews, their revenue factor was set at a baseline of one. From there, responding to reviews had a direct and almost linear impact on the number of hotel bookings. Interestingly, as the percentage of reviews responded to reached about 40%, the impact on the number of bookings levels off at just over a 100% increase. Yes, that's right. Businesses were able to double their revenue by responding to 40% of their reviews.

What is most interesting is how responding to more than 40% of reviews was not desirable. In the study, these Cornell researchers found that the number of bookings decreased as businesses responded to more than 40%

of their reviews on TripAdvisor. By the time a business had responded to 80% of their reviews, they had undone all the positives and sunk back down to the baseline revenue factor of one. Responding to more than 80% of reviews actually damaged revenues below the starting point, causing a loss of sales of about 50% when responding to 100% of reviews. See figure 4.4, which illustrates the sales impact of review response frequency.

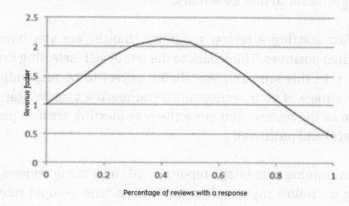

Net revenue effects of responding to reviews on TripAdvisor

Figure 4.4: The impact of review response frequency on sales is graphed. 40% is the optimal amount of reviews to respond to

This study confirms with a high degree of confidence that responding to reviews is good for your business. It confirms you want to respond to up to 40% of your reviews and you do not want to respond to all of them. However, the study did not come to a conclusive answer as to why responding to more than 40% of your reviews was a bad thing. Having personally responded to thousands of reviews across the internet, here's my personal explanation. Reviews are similar to social media. In both places, users create and post UGC. You could say these online locations are like the "public square of the internet" where users interact with each other.[7]

Responding to too many reviews feels invasive, controlling and overbearing to the community. In return, this causes loss of trust and feelings of annoyance and irritation among consumers whom you hope to influence.

Having managed online reviews for several years before finding this Cornell study, I was very pleased to see it lined up nicely with what I had trained my team to do. Essentially, we responded to all 3-star and lower reviews, all reviews with questions in them, and a few positives. The product catalog we managed at the time had over 200,000 reviews with an average rating of 4.32 stars. With my rule of thumb in place, we were responding to approximately 32% of our reviews. For my team, the takeaway from this study was the need to respond to a few more positive reviews to get closer to that 40% mark.

If you're just starting a review program, chances are you have more negatives than positives. Think back to the law of self-selecting extremes in chapter 3. In this scenario, you should expect to be responding to a higher percentage of your reviews until you reach a healthy star-rating equilibrium as the reviews you are actively requesting are also posted to your listing(s) and profile(s).

Rather than running percentage reports to see how many reviews you're responding to, follow my simple rule. Read as "the 3-cupid rule", this principle I've developed will help you easily know which reviews to respond to, and which to leave alone.

The 3QPD Rule (Pronounced "3 cupid")

- *Respond to ALL*   3-star or lower reviews

- *Respond to ALL*   Questions in reviews, regardless of star rating

- *Respond to SOME* Positives

  Dispersed throughout your reviews

In the Cornell study, Anderson and Han also confirmed that consumers appreciated constructive responses to negative reviews more than responses to positives. You want to fully showcase your high level of customer care in every response to negative reviews, which would be 3-stars or lower.

Any review with a question embedded in the text, regardless of star rating, needs a response. In this situation, consider yourself the moderator of a conversation. You want to provide the most helpful context and information so when your target audience reads both the review and the response, they come away feeling more positive and informed. Reviews with questions are softball tosses you should easily hit. Give the most helpful answer possible to showcase your high level of customer care.

Lastly, you want to respond to some positive reviews, not just the bad ones. This can help increase trust and purchase intent by showcasing your care for happy customers in addition to those with questions or concerns. In section 4.3 we'll discuss more specifics for responding to question-based reviews and positive reviews.

Make a review playbook

Establishing a playbook, or singular source of knowledge for a product, service or process, is critical to lasting performance.

A review response playbook can give you many benefits including:

- *A unified brand voice and customer message*
  - *With documented info, team members are less likely to post conflicting info.*
- *The ability to onboard new hired faster and with greater proficiency*
  - *You are not dependent on another team member remembering everything.*
- *Independence from turn-over knowledge loss*
  - *As someone leaves the team, you retain best practice knowledge.*
- *Enhanced and refined performance*
  - *Habitually updating and adding to a playbook informs future responses with greater precision.*

Your playbook should be a living document that is continuously updated and added to. As your entire team contributes to your review playbook, the entire team gets better collectively. New learning points are documented to help retain knowledge for the team. Just remember that this is not a list of responses to copy and paste. Every public response you post should be customized, but a well-built playbook can inform more strategically crafted responses.

Here's everything I'd recommend including in your custom review playbook:

1. A note from you regarding the importance of review responses for the company

2. File information for the document, including ownership and social norms and team member expectations for keeping it up to date

3. On-brand approved review intros and signatures

4. Login and password info for company profiles used to respond to reviews

5. List of recurring themes you start to observe in reviews and helpful information on how to respond to them. Include examples of stellar replies for bonus points

6. If your playbook also covers how to address private messages, you could list the most helpful templates to be used. (Remember, templates are ok to use in "behind-the-curtain" messages over email, direct message or chat.)

7. Links to helpful resources and/or lists of helpful contacts within your organization and contact at partner companies

8. Anything else specific that you feel is applicable such as product/service knowledge

Review hall of fame

If you're going to commit to responding to your reviews, you may as well make it fun. Take time to record the funny ones you come across. They will come up. With the help of my team, in my first two years of managing reviews I was able to build a 70-page review hall of fame document. Funny reviews were often shared with co-workers and in company meetings for a good laugh. You can organize your hall of fame any way you like. This is just a good way to make a sometimes-repetitive task more fun and exciting.

Section 4.3: Responding to Negative, Positive and Inquisitive Reviews

Take your public response strategy up a notch with these advanced techniques

In addition to leveraging all messaging strategies in section 4.2, these tips will help you fine-tune your public responses in a variety of situations from negative to positive and everything in between.

Responding to Negative Reviews

Oh negative reviews. They cause such stress and panic. In fact, negative reviews have given rise to scam artists who prey on business owners desperate for them to go away. Not that I'm proud of it, but in my early days managing reviews I fell for one of these scams and lost $2,000. That's a story for another day though. Just do not believe anyone that tells you they can make your negative reviews disappear.

Beyond that, don't fall into the mindset that negative reviews will ruin you. Some negatives are actually good. They give a measure of authenticity to your ratings that increase consumer trust.

In the rare case that you suspect damaging review fraud or manipulation on your listing, report it to the platform, whether it be Amazon, Google, or elsewhere. A known strategy is called review brigading. Do you remember the Reddit-fueled GameStop story of January 2021? Reddit users on the subreddit r/wallstreetbets coordinated a group effort to buy GameStop (GME) and sent the price soaring over 1,700% in a matter of days.

The same thing can be done with reviews, and it does happen. I've personally seen this. I was donating time consulting my local police department when a famous YouTuber came and live streamed confrontational conversations with the officers. Not only did this individual coordinate a live jamming of the entire department's phone lines by telling his live audience to all "call them and protect him", but many followers began leaving an unprecedented amount of negative reviews on Google and Facebook.

Days later, I made a detailed case to the Google My Business support team. I listed all the negative reviews that were poured on the profile in a compressed amount of time. As an example, I listed screen shots and links to 17 profiles that had collectively written 216 negative reviews of police stations across the country. Google acknowledged this coordinated behavior broke their terms of service and removed the reviews.

The likelihood that something so extreme happens to you may be low. The likelihood that you will get negative reviews is guaranteed. The following strategies have proven exceptionally effective in review responses to minimize the negative impact of negative reviews and increase purchase intent.

Mirror feelings, not "facts"

In chapter 1 we talked about the principle "perception is reality". Sometimes negative reviews embellish the truth. What if you need to mirror the message of a review, but you can't agree with the intensity of the claims made? The answer is mirroring feelings, not claimed "facts".

How do you do this? It's as simple as shifting focus from the claim to the word "feel". If the review says: "Horrible store! Their curbside delivery times are way too slow!" Instead of saying: "We're sorry our curbside delivery is slow," say this: "We're sorry you feel the curbside delivery was too slow." In situations like this, you could also use phrases like: "didn't meet your expectations" or "wasn't what you expected".

Why mirror a negative review this way? Because in truth, they do feel the delivery was too slow but it's unfair to say it is objectively slow when no socially-accepted delivery time labels exist. The next customer could get their items even slower and give you a positive review for fast service. Many negative claims are perception based like this one.

On a similar note, don't ever use the words: "We apologize..." when mirroring a perception-based complaint. After all, you aren't the source of the negative claim. The perception of the reviewer influenced this claim. Instead, say: "We're sorry...[followed by a mirroring of feelings]." You can genuinely be sorry that a reviewer isn't satisfied but apologizing for a perceived issue is being a pushover and taking it too far.

Selective inclusion of negative & positive words

The selective inclusion of negative and positive words is an advanced form of mirror messaging. Mirroring a message validates emotions and confirms understanding; however, it benefits you to filter the intensity of sentiment you reflect back to your target audience.

If someone tells you they had "the most awful experience" at your store, why on earth would you regurgitate the same intensity of feeling? You can showcase you've heard them while subconsciously deescalating the situation in a mirrored reply: "We're sorry for the experience" you've had. On the flip side, if someone is communicating to you that something went well, insert ownership over that positive thing and magnify the undertone of your response. Consider this example:

Review from Billy_Bison: (1-star) July 19th
I had the <u>most terrible experience</u> with FabPhones. <u>I waited on hold for an absurd amount of time. It had to have been like two hours.</u> Sure, *the lady that answered the phone was nice and took care of my question,* but <u>no one should have to wait that long on hold.</u>

Company Response: July 20th
Billy_Bison, we're sorry <u>the experience</u> you had while *receiving support from us* didn't meet your expectations. We are glad to hear *our team member who assisted you was nice and was able to fully resolve your question.*

Your <u>feedback about wait times</u> has been noted and is appreciated. Such <u>wait times</u> are not typical and certainly not what we aspire to. We care about your experience and are happy to address any additional questions you may have. Email us at:_____

Thanks! FabPhones

Notice the underlined text in the company response mirroring the negative underlined text from the review. The company mirrored the negative mentions but minimized the intensity by removing unnecessarily negative descriptive words. Likewise, the bolded text represent the mirroring of positive mentions. The company expanded and highlighted the good mentions made by the reviewer and emphasized the positive nature of the service provided.

The response is truthful, authentic, and empathetic. It is also strategic and favors the interests of the company. Artfully apply the selective inclusion of negative and positive words in a similar way you'd use passive and active voice. Minimize the negative and magnify the positive.

Discrediting negative claims

I once interviewed someone for my team who had direct experience managing online reviews. This somewhat rare work history intrigued me. I asked for details about this person's experience. They managed all Google reviews for a local dentist office. The topic of negative reviews came up and I asked if this person had responded to them and what their approach was like.

They went on to tell me a story. One time someone gave the dentist's office a 1-star review. This person clearly had a bad experience and was incredibly intense in their comments. It appeared it was the worst possible experience you could have at a dentist's office. The review mentioned many things, including the dentist acting so angry that he threw something across the room.

With my interest peaked, I asked the candidate how they responded to the scathing review. Their response went something like this: "Oh, we're so sorry for what happened! Don't worry, we'll take care of you. Call us and we'll get you free teeth whitening treatments and make sure you're completely satisfied!"

Now put yourself in the shoes of the target audience reading the review. If you read that response, would you think the dentist actually threw something across the room? Based on the overly apologetic tone of the response, many would say yes.

I went on to ask my interviewee: "So, did the dentist actually throw something across the room?" Their response? "No, he did not. He's a nice guy and wanted to make the customer happy."

What went wrong here? By not confronting the blatant lie, the company response passively agreed with the reviewer. What is the impact of this critical error? The target audience then believes that the dentist did indeed throw something across the room, when it never actually happened. This would undoubtedly cause lost sales.

How should the company have responded to this negative review? Something like this would work:

[Reviewer Pen Name]

We're sorry the experience you had didn't live up to your expectations.

After receiving this review, an investigation was made regarding the claim of something being thrown by Dr. Toothbert. Several individuals who were present at the mentioned time of your appointment were interviewed and we can now confirm that nothing was thrown across the room.

With this said, we want to fully address any remaining concerns or questions you may have. Please email us at:_____ and we will be happy to find a resolution for you.

Thanks! –Happy Tooth Dentistry

As the company representative responding publicly to reviews or social media comments, you have an obligation to set the record straight. You are a moderator of sorts. You must directly challenge any obvious misinformation, lie, or degrading claims in a truthful and respectful tone. Beyond directly challenging misinformation, another approach you can take is to draw attention to missing information. If a product requires assembly, ask if the assembly instructions were properly followed before fully agreeing that the unit is defective. If a product was damaged, first state that the item can be damaged if the care instructions are not properly followed. If someone claims they waited over an hour to be seated at your restaurant, ask if their party was over eight people. Let them know large parties in peak hours can be slower to seat, but that a reservation will address this issue next time. Control the narrative by adding more context and detail that will help the target audience have the most favorable interpretation of the situation.

This is discrediting negative claims and it is one of the most important techniques for public response strategy. Effectively discrediting negative claims casts a cloud of doubt over the review. Your target audience will likely not believe the reviewer's sensational claims after reading your informed and courteous response.

Promise the moon

The idiom "promise the moon" is generally believed to express a promise made that is unlikely or impossible to be fulfilled. In the world of reviews, this idiom becomes a mathematically significant business principle.

One of the many product categories I managed over the years was mattress protectors. A mattress protector is a thin waterproof covering that is placed directly on a mattress under a fitted sheet. There are all sorts of protectors, but most of them have one thing in common. They are sensitive to heat. If air-dried at high temperatures in the wash, the waterproof backing will melt and become useless. Of the tens of thousands of reviews we received over the years, this was the number one complaint.

We knew this was an issue that impacted not just our mattress protectors, but nearly all mattress protectors sold at the time. As you'll read in chapter 5, we used this harvested information to manage expectations. The listing and packaging both had care instructions provided and complaint rates decreased. Still, some customers would ruin their protector in the dryer. After all, we couldn't account for the variance in temperature settings of dryers being used.

So, we deployed another strategy. We promised the moon. Or more specifically, we openly promised a full refund or a replacement unit in our review responses. You may say this is a bold move. After all, what if people see your response and contact you for a replacement when they don't actually deserve one. Fair point, but let's look at a simplified equation of how this played out.

Let's say our mattress protectors were priced at $30 each and we sold 100 per day. That's 36,500 protectors sold per year and $1,095,000 gross income. An average review rate of 2% for 36,500 units sold means we would have collected 730 reviews in a year. If one out of five reviews were negative, we would have offered free replacements 146 times in negative review responses.

Let's stop there for a minute. 146 negative reviews X $30 = $4,380 refunded. That's 0.4% of your gross income. Would you be willing to pay 0.4% of your gross income to earn the perception of exceptional generosity? Think of it. Everyone who claims a bad experience publicly in your reviews could be taken care of. Every one of your review responses with a promised refund becomes a little billboard advertising- "We'll take care of you no matter what." That's a powerful message which we found increased purchase intent.

It actually gets better. In the case of the mattress protector, we never even came close to paying out 0.4%. You see, less than 6% of those we responded to contacted us for their promised refund. So in this example, we only had to pay out on nine protectors. That's $270, or 0.024% gross income refunded.

Now I'll ask you again with a different number. Would you be willing to pay 0.024% of your gross income to earn the perception of exceptional generosity? We were definitely willing. In fact, we'd go above and beyond by sending replacement units and giving a 100% refund in many cases.

You may be wondering how this principle applies to larger ticket products. Although the equation may be the same, it's likely much more than 6% will take you up on your offer if there's more than $30 in it for the customer. If you're selling furniture for example, you may not want to ship out a new couch every time someone says it's not soft enough. I get that. In such cases you can be "specifically vague," by specifically mentioning a solution while also being vague about the solution. For example: "We will make it right." or "We promise a quick solution." Both of these examples specifically offer help while keeping the offered solution vague.

You'll need to run the numbers for your situation and decide what you can give to customers. Regardless of how your numbers pan out, remember the principle here. It's cheap to be generous. Promise the moon and your target audience will love you more. The magic part is you'll never actually have to pay it all out.

Asking for review updates

This technique is one of my favorites and has evolved over the years to be more sophisticated. It is based on the principle of reciprocity. Stated succinctly, it means if you do something for me, I'll do something for you.

After promising the moon, you will have reviewers contact you for the promised refund, replacement, or whatever you offered. It's critical that you respond in a timely manner with good information and a smile on your face. After taking care of the customer, you've now earned the right to ask for something. That's when you ask for an updated review. Some people will update their review and others will not. I can promise though that you'll always get more positively updated reviews if you ask.

This principle is fairly simple but now I'm going to tell you how I've done this systematically across thousands of product listings with many team members involved. First, build a simple Google or Excel sheet like the one in figure 4.5.

In column A, you have a list of created "review case numbers". When your team member responds to a review and promises the moon to someone, they will include the next available unique case number in their public reply. This one technique alone will reduce the frequency of people emailing in claiming you offered them a refund. Why? Because people reading the review response are more likely to believe your offer is tied to their account info. In truth, it is not...yet. Your team member will go on to fill out the remaining items in the respective row, including (where available) the direct URL to the customer's review.

	Review Case #	Team Member	Date of Response	Reviewer PEN NAME	Review LOCATION	Date Review was Posted	Review URL	INITIAL Star Rating
	YOUR INFO				INITIAL REVIEWER INFO			
2748	1-R102656							
2749	1-R102657							
2750	1-R102658							
2751	1-R102659							
2752	1-R102660							
2753	1-R102661							
2754	1-R102662							
2755	1-R102663							

Figure 4.5: A sample spreadsheet of tracking review responses is shown

What comes next could be managed by your review response team if you're in a smaller organization. If you're in a larger organization, I'd recommend this be done by the customer service department.

When customers contact you at the email address you provided in your public review response, they will include the "review case number" you provided. At that moment, the communication is now "behind the curtain" in private conversation. You'll ask the customer for all their order details so you can look up their account and process the refund, replacement or whatever is needed.

After a solution has been provided, the customer service team can ask for an updated review and include the direct URL to the customer's review. This is because the customer included their review case number in their message, which the customer service team looks up in this sheet. BOOM! How cool is that?! Keep in mind that not all review platforms let you save a URL to a direct review link. In these cases, you'll have no URL to save and no URL to reference in your update request. In these instances, the review update request could be as simple as giving them the steps to find their review from their account. You will know what website they purchased from based on their account info.

Over hundreds of instances tracking what types of solutions customers liked, we found that customers liked receiving a free replacement more than a 100% refund. In fact, customers who received a free replacement were 20% more likely to update their old review favorably and give an average 0.4-star higher update compared to those who received a refund. Try offering different types of solutions and tracking which work best for you.

As you consistently respond to your reviews, including your email and being helpful and generous, you'll also notice something else start to happen. People will email you before they even leave a negative review. Your responses are like little billboards all over your listing(s) and profile(s) advertising that you are helpful. What I've seen is less than half of the emails you receive will have review case numbers. All other emails are customers proactively reaching out to you with support questions and even pre-purchase questions. The existence of these emails confirms a couple things. People are reading the reviews and your responses and your responses are actually preventing some negative reviews from ever posting at all.

Responding to Positive Reviews

Remembering the 3QPD rule, you don't want to neglect your positive reviews. Responding to some of these shows your target audience that you care about all your customers. Thankfully, responding to positive reviews is fairly simple and straightforward.

Don't just say thank you

Remember the principle of mirror messaging. It applies here as well. Responding with repetitive phrases like "thank you" will dilute the sincerity of your efforts. Mirror some components of the positive sentiment in positive reviews specifically to showcase your care for the reviewer.

Choosing which positive reviews to respond to

Since you don't respond to all positive reviews, you need to choose which ones you will or will not post a reply for. Focus on the most recent reviews. Many consumers filter reviews by the most recent first. You want your response time stamp on positives as well as negatives to be timely.

Next, consider the review length. Find the review that is short, but still mentions something specific. If a review just says: "Great experience, love it." There's not much to mirror in your message. Contrast that with this review: "My server was very kind and patient when we accidentally spilled a drink. Great environment and service." This one is still short and it's specific. Your reply could be as simple as: "We're happy you enjoyed the environment at [restaurant name] and appreciate the opportunity to serve you. There's no spilled drink we won't handle to put a smile on our diners' faces. Thanks! [restaurant name]"

Lastly, avoid responding to all-star reviews: These reviews may be longer form, include a photo or video and rave about your amazing product or service. Leave these ones alone. Don't respond and find a shorter one. Let the most influential positive reviews stand on their own. In some cases, responding to these reviews could be misinterpreted as manipulation or fake reviews. Would you think it looks fishy to get a glowing all-star review just to see a well-polished response from the company posted hours later? You'll receive plenty of shorter reviews, so this shouldn't be an issue.

Responding to Inquisitive Reviews

Inquisitive reviews are ones with questions in them. This is the "Q" in the 3QPD rule. Respond to all reviews that have a question or lacking info, regardless of star rating. Essentially, you're looking for opportunities to provide context to a review to help your target audience more favorably consider your product or service.

It's like you're the moderator of a conversation. However, since you're not the audience reviewers write to, questions typically aren't asked of you. They tend to be more rhetorical or addressed to the online community. You can still jump in and provide the right answer.

Directly answer the question

As silly as this sounds, I have to remind people of this. If someone is asking a question, they want an answer. Sometimes it's an uncomfortable question such as "I wonder if I can return this used?" or "Do they ever clean the bathrooms?". In these cases, respond with info that is useful for not just the reviewer, but for everyone who could read your response. State information about your return policy and where to get individual support. Apologize that the bathroom didn't meet the reviewer's expectations and assure them it is cleaned regularly. Let readers know what your bathroom cleaning schedule is like and what's included. Be direct and provide the info you'd want to receive if you asked the question.

Answer the unasked question

There will undoubtedly be times where the reviewer doesn't know everything they should ask. They're not the product expert, you are. When a review is discussing something incomplete or off course, take the time to provide all the relevant info to what is being shared. This is, again, for the benefit of your target audience. You don't want them to be misguided by an uninformed review. Steer them back on course. Here's an example of what this could look like:

> **Review from Jacob L: (4-star) May 7th**
> *"Love this action camera! It's simple to use and, honestly, takes high quality videos. I'd love to mount it on my car dash while doing some occasional Uber driving on the weekends. Haven't figured that out yet. For the price though, it's adequate."*

Company Response: May 7th

"Hello Jacob! Thanks for your feedback. We're thrilled that you love the quality of video this camera takes.

If you haven't yet seen our other accessories, we make 3 different dash cam mounts for cars. Considering you may only be using it occasionally, we'd recommend the model below. It's a quick release style mount featuring a commercial grade suction. It can easily be removed after a weekend of driving.

Quick Release Dash Cam Mount
Add the direct URL here

Contact us directly at: customerservice@actioncams.com if there's anything else we can help you with.

–Action Cams

In the response, information about the dash cam mount was provided. Instead of just saying it exists, the response includes the direct link, making it easy to find. When other readers find this review, they may also want to use this camera in their car. Since you replied with thorough info and a link to the dash cam mount, you may have just won a sale of both items. Your review responses are public and permanent. It's worth the time to do it right.

Section 4.4: Responding to Q&As
Answer questions to manage expectations pre-purchase

Questions and answers (Q&As) are typically found on product listings and company profiles. Consumers typically read Q&As on a listing pre-purchase. At this point in time, they are evaluating product quality and verifying if the product or service will meet their individual needs.

Power Reviews found that a conversion lift of 157.1% occurs when customers interact with Q&As on your listing.[8] That's not all Q&As are good for; they are great at driving traffic from search engines to your website's product page. For example, when someone asks a question on Google, if your product page has a question and answer that matches the search, that specific Q&A may be served as the best search result. When clicked on, the user is taken straight to your product page. Contrast some of the differences between Q&As and reviews in the following table.

Q&As	Reviews
Usually written pre-purchase, looking for details to confirm/validate a purchase. Tend to focus on personal application questions	Almost always written post-purchase, evaluating the product, service and/or experience
Sometimes written post-purchase, asking questions about how to use the product	Sometimes questions are asked in reviews but are usually rhetorical in nature
Generally not overly positive or negative content. Mostly inquisitive	Content can be very positive or very negative
Questions are posed to both the online community and the company. Responses from both are expected	Reviews are written primarily to the online community. Most platforms have no community replies. Companies are expected to respond by some
Replies are typically expected in 4 to 24 hours (Power Reviews, n.d.)	Replies are not expected at all by some; others expect a reply within a week

Many of the strategies in this chapter will translate directly to your Q&As responses. One additional layer to consider when responding to Q&As is the threaded responses. Unlike most reviews, Q&As encourage responses and reactions to the original post, aka the question. Answers from the community can vary widely. Some community answers are very helpful and will increase purchase intent. Others may dissuade customers from purchasing. It's your job to be the moderator.

The best practice I recommend is prior to writing your response to the question, first check for answers posted by the online community. Take them into account as you write your response. Sometimes your answer has to be so direct that you openly state that info from other answers are verifiably false. When needed, post additional responses in the thread directly responding to others who have answered the original question. You may end up posting several responses within a thread of a single question.

On some marketplace sites, other sellers can comment on these Q&As as well. If they are posting responses with misinformation, directly address these issues in a similar way to discrediting claims.

Section 4.5: Responding to Employee Reviews

Employee reviews merit special attention and a tailored approach

Responding to employee reviews matters just as much as responding to consumer reviews. Glassdoor found that 86% of job seekers are likely to research company reviews and ratings when deciding where to apply for a job. Most of these individuals will read at least five reviews and 80% of job seekers who read reviews say their perception of a company improves upon seeing the employer's response.[9]

So how do you respond to employee reviews? The first thing to realize is that basically all strategies mentioned in this chapter will aid you with your employee review responses, as they are also reviews. However, there are some subtle differences. I'll share my pro tips for employee reviews that go above and beyond what you've already read.

Who responds to employee reviews?

This question is up to you and your organization to decide. However, who your response is labeled from does matter. I'd recommend having your responses signed from HR, The Employee Experience Team, The People Team, or something similar. If that's not you, it's ok. Just collaborate with that team to ensure each response is reflective of what they would say. Remember, you are on stage when responding publicly. You need to have the right stage name for this audience.

Mirroring a bulleted list

Employee reviews can sometimes be more emotionally charged than customer reviews. After all, an employee's experience working for you is a significant portion of their daily and weekly life. Although I have seen negative customer reviews with lists of grievances, this pattern is more common among employee reviews. How do you respond to a review with 3, 5, 10 or more listed complaints?

Think back to the principle of mirror messaging. Although we do want to showcase our care for the reviewer and validate their concerns, writing back a 5-paragraph persuasive essay is not productive. It will take up your day, give you more opportunities to take a misstep, and most people will not read it anyway.

There are two response methods I'd recommend using for a lengthy list of complaints in a negative employee review:

1. *General acknowledgement*

Make a brief, several sentence response that acknowledges their dissatisfaction generally. Thank them for sharing and let them know their feedback has been noted by the HR team. Close with your standard invitation to continue the conversation privately. Here's an example:

> Thank you for taking the time to share your detailed feedback about working with us. Know that your opinion is valued and our HR team has taken note of the items you've shared.

> We care about you and would love the opportunity to fully address your concerns directly. Contact us at: Employee.Experience@companyname.com.

> Thanks! – [Company Name Employee Experience Team]

2. *Mirroring top grievances*

This approach is like general acknowledgement, except we'll also add a few direct mirrored messages of the most critical grievances. You'll never want to mirror a long list of complaints. That starts to look like a political debate. It also starts to make you look petty and intimidating. Choose the one to three most damaging complaints that could negatively impact your target audience. Mirror those in your response. Here's an example reply:

> Thank you for taking the time to share your detailed feedback about working with us. Know that your opinion is valued and our HR team has taken note of the items you've shared. Although we can't sufficiently address all the points made here, we'd like to address the following:
>
> Complaint #1 (GIVE A SUCCINCT FACTUAL LABEL TO THE COMPLAINT TOPIC.)
> (ADD A TAILORED BRIEF RESPONSE TO THIS TOPIC.)
>
> Complaint #2 (GIVE A SUCCINCT FACTUAL LABEL TO THE COMPLAINT TOPIC.)
> (ADD A TAILORED BRIEF RESPONSE TO THIS TOPIC.)
>
> Complaint #3 (GIVE A SUCCINCT FACTUAL LABEL TO THE COMPLAINT TOPIC.)
> (ADD A TAILORED BRIEF RESPONSE TO THIS TOPIC.)
>
> We care about you and would love the opportunity to fully address all your concerns directly. Contact us at: Employee.Experience@ companyname.com.
>
> Thanks! – [Company Name Employee Experience Team]

Closing contact

Just as you do when responding to customer reviews, you want to drive the continued conversation with the reviewer off-platform. Your target audience's primary concern is to see that you are providing the needed support to each reviewer, not exactly how you resolve a specific situation.

The contact request you make can be slightly different for employee reviews. Instead of a customer service email or phone number, you could use one of the following options:

- *A dedicated employee email address, such as HR@companyname.com or employee.experience@companyname.com*

- *A specific leader's email address such as the CEO, the HR Director or People Experience exec.*

- *A reference to use of an internal only contact method, such as an anonymous employee suggestion box (this would only be applicable if the review was written by a current employee).*

Consulting HR, legal and managers prior to responding

Some reviews will be straightforward and simple to respond to. Others may make claims that are more extreme or concerning. Realize that when you respond to reviews publicly, you are responding on behalf of your organization. For this reason, it's best to consult your HR and legal teams as needed.

Sometimes, you can use situational cues, such as the date, title, department and tenure associated with a review to guess where the review may have come from. If you determine a specific department or team manager might know who could have written a review, contact them. Let them see the review and ask if they believe they know who could have written the review. Sometimes, a manager will have a high degree of certainty of who wrote the review. In this case, collect background info about the review confidentially that could help you better form your public response.

Never cross the line of anonymity

There is no benefit to identifying and confronting an employee about a negative review. Even if you are 100% certain you know who posted a negative specific review, never confront the individual publicly in your response or privately. This is important because you won't always be able to figure out who posted a review. If you do and you openly address the individual, you undermine the trust of the review system for the rest of your employees.

Openly addressing an individual in a public response would be the equivalent to a public attack on an employee. It would certainly make you look bad to your target audience- some may think you're an aggressive employer that suppresses open thoughts and feedback. Others may think you're stupid for assuming you know who posted an anonymous review. Regardless, the platform is likely to delete your response for sharing personally identifiable info.

Confronting an employee privately about a negative review will also end poorly. Let's say you know who wrote the negative review, you invite them to meet with HR and ask them why they posted such negative content. This individual now has more reasons to share why they dislike you. They may tell other employees who may post additional negative reviews. If you happen to guess incorrectly who wrote the negative review, you then end up accusing someone who may be a happy or not happy employee. Either way, this interaction is likely to damage that employee's opinion of you.

If you want to confront the employee that possibly wrote a specific negative review, try this approach instead. Either in a scheduled 1:1 meeting with the employee or in casual conversation, ask the employee how they are doing. Use questions and follow-ups to guide the conversation towards some of the topics mentioned in the review. If a pre-existing relationship of trust exists, it's possible that the employee shares similar feedback that they voiced in their anonymous review. At that moment, you can now openly discuss the topic, still never addressing the review. They shared the topic with you directly, so it becomes appropriate to discuss, address and hopefully resolve. Still, you never want to insinuate in any way that you believe they posted the review in question. Don't even acknowledge it. The review is simply the informer of your questions to help an employee in need.

This approach saves you from accidentally associating the wrong person with a review. If the employee never brings up the topics in the review, neither should you. Congrats on avoiding a damaging and embarrassing situation.

Reporting employee reviews for deletion

There will come a time when you wish a review was simply deleted rather than needing to reply to it. This may happen if a review is overly negative or contains false information. There are two ways employee reviews can be reported for investigation and deletion:

- *Using the publicly available "flag" on the review, you submit the review for moderation through the platform's standard moderation process.*

- *You email your account representative a direct link to the review.*

In my experience, emailing your account rep is more effective. They can pass the review on for moderation with more influence than through the standard process. In your email, you will want to take a helpful tone, letting them know this review might not meet the website's community guidelines. Never demand that a review or other UGC get removed.

For your moderation request to be most successful, consider these things:

- *You actually have to know who your account rep is. Build a good working relationship with them.*

- *You have to know the community guidelines for Glassdoor, Comparably, Indeed, InHersight and/or whatever other employer review site you're dealing with. In my experience a review will never be deleted simply because you want it to. It must breach the community guidelines or terms of service of the website. When making a request for moderation, make a case of how the review might be in breach of these policies and request the platform take a second look. Common reasons for breach of policy would include sharing of personal info, vulgarity, hate speech and sharing confidential company info.*

- *You want to be selective with the reviews you report for moderation. If the frequency of your requests is too high, your account rep may not give as much weight to each review you submit. Pick and choose the most extreme and obvious breaches of policy to report.*

Chapter 4 Summary

Section 4.1: Impact of Responding to Reviews

Why responding to reviews is worth your time and attention

Why should you respond publicly to reviews and other UGC online?

There are three primary reasons for responding publicly to online reviews:

1. *Increase consumer trust:* Showcased customer care gives shoppers greater confidence in your business. This in turn increases purchase intent.

2. *Control the narrative:* By engaging with your reviews, you can discredit negative claims, answer questions and provide clarity for other shoppers who read reviews.

3. *Increase your ratings:* A consistent review response program gives you the chance to turn negative reviews to positives and prevent some negatives completely.

Section 4.2: General Mechanics of Strategic Review Responses

Learn the fundamentals of crafting powerful public responses

Who is your target audience when responding to public reviews?

It's not the reviewer. It's the entire internet. Some single product listings can receive 60,000 page views per day. They are your target audience. When you're responding publicly, you are on stage. Have a showcase mindset and tailor your response to be helpful for everyone who will read it.

What is mirror messaging?

Mirror messaging is a written form of active listening. You validate what the reviewer has said by mirroring some of their statements. There are two forms of mirror messaging: Exact repetition of a word or phrase and referencing a topic shared with specificity.

How many reviews should you respond to?

The optimal amount of reviews to respond to is 40%. The 3QPD rule will get you close to this volume with simplicity:

The 3QPD Rule (Pronounced "3 cupid")

· *Respond to ALL* **3**-star or lower reviews

· *Respond to ALL* **Q**uestions in reviews, regardless of star rating

· *Respond to SOME* **P**ositives

Dispersed throughout your reviews

Section 4.3: Responding to Negative, Positive and Inquisitive Reviews

Take your public response strategy up a notch with these advanced techniques

How should you respond to negative claims made in reviews?

Mirror feelings, not claimed "facts" a reviewer might share in a negative review. Use passive voice to distance yourself and the reviewer from the problem and active voice to take ownership of the solution. Directly address false claims to set the record straight using passive voice. Invite the reviewer to contact you privately for a solution.

Section 4.4: Responding to Q&As

Answer questions to manage expectations pre-purchase

What are Q&As and why should you care about them?

Most product listings and review profiles also have a Q&A section. Here, shoppers ask questions and the online community gives answers. You can also engage with and positively influence consumers by answering Q&As. Most techniques used for reviews also apply to Q&A responses.

Section 4.5: Responding to Employee Reviews
Employee reviews merit special attention and a tailored approach

How is responding to employee reviews different from responding to customer reviews?

Employees are the "customers" writing the reviews. These reviews can be more emotionally charged and can often merit the consulting of legal, HR and/or people managers prior to responding. Your responses should be written with great care and should have a dedicated contact method you can share publicly such as an employee feedback email address.

Section 4.3: Responding to Employee Reviews

HARVESTING INSIGHTS

Improve experiences and ratings with review data

QUESTIONS TO CONSIDER:

Why is a star rating more important than a net promoter score (NPS)?

What two types of data should you harvest from your reviews?

What is a review audit and how do you perform one?

Why is it important to continuously track review KPIs?

What is a perception matrix analysis?

Where are employee feedback insights harvested?

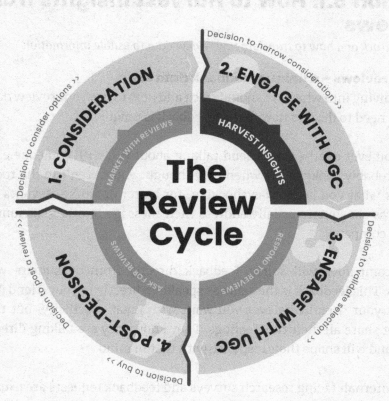

Figure 5.1: Harvesting insights is the element of owner influence associated with stage 2 of The Review Cycle: engage with OGC

Harvesting and applying insights from your reviews is the element of owner influence associated with stage two of The Review Cycle. After a consumer has made the choice to evaluate your offering among the many available options, they click into your product listing or profile. Here, they engage with your OGC content. Your OGC content can be reverse-engineered from the review insights you've gained in order to increase purchase intent. Applying the knowledge you've collected from your review data can also be used to improve your products and services, which increases your ratings.

Section 5.1: How to Harvest Insights from Reviews

What to track and how to translate raw review data to usable information

Online reviews – a unique feedback data set

Before diving into what you should track and how to use your review data, we first need to discuss how review feedback is unique.

Have you ever overheard a friend talking about you with someone else? They probably spoke freely when they thought you weren't in the room. Perhaps what you heard was shocking, for better or worse. Reviews are similar as consumers usually address their message to other consumers about a company.

Many companies will solicit feedback directly from consumers with surveys. This feedback is the same as speaking directly to your friend. You can ask your friend whatever you want with great specificity, but they may not share all their true feelings. They know they are talking directly to you and will shape their response with that in mind.

These internal-facing research surveys and feedback requests are usually tied to a *net promoter score*, typically referred to by the acronym NPS. A standard NPS question looks like this:

On a scale of 0 – 10, how likely are you to recommend _____ to a friend?

Not at all likely   Extremely likely

| 0 | 1 | 2 | 3 | 4 | 5 | 6 | 7 | 8 | 9 | 10 |

Figure 5.2: A Net Promotor Score (NPS) question shows
a scaled response from 0 to 10 for the likelihood of a
customer recommending a product or service

From this question, a score between 0 and 100 is calculated. Responses from 0 to 6 are considered "detractors" and count as a negative response. These are the people who are likely to say negative things about your product or service to others. A seven or eight response would be considered "passives". These individuals will likely say nothing as the experience was good enough. Those responding with a nine or ten are labeled "promoters" and will likely say good things about you.

Your NPS score is calculated by subtracting the detractor percentage from the promoter percentage, leaving you with the net percentage of promoters. If you had 15% detractors, 10% passives and 75% promoters, your NPS score would be 60. 75 − 15 = 60.

If you want to pause here and search the internet for NPS, you'll find tons of articles about it. Many businesses use NPS as a fundamental key performance indicator (KPI) of success.

I disagree with focusing on NPS as the primary indicator of customer loyalty and satisfaction.

While true that an NPS score can accurately reflect the legitimate customer experience. However, it is generally an internal-only metric of customer loyalty and happiness. Customers can't see your NPS and therefore don't make purchasing decisions because of it. Publicly visible ratings and reviews directly shape purchasing decisions, even when ratings are not aligned with an NPS score.

While working at Malouf, my team managed reviews for many different mattress protector models sold online. In some cases, we had product listings struggle to sell enough due to many negative reviews claiming the product was not waterproof. When looking at actual failure rates and internal feedback data, the claimed problem simply was not there. Defect rates were well below acceptable thresholds. So, why then were we getting so many negative reviews claiming they weren't waterproof?

A protector failing in a moment of child bed-wetting would make any parent angry. Pee going through the protector = 1-star review. Because a rare product-failure of this nature accompanied a highly uncomfortable experience, it was over-represented in reviews compared to positive experiences. The problem on the listing wasn't tied to many product failures; it was tied to an under-representation of product successes. After all, who's going to write a review at 3:00 a.m. when that $20 protector worked?

Internal-only data may not have flagged this issue, because it was not a legitimate issue. The protector had a very small actual failure rate. Yet product failures became a perceived issue as the ultra-small minority that experienced pee going through it shared negative reviews more frequently than those with positive experiences. This created a perception of a failure rate much higher than it actually was.

Any type of problem that impacts sales is real and should be addressed. In the case of the protectors, we reinforced our listing content with information on how to care for the product and not damage the waterproof layer in laundering. This did help lower the rate of negative reviews.

Just like the general public wouldn't know about the protector's actual defect rate, they wouldn't have access to see NPS survey data. If a sample size is big enough, you may assume sentiment in public reviews and internal NPS surveys would be the same. You would likely be right. However, sometimes the two data sets can be different. For example, some people read reviews before they buy and then look for certain things they read about.

I saw this a lot with memory foam pillows. One review would say the foam smelled funny, then the next thing you know every other review was saying, "The reviews said this pillow smells bad. I opened it up, stuffed my face in it and they were right! It smells horrible!" Public access to the feedback (online reviews) can create self-fulfilling prophecies. People find what they look for and end up reinforcing an experience driver that others mentioned before them.

Should you disregard internal surveys and NPS? No. Direct consumer feedback, including NPS can be immensely valuable and can help you engineer better experiences for customers and employees. It is important to understand how this data set differs from your online reviews.

Should you prioritize ratings and reviews above NPS? Absolutely. Reviews are a unique form of customer feedback in which customers influence customers publicly. Remember, customers can't see your NPS and internal surveys. Those things are "behind the curtain". Ratings and reviews are on the public stage of the internet. For this reason, they directly shape perceptions and affect purchase behavior.

Quantitative and qualitative review data
Your reviews contain a wealth of insights and knowledge that can help you better align your offering with consumer preferences. So what type of data is found in your reviews specifically and what metrics should be used to measure your performance? Let's first discuss the two types of data, quantitative and qualitative review data. Here is how I distinguish between the two:

Quantitative review data: Any form of review data that is in number form and can be analyzed and evaluated with numbers and percentages.

Qualitative review data: Any form of review data that is in word form and can be evaluated by reading and human reasoning.

Quantitative review data includes your star rating, total number of displayed reviews and any number or percentage derived from your analysis. To measure how healthy your listing is, you'll want to evaluate at least these two quantitative metrics:

Review pace: The number of new reviews received over a standard time frame. I measure this weekly as (X) new reviews per week. This is different from the review rate (RR) discussed in chapter 2 because no contrast with sales volume is made. Think of this as the raw volume of reviews coming in, regardless of sales volume.

If your review pace is greater than your competition, you're winning. Even if they have more total reviews than you today, you'll eventually catch up and surpass them.

Rate of star-rating change: The positive or negative rate of change to your star rating over a standard time frame. I measure this weekly as: (X.XX)-stars per week.

If you are dealing with a listing that has a low star rating, you'll want a positive rate of change. This will be achieved primarily by asking for reviews, as we learned in chapter 3. However, there reaches a point of desired equilibrium where you don't want change. Generally, when a star rating is between 4.3 and 4.7 stars, it's optimized. You don't want to keep increasing to a perfect 5-star as it can be viewed as fake or untrustworthy.

This metric matters less as a comparison to your competition. You want to be aware of your own listings' changes and strive for consistent improvement up to the optimized range of 4.3–4.7. After that, you want to maintain ratings and have little to no change.

A third type of quantitative review data exists. I call it translated quantitative data.

Translated quantitative data: Translated quantitative data is qualitative data turned from words to numbers for quicker analysis. For example, if you read 100 reviews of a product and count how many times reviews mention poor customer service, you'd end your reading with a number. That number is the percentage of reviews citing the single problem of "customer service" and allows you to understand how significant the issue is as a percentage of all reviews.

This section will dive deeper into this translation process. It is more time-intensive, but greatly worth the effort. I had a good friend of mine, an Excel wizard, once tell me: *"You have to slow down to go faster."* This guidance came when he was teaching me methods of manipulating data in a spreadsheet. Indeed, he was correct. Taking the time to learn new spreadsheet functions and apply them to entire datasets was much faster than making changes to the data one cell at a time. The same principle applies to reading reviews for insights. It feels slow, but in a matter of hours you can have a reliable view of public-facing consumer insights. Because online reviews are publicly accessible, you can also follow this same process on your competitors' reviews to understand their strengths and weaknesses.

Now let's discuss the qualitative review data labels. Your qualitative review data is found in the actual text of your reviews. Labeling components of your qualitative data helps you translate the info to quantitative metrics for efficient decision making. As you read and evaluate review text, consider these labels.

Mention tag: When you read reviews, you want to concisely label topics. Then, as you read reviews, you can tally mentions and effectively translate your review text to numbers for analysis. For example, a mention tag could be: "customer service".

Specific mentions: When reading reviews, you'll likely want a short list of words or phrases that give context to each mention tag. Specific mentions for the tag "customer service" might include: slow, rude and unhelpful.

Exact quotes: Also found when reading reviews, you can save exact quotes from the reviews that illustrate a mention tag. For the tag "customer service", perhaps you found this quote in a review: "Slow email responses. I waited 3 days for a reply." Another review said the following: "The agent on the phone was rude and unhelpful." These exact quotes give even greater context to your original mention tag.

A translated review data set takes you from a list of raw reviews to a spreadsheet of mention tags, sorted from most to least mentioned. Each mention tag would have specific mentions and exact quotes for additional reference. This spreadsheet drastically increases the speed and reliability of interpreting what your reviews are telling you. It allows you to make decisions more efficiently.

Both quantitative and qualitative review data are important. When paired together, you're able to understand the experience of reviewers with context and scale. You will be more equipped to make informed changes to your product(s), service(s) and company that will lead to even better ratings and increased sales.

Recording and accessing your review data

In chapter 3 we discussed monitoring and tracking reviews. If you're going to mine your review data for valuable insights, you first have to access them. Take a look back to section 3.1 under "Monitoring Your Reviews" to see how you should first establish review tracking processes for your products or services.

If you have access to a review management service that centralizes your reviews, the first step to harvesting insights from your reviews is to export them into a spreadsheet format, like Excel. For product reviews, one of my favorite companies, Reviews.ai (formerly known as ReviewMonitoring. com), is able to scrape over 40 unique identifiers per review including these key identifiers:

- *Source (website the review is displayed on)*

- *Product name*

- *Rating*

- *Reviewer pen name*

- *Review title*

- *Review text*

- *Number of helpful votes on the review*

- *Review status (active on the site vs previously deleted)*

- *Time stamp of review post date*

- *Syndicated (organic vs syndicated review status)*

- *Includes media (identification of reviews with photos or videos)*

- *Sentiment score (rating from -1 to +1 algorithmically noting the positive or negative sentiment of the review text itself)*

- *Sentiment magnitude (rating of the intensity of the sentiment score)*

- *Link to the individual review (when available)*

Having these and other items exported to excel with the click of a button makes analyzing your reviews much more efficient and robust. Other review services will give you the ability to export key identifiers for your reviews as well.

Even if you don't have access to review management software, this chapter will be beneficial. As we read in section 3.1 under monitoring your reviews, you should at least be recording your total number of reviews and the displayed star rating on your profile(s) and/or product listing(s) weekly. If you have access to review management software, you may not need to manually record these items weekly, depending on what the software provides you.

As we proceed to the next topics in section 5.1, we'll specifically discuss how to harvest insights from your quantitative and qualitative review data.

Harvesting quantitative data from your reviews

From the consistent tracking of review activity on your listing or profile, you can calculate key performance indicator (KPI) metrics that help you measure review performance. Live star ratings and total number of reviews displayed on your profile are of highest importance. Whatever these two numbers are will have the greatest and most direct impact on sales volumes.

Assuming you have full access to your review data and your sales data, you could build a review KPI dashboard similar to what is shown in figure 5.3.

	A	B	C	D	E	F	G	H
1	Quantitative Review Dashboard - Frying pan - Walmart.com		1 Week	4 weeks	12 weeks	26 weeks	52 weeks	All Time (128 weeks)
2	Sales	Sales pace	234	740	2702	6596	11574	27100
3		Sales rate % change	26%	4%	-8%	5%	11%	-
4	Review Rate	Review pace	6	13	52	140	218	569
5		Review rate %	2.56%	1.76%	1.92%	2.12%	1.88%	2.10%
6		Review rate % change	0.80%	-0.16%	-0.20%	0.24%	-0.22%	-
7	Star Rating	Calculated star rating	4.50	4.12	4.03	4.21	4.32	4.37
8		Star rating change	0.38	0.09	-0.18	-0.11	-0.05	-

Figure 5.3: A sample review dashboard show important KPIs for quantitative review data

Let's dissect the example dashboard in figure 5.3.

Cell A1:B1: This is where you identify the dataset. In this case, we're looking at a dashboard for a single product (frying pan) on a single website (Walmart.com). You could use this same dashboard approach for many combinations including summary data of all reviews across many websites for a single product, summary data for all individual products in one category, or all your reviews across all products on all websites. I recommend having a dashboard like this for each individual product listing, then have that data feed other summary dashboards. This allows you to see both the big picture and the specifics on a single listing as needed.

Cells C1-H1: These are your time frame column headers. Cell C1 shows your review KPIs for the most recent single week. Cell D1 shows your review KPIs for the most recent four weeks, and so on. If preferred, you could build your dashboard on a rolling weekly or monthly basis. This is customizable based on your needs.

Column A: Here, your three primary functions of sales, review rate and star rating are listed as primary categories for your dashboard.

Column B: Your individual KPIs pertaining to each primary category are labeled. Let's go through them one by one.

Sales pace: This is the raw number of units sold in the given time frame labeled in the column headers. For physical retail, this would be the number of transactions. The number of transactions most directly correlates with the number of opportunities to collect reviews in a setting where many different items can be purchased from the same location. Numbers found in cells C2:H2 are whole numbers, indicating individual sales or transactions.

Sales rate % change: This is the calculated change in sales volume compared to the previous time frame. When building your dashboard, ensure that percentages are calculated correctly with the corresponding number of weeks. For example, cell D2 tells us 740 units were sold in the past 4 weeks. 740 sales / 4 weeks = 185 average sales per week the past 4 weeks. Cell C2 tells us 234 units were sold in the past week. 234/185 = 1.26, or an increase of 26% this past week compared to the 4 week average. +26% is displayed in cell C3. Notice that cell H3 is blank because you can't have a comparison rate of change from when the listing first launched.

Review pace: This is the raw number of reviews received in the given time frame as labeled in the column headers.

Review rate: This is the percentage of sales/transactions that end in a review. In column C we see that 234 units were sold in the past week. In that same time frame, 6 new reviews were posted on the listing. 6/234 = 0.0256 (2.56%).

Review rate % change: This is the calculated change in review rate compared to the previous time frame. Because the review rate is already a calculated percentage for the given time frame, getting the rate % change is easy. Simply subtract the current rate from the previous rate. For example, cell C5 tells us our review rate was 2.56% this past week. Cell D5 tells us our review rate was 1.76% the past 4 weeks. 2.56% – 1.76% = 0.80%. The increase of +0.80% is displayed in cell C6. Cell H6 is blank because you can't have a comparison rate of change from when the listing first launched.

Raw average star rating: This is the average rating of all reviews for the time frame indicated in the column headers. This is not a displayed star rating. Frequently, review sites use an algorithmic calculation to determine a displayed star rating. Here, we are calculating the raw star rating based only on the reviews from the indicated time frame. This allows us to see how ratings are going up and down, regardless of what the website displays. Typically, the trends you see in a calculated raw average star rating will mirror what ends up being displayed live on a listing.

Star-rating change: This is the calculated difference in star ratings compared to the most recent time frame comparison. For example, we see the average star rating from the 6 reviews received this past week is 4.5-stars as listed in cell C7. In cell D7, we see the average star rating for the 13 reviews received in the past four weeks is 4.12. 4.5 − 4.12 = 0.38. As indicated in cell C8, the reviews from this past week are averaging 0.38 stars higher than all reviews from the past 4 weeks. Cell H8 is blank because you can't have a comparison rate of change from when the listing first launched.

This sample dashboard may be difficult to build, depending on your access to sales and review data. It may be difficult to build due to time and resource constraints. However, this example shows the metrics that matter. As you make changes to your review requests, you'd use a dashboard like this to verify if your efforts made an impact in your review rate. You'd also see the correlation between sales and star ratings over time. Prioritizing the accurate tracking of your review KPIs can lead to measured improvement.

Translating qualitative review data with the use of sentiment analysis software

In the many years I've managed reviews, lots of companies have tried selling me their sentiment analysis software. Using algorithms and machine learning, they would run a text dataset through their system and translate words to numbers with positive and negative sentiment mention tags. For example, you could put a set of 10,000 reviews through one of these tools and it would give you a report of the top positive and negative mentions, with percentages.

Besides being generally expensive, these tools are not always accurate. They also require you to have a way to export your reviews in order to input them in their system. Without human reasoning, some mentions may be taken out of context and mislabeled as negative when a positive mention is being made. Other challenges of computer interpretation include similes, metaphors, idioms, references to pop culture and current events that may be misinterpreted.

The better sentiment analysis tools have ways of training the algorithm over time to be more accurate. For example, the tool may tag a review mentioning "gun" as negative and communicating violence. But what if you're a gun manufacturer? The context of the entire data set changes. You can provide examples to the tool of what it should label positively and negatively to improve accuracy over time.

If you have immensely large datasets, these tools can be helpful in identifying general trends with some reliability. To find service providers in this space, go to Capterra.com and/or G2.com and search for "qualitative data analysis software". These two sites are review websites for software companies.

Another critical weakness of sentiment analysis tools is their inability to provide robust lists of specific mentions and exact quotes relating to a mention tag. For example, the negative mention of "suction power" may be highlighted in a word cloud report for a vacuum cleaner. Although the tool did accurately identify "suction power" as a negative, reading exact quotes is still required to best understand what is happening. Additionally, references to suction power that don't use the exact words "suction power" are less likely to be surfaced by the tool.

Beginning my work in the review management space at a startup meant I had to be scrappy and resourceful. We didn't have the budget for large, sophisticated software tools. Over the years, I developed and refined a specific approach to manually interpreting text datasets, especially review datasets. On one occasion, I was able to compare the interpreted results of a high-end sentiment software tool to my manually calculated findings for the same dataset. Contrasting the findings from the two approaches confirmed the following for me:

- *Good sentiment analysis tools give you trend data fast and somewhat accurately with some examples.*

- *Manual analysis is more in-depth, has greater context, and greater accuracy.*

- *The individual doing the manual audit gains insight and context that are valuable beyond simply reading the report a software tool would produce.*

If you're considering paying for sentiment analysis software, consider the volume of reviews needing to be analyzed, your time availability and your budget. Even with a tool, time and energy must be dedicated to properly using it and applying findings for real change. Now let's talk about how to translate qualitative review data manually.

Translating qualitative review data manually

Whether you need to do a manual analysis of your reviews due to budget limitations or your desire for the more in-depth results, I recommend learning this approach before using software tools. Here, you learn the mechanics of reasoning associated with data translation. This section could help you interpret any text-based dataset, but our example will be focused on interpreting review comments. Conducting a review audit is the label I use to refer to this process of manually translating qualitative review data.

The premise here is to count mentions of all unique topics that you find while reading reviews. This is done by labeling each new topic with a concise mention tag. Then, as you read you can add specific mentions and exact quotes that give greater context to each mention tag. Each mention tag can be labeled positive or negative to communicate sentiment.

After reading the reviews and tallying mentions as you go, you sort mentioned tags by most mentioned to least mentioned. The result is a polished list of top positive and negative mentions, ranked by percentage with contextual examples. Spending the time to systematically record what you read in reviews gives you unbiased data that reflects the perceptions of your reviewers and those viewing the reviews on your profile or listing. Presenting such information to teams and leadership within your company will be far more trustworthy and influential than you sharing your "gut feeling" after casually reading some reviews.

Let's now discuss precisely how to manually translate your review text as you perform your first review audit. This may be easy for you, or foreign, depending on your familiarity with spreadsheets. Either way, I'm going to walk you through this. If you want a cheat sheet, my review audit template can be downloaded at TheReviewCycle.com, along with other helpful resources. Take a look at figure 5.4. This is an example review audit of a plastic storage container. Although this example is for a single product on a single website, the same principles can be applied to auditing reviews of many products within a category or many brands in a company, etc.

Storage Container - Walmart.com - 11/19/21	Mention %	Total #		Absolute # of Ratings							
	142%	98	50	34	8	2	4				
Mentions	**%**	**Total Tally**	**5 Star**	**4 Star**	**3 Star**	**2 Star**	**1 Star**	**Specific Mentions**	**Exact Quotes**	**Exact Quotes**	**Exact Quotes**
Durability	50%	49	37	12				Strong, tough, weather-proof, nice lid	I like how strong	Very	The lid is nice
Size	22%	22	13	7	2			Large, Good fit in trunk, big	Used in my	Large and	Fit lots of
Color	17%	17	7	7	2	1		Variety of options, black is nice, gray,	Good options	Black is classic	Lid colors are
Lid	12%	12	2	3	3	1	3	Tight, hard to open, kids can't open	Way too tight	Hard to open	Kids got mad
Price	12%	12	7	4	1			Good value, cheap, good deal	Good deal for a	Very cheap	
Durability	7%	7			3	1	3	Broke, cracked, split, in cold	Broke after one	Split on corner	Cracked in cold
Customer Service	6%	6	3	3				Quick, gave replacement, helpful	Got a new one	They were nice	Quick to
Lid	4%	4	3	1				Tight	Very tight		
Price	4%	4			1	1	2	Too cheap for price paid, not worth it,	Broke, not	Too much for	
Size	3%	3			1	1	1	Akward shape	Didn't fit in my		
Customer Service	3%	3			1		2	Rude, not helpful	Didn't listen to	No support	

Figure 5.4: An example review audit of a storage container. This spreadsheet shows the tally of various mentions about the product, sorted by frequency of mention

Cell A1: List the name of the applicable product, website, and date of the audit. I recommend hyperlinking this text to the actual product listing for quick reference.

Column A: Place topic-specific mention tags that you'll find while reading reviews here. Make sure you're using mentions that are materially reflective of what reviewers say and keep them brief. One or two words is best. As you audit more and more reviews across different products, you'll find value in using the same mentions across all your audits. In this example, the mention "durability" is listed twice, one highlighted green and one highlighted red. Green indicates positive mentions of "durability" and red indicates negative mentions of "durability".

Column B: The percentage of reviewers talking about the respective mention in column A. To calculate the percentages in column B, divide the total # of reviews (C2) by the mention-specific tally in column C. So if I were writing the formula for cell B4, I'd write it as follows: =C4/C2, then copy the formula down to the bottom of column B.

Cell B2: This is the total percentage of mentions. You may wonder why it is greater than 100%. Typically, each review will highlight more than one mention. In this example 142% would mean on average 1.42 unique mentions were made about the storage container per review.

Column C: The total tallies of mentions across all 5, 4, 3, 2, 1-star ratings. Use a sum function to total the number of tallies manually entered from the adjacent cells in columns D-H.

Columns D-H: Individual tally counts indicated by star rating for each respective mention in column A. These are manually entered as you read reviews and tally mentions.

Cells C2-H2: The total number of reviews across each star rating is listed. These numbers should be manually entered from the product listing as absolute references, NOT as sum functions of the numbers below in their respective columns.

Column I: Specific mentions are listed that briefly give greater context to the primary mention tag in the respective cell from column A.

Columns J-L: Exact quotes are copied and pasted from the reviews to exemplify the respective mention in column A. It is best to copy only the portion of the review that exemplifies the mention. If you copy an entire review each time, this creates more work for the person who will read your audit report, especially if the reviews copied are really long.

From this example, we learn a few things after reading the 98 total reviews on this storage container listing. If I were in the research and development department and given this report, I would instantly know the greatest strengths and weaknesses of the product by looking at the mentions and their percentages and tally totals in cells A4:C14. I could easily look in columns I – L to get greater context for each mention.

Based on these findings I'd recommend that we never compromise on our plastic thickness to save cost. This is because the durability of our container is the top reason people like it. We need to protect that positive experience driver. If anything, we'd want to make it more durable and possibly more resistant to cold temperatures as indicated by the negative mentions of durability.

I'd also have confirmation that our sizing is agreeable to customers and the current variety of colors we offer is great. Perhaps experimenting with additional color options could create new revenue opportunities.

Although some mentions of the lid are positive, it appears the lid is too tight and difficult to open. This specific negative mention is a pain point for all customers, even those giving positive reviews. Making an easier-to-open lid would likely increase customer satisfaction and improve ratings and sales. Negative mentions of price are negligible, as are negative mentions of size and customer service.

All these observations could be made in a greatly condensed amount of time for decision makers. By conducting an audit of this storage container listing, you're essentially translating the voice of 98 consumers into a concentrated list of items to be evaluated and acted on. You are a words-to-numbers translator, turning qualitative data into quantitative data.

When you're ready to attempt a review audit of your own, you'll need four things:

1. Your own spreadsheet like the one in figure 5.4.

2. The list of reviews you'll be reading, either from an export or directly on a product listing's web page.

3. Some music or snacks to keep you focused.

4. Some thick skin.

Number three is somewhat comical, but I remember times of doing large audits, rewarding myself with a single M&M after each tenth review I read. You do what you gotta do to stay focused.

Number four is important. Remember that all feedback is a gift. Even if it is a poop emoji inside a horribly wrapped box, it is still a gift that can benefit you. Do not take the feedback personally. You literally have to turn off your emotions and think about how the data can benefit you. If you were the product designer that made the storage container, you might be upset to read the negative reviews of the lid being too tight. It is human nature to care like that. However, we're looking to harvest value that will result in greater profitability, not compliments. Understanding why the lid is frustrating customers empowers us to fix it and ultimately make more money.

As you begin reading the first review, keep an open mind. Read the whole review and think about the mentions that could be tagged in column A. Create your first one or more mentions as appropriate. Be sure to tally "1" for each unique mention under the appropriate star rating in columns D – H. Follow the same pattern for your second review, creating additional mention tags in column A as new topics surface. When a reference to a pre-existing mention is made, you are simply adding a tally to that row under the matching star rating in columns D – H.

For mention tags in column A that are positive, highlight them green. For negative mentions of the same tag, highlight them red. I always read both the review headlines and the body text of reviews when doing an audit. Sometimes mentions will be made in both places.

Make sure you don't start this process with mentions on your sheet. Being open minded to what the reviews will tell you means not having predispositions of what you will find. You are doing this to represent what reviewers say, not what you want them to say. Having a mindset of looking for something specific will introduce bias to your results. An exception to this recommendation would be if you're repeating an audit of a product you've already audited in the past. In this case, you have mentions to build upon as they come up in your reading. I have conducted review audits of the same product with a pre-existing list of mentions. There was value in seeing that some negative mentions were not found at all. This was evidence of previous efforts effectively addressing negative mentions. In the same way, seeing no tallies for a previously present positive mention would be important.

Keep in mind that negative mentions can exist within positive reviews and vise versa. Think of the storage container example. Negative mentions of the lid were present across all star-ratings. Putting your tally under the matching star rating in columns D – H for positive and negative mentions allows you to highlight the pros and cons, regardless of star ratings.

As you continue reading reviews, you'll add more and more tagged mentions in column A. You'll also add words or short phrases in column I and exact copied and pasted quotes from reviews in columns J – L. You can make more columns for exact quotes if desired. You'll probably notice some themes start to surface. Don't stress about reordering your rows as you read. You can do that after you've finished reading all the reviews. Simply add a filter to row 3, then sort the whole spreadsheet by mention percentage from most to least when you're done reading reviews. Sorting the data at the end is the moment of truth! It's super exciting to see the translated data pointing out what's going well and what can be improved.

Your ability to affect change on the product is a function of two things: your ability to effectively communicate your findings and the ability of the decision maker to listen and apply your findings. Perhaps you're a small business owner doing this on your own, in which case, I'd recommend listening to yourself. But if you're needing to use this report to persuade and inform decision makers, I'd recommend writing a summary to accompany your findings. Highlight the most important pros and cons, giving the context of percentage and number of mentions. Give examples and provide quotes as appropriate. Most importantly, if you are in a position to provide recommendations, do it! You are now the feedback expert on that particular dataset. Represent the voice of the customers and tell your team what can be improved that will lead to better experiences and increased sales.

At this point you may be thinking this is a process you can follow, but there are 1,789 reviews on the product you need to audit. Do you buy a ten-pound bag of M&M's or is there another way other than reading all the reviews?

That's a question for you to answer. Are those 1,789 reviews on the single product your whole business is built upon? If yes, get the M&M's and go to work. There's too much at stake to risk not knowing what all your customers have to say. If it's one of 100 products in your catalog, you might opt for the sampling approach. Sort your reviews by most recent and audit a minimum of the first 100 reviews. That's enough to give you a decent perspective on things.

If you want to read more consumers' opinions in less time, try this: Export your reviews into excel. Add a column and label it: "Character count". Add a character count function for the length of each review. In excel, the formula is: =LEN(cell). Copy the formula down the column. Next, sort all reviews from shortest character count to longest. Finally, sort by date with the most recent at top. Now you are reading all the recent reviews sorted by character count. You can get through more consumers' reviews in less time because you're reading the shortest most recent reviews first. There is value in longer reviews as well. This is just one approach you could take.

Designing your library of reports

As time goes on, you'll do more and more of these review audits. You, or others on your team will want to reference them. Perhaps each year you'll want to redo a review audit of the same product and compare findings year over year. You may want to take three different individual product review audits and build a unique report comparing them against each other. In any of these cases, keeping your files organized and accessible will help you succeed. Here is what I recommend:

Create a folder for each audit you do. Within this folder you'll have your spreadsheet audit and the correlating word doc summary report. For all three, use obvious labels with standard formatting for ease of future searchability. Here's an example.

FOLDER: [Product Name]_[Product #]_Review Audit_MM_DD_YY

EXCEL FILE: [Product Name]_[Product #]_Review Audit Spreadsheet_MM_DD_YY

WORD FILE: [Product Name]_[Product #]_Review Audit Summary_ MM_DD_YY

From there, you can organize folders by product category, year, store location, or other category identifiers that make sense for your situation. Be purposeful and consistent in your file naming and organization. It might not be a bad idea to have backup files, locked files with restricted editing rights for team sharing, and other protections on your files. Although the reviews themselves are still publicly accessible, your reports took time to build and now have refined value. It is worth protecting them.

Section 5.2: Interpreting and Applying Harvested Insights from Reviews
Turning observations into better experiences and increased sales

Interpreting and applying quantitative insights from your review dashboard

Your review dashboard, like the one in figure 5.3, displays important review KPIs. Tracking the health of your product listings and profiles with these metrics helps you know when things are going well and when problems arise. You should always strive to improve the quantity of reviews you collect and get your ratings up to the 4.3 to 4.7-star range. Keep your eyes open for unusual changes in your KPIs. Of course, some variance in your star rating and review pace is to be expected. But when a large or sudden change occurs, this is your signal to investigate.

On one occasion, I was working to collect new reviews for iFIT's Google profile. When I joined the company, it had a 2-star rating and 146 reviews. This was a direct result of the law of self-selecting extremes, as discussed in chapter 3. Since no strategies were in place to ask for reviews, the only ones posted were from those with polarizing extreme positive and negative experiences. In this environment, you can expect the negatives to outweigh the positives.

Soon after discovering this profile, I spoke to the sales team and asked if I could send a review request email to customers after they purchased directly on our site. They agreed. I turned on a basic review request email using a software tool. Almost instantly, we started collecting reviews. Of the new reviews being collected, we were averaging 4.6 stars. Within three months, the listing had improved to 3.5 stars with 350 reviews. Nothing had changed to the customer experience. We just asked for reviews.

With this new review email in place, we were averaging about 16 new reviews per week. Then suddenly, our review pace dropped to about two reviews per week. After a couple weeks of seeing this same volume on our review dashboard, I decided to investigate. It turned out that the settings on the software tool we were using had been changed somehow. Review emails were not being sent. I reset the tool properly and the review pace increased back to the expected 16 per week. About seven months after starting this process, the listing was up to 4.1 stars with over 900 reviews. If I wouldn't have been tracking our review pace as a KPI, I would not have noticed the emails got turned off.

Here is another example of identifying something significant from review KPIs and finding a solution. While working for Malouf, I managed reviews for many mattresses sold online. These mattresses are rolled up like a burrito and compressed for economic shipping. On one occasion, a top selling mattress of ours had a decreased average star rating for about two months. Before this period, it averaged about 4.3 stars. After the two months, the mattress averaged 4.2 stars. The average star rating during that short 2-month time frame was about 3.7-stars. This was cause for concern, so I investigated.

I performed a review audit and read all the reviews of this mattress over that two-month time frame. One obvious trend emerged. Almost all the negative reviews said the mattress didn't fully expand after they opened it. Pictures in some of the reviews showed sections of the mattress that just stayed compressed and flat. After sharing this with our product development team, they agreed it could have been a defective batch received from the manufacturer.

We put all the reviews citing this expansion issue in a report and sent it to our manufacturing partner. We noted the impact on our ratings and customer dissatisfaction, both damaging profitability. Their response was just crazy. They admitted to knowing this issue was highly likely for a large purchase order that matched this time frame. They said unusually cold temperatures were present at the factory when that batch was manufactured, which likely damaged the foam quality. They offered to reimburse the order to make up for lost revenue. We proceeded to share this news with our customer service team so they could aggressively offer refunds and exchanges for customers who encountered this issue.

This example also demonstrates the importance of tracking your review KPIs on an ongoing basis. We were able to hold our partner accountable using review data. The outcome resulted in new revenue from the factory and a proactive customer service plan that helped us improve our ratings back to 4.3-stars.

Interpreting qualitative insights using the perception matrix

Monitoring your review KPIs is fairly straightforward. You track percentages and trends, watching for anything that is inconsistent or unexpected. When you find something concerning, you investigate and perform a review audit. Translating your qualitative review data is a time commitment, but it's simple to do with the framework provided in figure 5.4. You read all the reviews and tally mentions.

Then what do you do with the results of a review audit? How do you interpret what you tallied and make things better for your customers? Having gone through this process many times, I've developed the perception matrix to help you more efficiently connect observations to solutions. Categorizing mentions from your review audit with the perception matrix will help you address each topic more appropriately and strategically.

The Perception Matrix

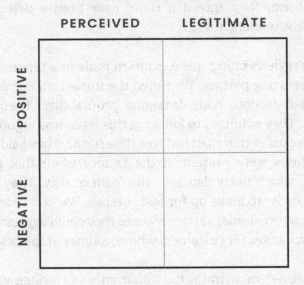

Figure 5.5: The perception matrix is a four-quadrant chart. It marks the overlapping intersections of positive and negative with legitimate and perceived experiences

Look at the perception matrix in figure 5.5. On the Y-axis, you will find positive and negative drivers. A positive driver is something that results in greater satisfaction with a product, service or experience. A negative driver is something that results in decreased satisfaction with a product, service or experience. A single positive or negative driver can be found in any review from 1 to 5 stars. The sentiment of these individual drivers emerge through the review audit process as shown in figure 5.4.

On the X-axis in figure 5.5, perceived and legitimate drivers are displayed. A legitimate driver is something that is objectively good or bad for most customers. This would be something measurable and not subject to individual opinion. For example, if an acceptable product defect rate is 1%, a defect rate above 1% is a legitimate negative driver. Contrast legitimate drivers with perceived drivers. A perceived driver is something that is believed to be good or bad, regardless of being legitimate or not. Examples of perceived drivers could include believed quality, value or outcomes provided by a product or service. It could be the level of satisfaction associated with an experience, color or price of a product.

Building from the storage container example referenced in figure 5.4, let's see where each of the discovered mention tags fit in the perception matrix. Figure 5.6 shows mention tags added to the perception matrix. I also included the mention percentages for added context. All positive mentions labeled green from our review audit are in the positive row. All red-labeled negatives are in the negative row. You may wonder why all mentions are under the perceived column. Aren't some of these mentions legitimate drivers?

We have not yet determined if any of these mentions are legitimate drivers. Let's consider the specific mention of "durability". "Durability" is a legitimate product quality, right? Yes, the durability of the storage container has a legitimate measurable level of quality. However, no quality control thresholds will ever be mentioned in reviews. Customers writing reviews don't have access to that data.

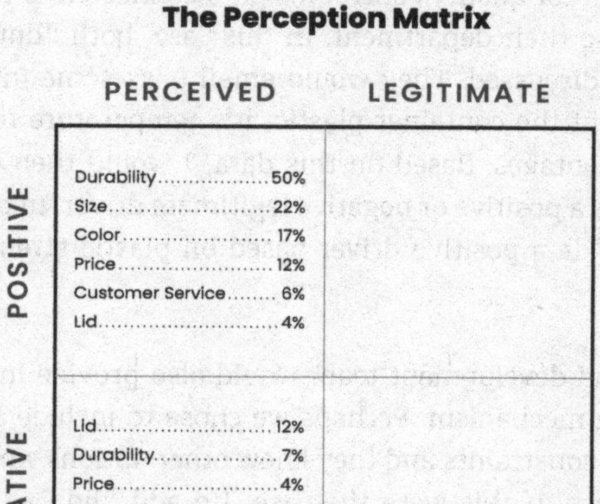

The Perception Matrix

	PERCEIVED	LEGITIMATE
POSITIVE	Durability.................50% Size............................22% Color.........................17% Price...........................12% Customer Service........ 6% Lid...............................4%	
NEGATIVE	Lid...............................12% Durability.....................7% Price.............................4% Size..............................3% Customer Service........ 3%	

Figure 5.6: All positive and negative drivers from the storage container example are listed in their respective quadrants of the perception matrix

198

While the row assignment of a driver is determined by sentiment (positive or negative), column assignment is determined by data source. Review data will always fall in the perceived column of the perception matrix because it is opinion-based and publicly accessible. It is not absolute knowledge. Legitimate drivers are determined by measured, researched and complete data that is typically only available inside an organization.

Once you've filled in your perception matrix from all mentions found in your review audit, it's time to evaluate each perceived driver to determine if it is also a legitimate driver. Essentially, we want to determine if the public's perception is real and legitimate. This process may require some collaboration with other departments or team members, depending on how your company is organized.

In my experience, the process went something like this. I'd send an email to a colleague in research and development with my review audit report. I would ask them for quality control insights connected to the perceived drivers related to their department. In this case, both "durability" and "lid" would be discussed. They would email back some info about the actual strength of the container plastic, it's temperature tolerance and defect rate percentages. Based on this data, I would then determine if "durability" was a positive or negative legitimate driver. In this example, yes "durability" is a positive driver based on plastic strength and low defect rates.

The research and development team would also provide insights about the lid's closing mechanism. Perhaps we chose to include a cheaper lid design for price constraints and they knew other options would be easier to open and close. If this were the case, I'd add "lid" as a legitimate negative driver.

I would follow this same pattern of consulting internal stakeholders for the mentions connected to them. After sharing the report with the customer service team, I might have discovered that we always give replacement units upon request. That's very positive. If wait times for calls, emails and chats are all averaging faster than our performance metrics, I'd for sure list "customer service" as a legitimate positive driver. Lastly, I would contact the marketing team to discuss size, color and price. In an ideal situation, they would have market research to back why those variations were selected. By this point, your perception matrix would look like figure 5.7.

The Perception Matrix

	PERCEIVED	LEGITIMATE
POSITIVE	Durability..................50% Size.........................22% Color........................17% Price.........................12% Customer Service........6% Lid.............................4% N/A	Durability Size Color Price Customer Service N/A Shipping
NEGATIVE	Lid...........................12% Durability...................7% Price.........................4% Size..........................3% Customer Service........3%	Lid N/A N/A N/A N/A

Figure 5.7: A perception matrix graph is filled out with all verified perceived and legitimate drivers

All perceived drivers verified as being legitimate are listed in the legitimate column. If a perceived driver was not found to be legitimate, it is marked with an "N/A". Also note that the process of verifying legitimate drivers led to the discovery of "shipping" being a positive driver. This was because the marketing team shared research confirming our storage container shipped faster than all the competition. Although this was not mentioned in the reviews, it is a legitimate positive driver that should be acknowledged.

Applying observations from the perception matrix

Now we know how to add perceived drivers to our matrix with findings from a review audit. We also know that legitimate drivers are verified and identified by referencing internal company data. So, how do we protect our positive drivers and fix negative drivers? There are seven driver combinations you should be prepared to address. Reference figure 5.8 and let's go through each of them.

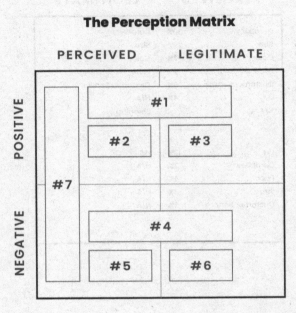

Figure 5.8: The seven most common experience driver combinations of the perception matrix

#1- *Perceived and legitimate positive driver:* This is the most desired scenario. A specific driver for your product or service is publicly perceived as being positive and can legitimately be verified as positive. You will sell more and have greater post-purchase satisfaction because of this driver.

Drivers in this category should be protected by your organization. Do not compromise on these drivers. Additionally, these drivers are things you should highlight in advertising. You can have the highest degree of confidence that consumers will experience what you promise when these drivers are marketed.

#2- *Perceived, not legitimate positive driver:* This scenario is desired, but without intervention will cause a decrease in both customer satisfaction and profitability. Essentially, the public falsely believes this driver to be real, but it cannot be backed up legitimately. If left unchecked, this driver may bring you increased sales in the short term, but it will cause post-purchase headaches.

In order to move this driver from #2, to #1 (see Figure 5.8), you must also make this driver legitimately true and positive. If this is not accomplished, this driver will either be reduced to nothing, or evolve to #5 (see Figure 5.8).

#3- *Legitimate, not perceived, positive driver:* This scenario is desired, but without intervention will not benefit you much. This driver is legitimately positive for consumers, but they don't know about it. There is not significant understanding among the public that this driver exists and benefits them. If left untouched, this driver is a wasted opportunity.

To move this driver from #3 to #1 (see Figure 5.8), you must proactively educate your consumer base about this driver. Tell them that it exists and why they should care. This will foster the growth of positive perceptions of this driver which will increase sales.

#4- *Perceived and legitimate negative driver:* This is the most undesired scenario. A driver in this state is both well known to be a problem and is legitimately a problem. You will sell less and have less post-purchase satisfaction because of this driver.

Drivers in this category should be acknowledged and addressed both publicly and internally. You must legitimately fix the issue and showcase your fixing of the issue. If you fail to publicly showcase how you are making it right, you may completely resolve the legitimate driver, but end up in scenario #5. Lingering negative perceptions may still cause lost sales even after the actual issue is corrected. Be thorough and complete in addressing these drivers publicly and legitimately.

#5- Perceived, not legitimate negative driver: This is an undesired scenario. Although the driver is not a legitimate concern, the false belief in this driver causes lost sales. The good news here is the driver isn't actually real. There isn't a need to address a legitimate root problem.

The way to address this scenario is with public re-education. Address the false perception with accurate information. Provide context, examples and other resources appropriate to the situation to debunk the false belief. If you are successful, you will eliminate this scenario and increase sales. In some cases, you may even turn this #5 scenario into a #2 or even a #1.

#6- Legitimate, not perceived negative driver: This is an undesired scenario and without intervention, it will damage your success. Because this driver isn't perceived as being negative, it may not decrease sales. However, post-purchase customers will encounter this legitimate negative driver. Satisfaction will decrease products will be returned, and with more new reviews this may turn into a #4 scenario (see Figure 5.8).

In its current state, this is easier to deal with than #4. You may not need to publicly acknowledge and address the issue. You can simply focus on fixing the problem, legitimately.

#7- Perceived as both a positive and a negative driver: This scenario is typically undesirable. The presence of conflicting opinions about a driver lowers consumer confidence in your product and causes a decrease in sales. Most often, this scenario occurs for products or services that are highly preference based. For example, is the pillow soft enough or is the salsa spicy enough? These questions produce a wide spectrum of answers, both positive and negative.

To address this scenario, you must manage expectations. Clearly define what the product or service is. Sometimes you must also clearly define what it is not. Satisfaction increases when consumers receive what they expect to receive, even if the quality is lower. Effectively addressing #7 can turn it into a #2, and sometimes even #1.

For all seven scenarios, you be the judge if a driver is significant enough to take action. Some drivers may be so small that they are not worth your time and energy. Others may be so large they demand your attention.

At this point you may be wondering why this model is called the perception matrix and not the legitimate matrix or something else. It's because perception is generally the lead influencer of consumer behaviors. Most of the time, individual drivers in the perception column will also be in the legitimate column. Sometimes individual drivers will only be in the perception column. It is very rare for a driver to only be on the legitimate column because people share opinions online.

In a similar way, if it appears there is a conflict in sentiment of a driver, the perception driver wins. Example: Company data says a product feature is a legitimate positive. Online reviews cite the same feature as a perceived negative. The perceived negative driver is crowd-sourced social proof. It's the community disagreeing with the verified data the company has. The company can believe whatever they want, but if the driver is causing a loss in sales and customer satisfaction, the results are reflective of reality, even if it is only perception based.

The magic of managing expectations

As you go through your own perception matrix analysis, you will find legitimate changes to address with products and processes. You will also find things that only have to be addressed on the perception side (primarily scenarios #5 and #7). I'd like to share one powerful example of how satisfaction and sales can be improved by addressing perception-based drivers by managing customer expectations.

In 2015, I experienced firsthand the impact managing customer expectations could have on business. I graduated college the year prior and was six months into my job at a startup bedding manufacturer. Most of the pillows, sheets and other bedding products were sold to retail stores, but I was hired as the second member of the online operations department. We managed a small and growing catalog of products sold online.

That first year of employment we launched over 50 new products. Some succeeded and some failed. There was one product that launched well, then took a sudden nosedive for the worst. It was a reading pillow as seen in figure 5.9.

Figure 5.9: A gray reading pillow[1]

As was allowable at the time on Amazon, we gave away a handful of these pillows in exchange for a few reviews. This got the listing started and sales trickled in. The star rating was 4.5, then dropped to 4.4, then 4.3. Remember, Amazon rounds 4.3 stars to a 4 ½-star image and 4.2 stars down to a 4-star image.

The pillow dropped to 4.2 stars by the time it had 40 total reviews. That same day, sales dropped over 100% and held at a slow crawling pace. A couple days passed, and my boss asked me to figure out why our ratings dropped. I proceeded to read all 40 reviews and took notes of what people mentioned (my first review audit).

There were a couple random complaints and one very clear problem mentioned in the majority of the negative reviews – people didn't know how big the pillow was. Some said it was big while others said it was small. Some people liked the size, while others did not. Size, as an experience driver, was being perceived as both a positive and a negative, precisely in line with scenario #7 of the perception matrix.

To be fair, would you know how big this pillow is based on figure 5.9? For all you know, it could be a Barbie-sized pillow, or a king-sized pillow. Once we understood that customers didn't have a way to know what size the pillow was, I was asked to find a solution. At first, I was really stumped. There is no standard sizing chart for a product like this. I could make a comparison to other household items like a couch or a chair, but they also vary in size and style.

Eventually I realized we just needed to communicate the dimensions exactly as they were. Who could argue with that? There would be no ambiguity around comparisons and customers could accurately gauge if the size would meet their needs. We measured the length of the arms as well as the width and height of the pillow and came up with the image you see in figure 5.10.

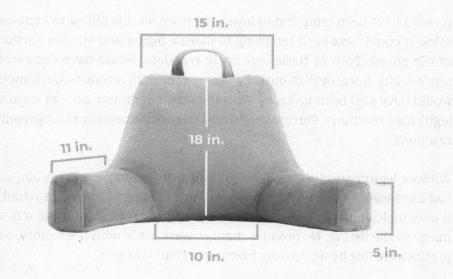

15 in.

11 in.

18 in.

10 in.

5 in.

Figure 5.10: The reading pillow with displayed dimensions[2]

After adding this image to the product listing, almost no bad reviews were posted complaining about the size. By defining the size, customers were no longer comparing the pillow size with an arbitrary size they had in their head. We left no room for them to claim it was too big or too small, because they knew precisely what to expect. The star rating popped back up to 4.3 stars within a few weeks and sales jumped back to where they were previously.

This reading pillow went on to be the number one category best seller on Amazon. Not only that, but many other competitor listings for gray reading pillows started to appear. And guess what? They all had an image similar to ours with the measurements of the pillow. Luckily, we already had the lead over these copycat products. Both our sales and review momentum kept the product consistently ranking high for many years.

Why was this new sizing image so successful in increasing our ratings and sales? It's because the negative driver, "size", was only a perceived driver and therefore needed a perception management solution. With this new image, we had found a way to eliminate "size" as a perceived negative driver and ensure it was only a positive driver. This was accomplished by managing expectations with accurate sizing information.

It could have been tempting to lower the price on this pillow to increase sales. It could have been tempting to make a bigger and smaller version of the pillow. Both of these legitimate reactions would have decreased profitability. Not only that, but they were not the right reactions. Customers would have still been unhappy with the size. Legitimate drivers require legitimate reactions. Perception drivers require perception management reactions.

Without legitimate changes like a price drop or product modification, we had increased the star rating and sales of this reading pillow. And to think, it only took some time to systematically read the reviews and add a new image to the listing. No product changes were made with the factory. No profits were lost by liquidating inventory. That's magical.

This principle of delivering what consumers expect is much more far-reaching than a reading pillow sold online. A 2019 Harvard Business Review article found that aligned authenticity could equate to both better ratings and willingness to pay more. The study evaluated two forms of authenticity – social category representation (accurately reflecting an expressed label like authentic New York pizza), and value-based authenticity (a true expression of a core belief) as it applied to 24 restaurants. Diners were asked to rate their overall impression of the restaurant and their willingness to pay for the same meal in the future.[3]

This study revealed a couple key takeaways:

- *If diners felt a restaurant "fit" a certain category of food such as Italian or Barbecue, they were willing to rate it higher.*

- *If diners felt a restaurant was true to its values such as farm-to-table sustainability or a family-friendly environment, they were willing to pay more.*

This study was repeated again with musicians. The same correlations were discovered. If a musician's music was viewed as authentically representing a social category, such as country or pop, it was rated higher. If a musician was believed to be authentic to the values they portray, consumers were willing to pay more for their music.[3]

Interestingly enough, these two connections of authenticity were distinctly tied to increased star ratings and willingness to pay respectively, without crossover. If you want to know how to best represent your product, service or company for both higher ratings and greater profitability, it requires you to:

1. Know how your audience (consumers, job seekers, etc) views you today.

2. Know what your audience values from your offering.

3. Deliver what your audience needs to know and expects to receive.

Section 5.3: Harvesting and Applying Insights from Employee Reviews

Where to find perceived and legitimate data for an employee perception matrix analysis

Some other chapters have substantially different approaches to managing employee reviews compared to customer reviews. In chapter 3, we read that most employee review sites allow the submission of multiple reviews over time from the same employee. This factor alone makes your review request strategy different from customers. In chapter 4, we read about the need for first communicating with managers and HR prior to responding publicly to an employee review online. Other key differences in how to approach employee reviews were also listed.

As far as this chapter goes, the methodologies for harvesting and analyzing employee data are largely the same. Consider both quantitative and qualitative data. Translate your qualitative data through the same review audit process. You can also conduct a perception matrix analysis in the same way you would for a product using customer reviews and insights from various internal teams.

So, what's the edge you need to succeed when harvesting and applying insights from employee feedback? It is the data source.

Employee reviews posted on websites like Glassdoor and Comparably will be your perceived experience drivers in your perception matrix analysis. As customer reviews shape perceptions of shoppers, employee reviews shape perceptions among job seekers, investors, the community and even current employees.

Your data source for the legitimate column of your perception matrix won't be found by contacting the marketing or customer service departments. Research and development won't know the state of employee wellbeing.

The way to get this data is by asking all your employees directly. This could take the form of a company-wide employee engagement survey, ongoing pulse surveys, feedback collected in an anonymous suggestion box, or other internal-only feedback mechanisms. The important part is for this data set to be statistically significant. You need to have a majority of employee opinions represented in this dataset for it to be considered the "legitimate" reflection of employee happiness.

Contrasted with online employee reviews, your internal surveys will more accurately represent the state of your workforce. Internal employee feedback will inform legitimate experience drivers. Public facing employee reviews will inform perceived experience drivers. The same seven scenarios described in figure 5.8 will emerge in your perception matrix analysis of employee feedback by evaluating these data sets.

How you specifically respond to employee experience drivers will be different than responding to customer experience drivers, but the same general needs listed in section 5.2 are the same. For example, if an employee experience driver is in scenario #4 (see Figure 5.8), you will need to publicly acknowledge the issue, address it legitimately, and follow up publicly over time to uproot negative perceptions. However, public acknowledgement may not be externally facing. Depending on the type of experience driver, your public acknowledgement may be an internal-only communication to your employees. This could be a company-wide email or a company-wide town hall meeting with the CEO. In the meeting, the CEO openly addresses the negative driver, fields questions from employees, and shares how things will improve.

Here's another way experience drivers would be applied in the employee setting. After a thorough audit of all employee reviews, an internal only engagement survey and a perception matrix analysis, you know precisely what drives your company culture. You know that job candidates searching for the experience drivers you offer will be more likely to succeed in your organization. Incorporating questions around these drivers in your interview process will result in hiring more people that are aligned with the employee experience you offer and decrease turnover.

The same concept could be used for building out the content on the career page of your website or an employer profile on Glassdoor or elsewhere. Use the identified drivers in your perception matrix analysis to reverse engineer the depiction of your culture. Not only will this attract the right candidates to your company, but this content will resonate with current employees better. They will know you're showcasing the company in a fair light and not trying to be something you aren't. This will result in greater employee advocacy.

Chapter 5 Summary

Section 5.1: How to Harvest Insights from Reviews
What to track and how to translate raw review data to usable information

Why is a star rating more important than a net promoter score (NPS)?

A *net promoter score (NPS)* is a ratio of customer loyalty and satisfaction. It is often collected through internally facing feedback mechanisms. A star rating is a public-facing measure of loyalty and satisfaction. Because star ratings are visible to shoppers, it will directly impact purchase behaviors. NPS is not generally visible to the public and therefore only informs internal metrics.

What two types of data should you harvest from your reviews?

There are two primary types of review data that should be harvested: quantitative data and qualitative data. Quantitative review data is any form of review data in number form and can be analyzed and evaluated with numbers and percentages. Qualitative review data is any form of review data in word form and can be evaluated by reading and human reasoning.

What is a review audit and how do you perform one?

A review audit is the process of manually translating qualitative review data (actual review text) to quantitative data (numbers and percentages). This is done by manually reading the reviews and systematically recording all topics with labels, called mention tags. Software tools exist that can also do this, but there are tradeoffs to using them.

Section 5.2: Interpreting and Applying Harvested Insights from Reviews
Turning observations into better experiences and increased sales

Why is it important to continuously track review KPIs?
Review KPIs are closely connected to sales KPIs. Correlating review KPIs with sales KPIs will better inform product and marketing decisions to help maximize long-term revenue. Tracking review KPIs also empowers you to investigate sudden drops in sales efficiency that previously may have gone unnoticed.

What is a perception matrix analysis?
A perception matrix analysis is the categorizing of experience drivers. Experience drivers are things that positively and/or negatively impact a customer's satisfaction with a product or service. Experience drivers can be perceived and/or legitimate. Taking the time to identify experience drivers and label them appropriately empowers you to more efficiently address negative drivers and protect positive drivers.

Section 5.3: Harvesting and Applying Insights from Employee Reviews
Where to find perceived and legitimate data for an employee perception matrix analysis

Where are employee feedback insights harvested?
Employee reviews are posted publicly on websites like Glassdoor and Comparably. These reviews make up the data that will determine the perception drivers of your perception matrix analysis. Legitimate drivers for employee experience are collected through internal only surveys and feedback forms. These insights can be interpreted and addressed by following a complete perception matrix analysis.

MARKETING WITH REVIEWS

Super-charge your marketing with review content

QUESTIONS TO CONSIDER:

What is social proof?

What legal considerations should be known before marketing with reviews?

What is the best way to refer to ratings and reviews in static ads?

How do you identify an ideal review for an ad?

Why is A/B testing important?

What is employer branding?

What is employee advocacy?

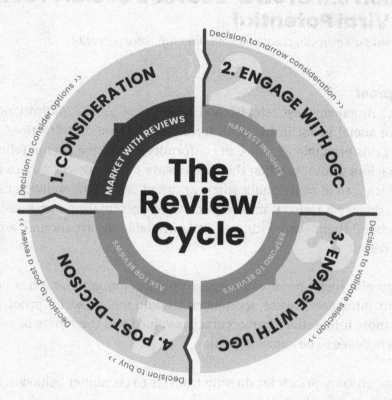

Figure 6.1: Marketing with reviews is the element of owner influence associated with stage 1 of The Review Cycle: consideration

Marketing with reviews is the element of owner influence associated with stage one of The Review Cycle. At the consideration stage, a consumer is deciding between many options. A strategically designed ad may get a consumer to consider your offering. However, what you say about your offering will always be taken with a grain of salt. After all, you have something to gain. Consumers trust consumers much more than companies. By advertising with user-generated content, like reviews, you can increase the effectiveness of your ads and get more people to consider your offering.

Section 6.1: Crowd-Sourced Social Proof and Viral Potential

How reviews act as social proof and have viral influence potential

Social proof

In 1984, American psychologist and academic Robert Cialdini coined the term **social proof** in his book Influence: Science and Practice.[1] He explains this principle as a type of conformity in which a person follows the behaviors of others when they are unsure of the correct way to act. Also referred to in some publications as "herd behavior," individuals in a group display a rational motive to consider information possessed by those around them even with very little available information as group size increases.

Interestingly, social proof can surpass public compliance and has been found to influence private acceptance.[2] Additionally, social proof has proven more influential when accuracy is valued and the source of social proof is believed to be knowledgeable.

These psychology principles directly transfer to consumer behavior. Ask yourself these questions:

1. Do reviews you read impact your personal opinions of products, services and companies?

2. Do you believe the purpose of online reviews is to share accurate experiences?

3. Do you believe reviews collectively represent reliable knowledge about the considered subject?

I know reviews have impacted my personal opinions. This is true for many people I know and is likely true for you. I believe the purpose of online reviews is to share accurate experiences. Sure, there are fake reviews out there, but most people keep using reviews. That means most of us also believe most reviews are trustworthy.

That third question reminds me of a quote from "Men in Black." Kay, played by Tommy Lee Jones, is sitting on a park bench in New York City with Jay, played by Will Smith. Kay, a government agent, is explaining to Jay, a new recruit, why people don't want to know about the aliens living on earth. When Jay says that people are smart and can handle the truth, Kay replies with a profound statement: "A person is smart. People are dumb..." Kay goes on to tell Jay "Fifteen hundred years ago everybody knew the Earth was the center of the universe. Five hundred years ago, everybody knew the Earth was flat, and fifteen minutes ago, you knew that humans were alone on this planet."

Kay's logic that a single person is capable of elevated understanding is reasonable. Single individuals have achieved exceptionally high levels of intelligence. Kay's statement regarding collective intelligence aligns with the principle of social proof. In masses, people tend to go with the flow, acting and believing like those around them.

But do most consumers believe reviews collectively represent reliable knowledge? As the number of reviews increase, yes. It has been well-documented that sales increase as the number of reviews increases on a listing or profile. In one study, Bazaarvoice found that sales increase by 44% when a listing collects 200 reviews compared to a listing with zero reviews.[3]

Although many consumers may agree with Kay that a single person is smart, online reviews wear a cloak of anonymity, rendering any single review less reliable. Anonymity removes verification of expertise or reliability of a person's opinion. As more reviews are written, the sum voice of all reviewers becomes more trustworthy. They couldn't all be wrong, right? Crowd-sourced information is often perceived as reliable today, even when each individual contribution is anonymous. Reviews therefore act as social proof and impact consumer behaviors among the masses. This fact makes your ratings and reviews highly influential content for marketing purposes.

A viral t-shirt review

Although most individual reviews reinforce the crowd-sourced opinions we see online, some reviews go viral to one level or another. In March of 2007, a New Hampshire based clothing company launched a new T-shirt design on Amazon. It was a black T-shirt featuring three wolves howling at the moon. A year later, a law student decided to post his tongue-in-cheek review:

> Pros: Fits my girthy frame, has wolves on it, attracts women
> Cons: Only three wolves (could probably use a few more on the 'guns'), cannot see wolves when sitting with arms crossed, wolves would have been better if they glowed in the dark.

Figure 6.2: The three-wolf moon t-shirt by The Mountain Corporation went viral in 2008 after a comical and sarcastic review gained attention and sparked an internet phenomenon[4]

This single review sparked additional comical and sarcastic reviews claiming the t-shirt attracted women and had magical powers. The three-wolf moon shirt inspired countless memes and pop culture references in every direction from business to politics. Many clothing brands have created renditions of the three-wolf moon shirt, substituting different animals and characters in the iconic three wolf moon design. Business Intelligence labeled the three-wolf moon shirt an internet phenomenon.[5] The hype grew so big that the New Hampshire Division of Economic

Development made the three wolf moon shirt their "official New Hampshire T-shirt of economic development".[6]

It is clear this single review dramatically increased sales, considering how many variations of the shirt have been made.

I've seen many examples of comical reviews leading to sales. Just in my first two years of managing reviews my team and I compiled 70 pages of funny reviews in our "review hall of fame." Many comments from other shoppers on these reviews openly acknowledged that the single funny review convinced them to buy. Although the sum voice of all reviewers is typically the most influential, never underestimate the impact a single voice can have when given the right attention.

If you want a good laugh, search for the below products on Amazon.com. These are my top three favorite products that have gone viral because of funny reviews:

- *Three wolf moon t-shirt by The Mountain*

- *Hutzler 571 banana slicer by Hutzler*

- *Haribo Goldbears Gummi Candy by Haribo*

Section 6.2: Legal Considerations of Using Reviews in Marketing

Understand which reviews can be used in marketing and how to use them

Is it legal to use reviews in marketing and advertising? Before deciding to use reviews in your ads, this question must be addressed. The short answer is yes, when done properly. There are a few things you should know first, at least as it applies in the United States.

In 1914, President Woodrow Wilson signed the Federal Trade Commission Act into law. This law included the creation of a new independent agency of the United States government known as the FTC or Federal Trade

Commission.[7] As the defending body of fair commerce, this is the mission of the FTC:

Protecting consumers and competition by preventing anticompetitive, deceptive, and unfair business practices through law enforcement, advocacy, and education without unduly burdening legitimate business activity.[8]

You can thank the FTC for things like the Telemarketing Sales Rule, which protects you from getting spammed by phone calls after asking to be put on the "do-not-call" list.[9] They also founded the Equal Credit Opportunity Act, which outlaws credit discrimination based on race, color, national origin, sex, marital status, age, or because a consumer received public assistance.[10] At the time of this book's publication, the FTC employs over 1,000 team members[11] stationed in DC and across eight other regional offices throughout the U.S.[12]

One of the FTC's primary strategic goals is to "Protect consumers from unfair and deceptive practices in the marketplace."[8] Over the years, methods of upholding this goal have evolved with business practices. A key predecessor to the FTC's regulations about online reviews is the use of expert and celebrity endorsements.

Figure 6.3: Famous opera singer Lillian Nordica endorses Coca Cola in a 1905 edition of The Booklovers Magazine[14]

As seen in figure 6.3, the use of celebrity endorsements in advertising expanded greatly in the early 1900's. In this famous ad, Lillian Nordica, a famous opera singer of her day, was featured in "The Booklovers Magazine" in 1905.[13] Only four years after an advertising budget of more than $100,000, this was The Coca Cola company's first year of national magazine ad placement.[14]

Wheaties is another great example of early endorsement marketing. After first launching the breakfast cereal Wheaties in 1924, the Washburn Crosby Company (later General Mills) made history when it ran the first-ever pre-recorded commercial jingle on radio on Christmas Eve, 1926. Then in 1927, Knox Reeves of a local Minneapolis advertising agency coined the slogan: "Wheaties- The Breakfast of Champions". This was used on a billboard in a local minor league baseball stadium. Wheaties was transitioning from generic ads to sports related ads and over the next few years, Wheaties began to be heavily advertised on hundreds of radio stations throughout the nation at sporting events. In 1934, Lou Gehrig became the first athlete to be featured on the front of the Wheaties box.[15] Aviator Elinor Smith was the first woman featured on the Wheaties box that same year.[15] The tradition of featuring prominent athletes continues to this day.

Figure 6.4: Lou Gehrig was the first athlete featured on a box of Wheaties cereal[15]

So, what does the FTC say about using endorsements in advertising? The following simple rules can be found within the lengthy regulations:[16]

· *Endorsements must reflect honest opinions of the endorser.*

· *Endorsements must not convey information that would be deceptive if said by the advertiser.*

· *The advertiser can't present an endorsement out of context to distort it from the endorser's opinion.*

· *The advertiser can continue to use an endorsement if the endorser still subscribes to that point of view.*

· *The endorser must be a true bona fide user of the product or service at the time the endorsement was given.*

· *"Material connections", such as payment or free product, between advertisers and endorsers must be disclosed.*

· *Advertisers are liable for the statements made by endorsers.*

· *Endorsers may be liable for their endorsement statements.*

These things matter for endorsements, but are reviews considered endorsements? The answer is, sometimes. An organic review—one posted without incentive and not used by the company in advertising)is not classified as an endorsement. That means a review posted to a website not owned or controlled by you in any form is not held to these standards. However, if a review meets one or both of these considerations, it is classified as an endorsement and subject to the same FTC regulations.

1. The moment a review is used in an ad, it becomes an endorsement.

2. If the review is incentivized in any way, it is also classified as an endorsement, regardless of where it is displayed. This is true even if you never use that review in an ad and it only exists on a product listing page or company profile.[16]

In addition to following the general guidelines regarding endorsements, the FTC specifically outlines regulations that pertain to consumer endorsements. Online reviews or other UGC found on social media and blogs would fall under these parameters. Consider the following critically important considerations:

FTC regulation: Disclosure of material connection

If any connection between an endorser (or a reviewer) and the seller/advertiser exists that might materially affect the weight or credibility of the endorsement, this must be fully disclosed.[16]

Explanation:

If you were reading reviews of a product and later found out they were all posted by employees of the company, would it affect your decision to buy the product? What about if the reviews were written by friends and family members of employees? What if those who posted reviews were paid to do so? These and any other material connection between the reviewer and the company must be disclosed in the review itself and in any ad that features part or all the review.

Action:

If a review is incentivized in any way (e.g. a free or discounted product, or entry to a giveaway), you must instruct the reviewer to openly state that fact in their review. This could be as simple as them writing: "The company gave me a discount on this product in exchange for my honest feedback in this review."

If an employee, family member, or other individual who is directly connected to the company is posting a review, that relationship should be disclosed as well. Example: "I work for _Company name_and they give all team members a free _ product name___ to test and share our opinions online. Here's what I like about it...."

Additionally, the FTC requires the company to track reviews posted by incentivized reviewers and those with material connections and ensure proper disclosures are included. When not included, the company is required, within reason, to instruct reviewers to edit their reviews and add a proper disclosure of material connection.

FTC regulation: Substantiation of truthfulness

The same level of substantiation (or proof) must validate the truthfulness of claims in a consumer endorsement (including a review) when an advertiser uses it in advertising.[16]

Explanation:

If you as the company choose to use an online review in an ad, you must be able to prove that those claims made by the consumer are a true reflection of the expected consumer experience. Now you can't control what consumers say in reviews, nor are you liable for what is said about you if it's not true in a review on an online platform you don't control (Amazon, Google, Facebook, Glassdoor). However, if you choose to hand-pick a specific review and use it for ads of any kind, now you are just as liable for the claims made in that review as if you said them yourself.

Action:

Be selective with reviews you choose to feature in ads. The review must be as truthful as if you said what the review says.

FTC regulation: Disclosure of expected results

If the consumer endorsement you choose to use in an ad makes claims that are not reflective of what most consumers would expect from the product, you must clearly disclose that fact in your ad.[16]

Explanation:

Let's say you sell a weight loss supplement. One review on your website claims the user lost 50 lbs. in three months. It's a great review, and truthful. This user lost 50 lbs. in three months. However, from scientific studies, the average user of the product loses only 10 lbs. in three months. Although losing 50 lbs. is possible and did happen, it is not a reflection of the average outcome of using the product.

Action:

If an ad features an abnormally positive outcome, you must clearly and conspicuously disclose what the average user should expect to experience. You are much safer by using reviews that are specifically vague. A review that is specifically vague makes a claim, but not a measured claim. So instead of using the review that said: *"I lost 50lbs. This stuff is amazing!!"*, use the one that said: *"I lost a lot of weight. This stuff is amazing!!"*

FTC regulation: Can't make claims that aren't verifiable

A review used in an ad cannot make claims about a product that would require proof the advertiser does not have.

Explanation:

If you were selling a pest control service. You can't use a review that says the service kept spiders out of the house for six months if you as the advertiser have no proof that the service is guaranteed to produce this outcome.

Action:

Do not use reviews that make claims that can't be verified by you as the advertiser.

FTC regulation: Reviewer retention of intellectual property rights for their own reviews

In 2016, President Barack Obama signed the Consumer Review Fairness Act. One of three primary provisions of this law is the protection of reviewers' rights to the content they submit in reviews. It is illegal to solicit a review and require the reviewer to forego their intellectual property rights to that content ("Consumer Review Fairness...", 2017).

Explanation:

To use reviews in advertising, written permission from the reviewer must first be acquired. When asking for permission to use a review, it is not allowed to ask the reviewer to forfeit rights to the content.

Action:

There are four ways you can acquire permission to use a review in advertising:

1. You find a review on a site and can identify who wrote it. You contact the reviewer and they give you written permission to use the review in advertising.

2. You collect reviews on a site you own or otherwise manage. In your review request form (whether in email, text or something else), you ask reviewers to check a box granting permission to use their review in advertising. All reviews collected by these means with a check box are usable in advertising. Many review management vendors have templates for this check box consent request.

3. A check box consent in a review form can segment consent to multiple questions. For example, one check box would ask if it is ok to use the reviewer's first name with the review in marketing. Another consent check box could ask for permission to use related images, or specific certain uses of the content such as on social media. When full consent is granted by a reviewer, you can use the following attributes in marketing:

    · *Review headline text*

    · *Review text*

    · *The star rating given*

    · *The pen name*

    · *The location (if provided by the reviewer)*

    · *Any photos or videos (if provided by the reviewer)*

Just as an advertiser cannot use a celebrity endorsement out of context, you may not use part or all a review out of context. However, it is allowable to use part of a review as a quoted excerpt if doing so does not change the context of what the reviewer originally shared.

4. You find a review on a platform you don't own or manage like Google, Facebook, Amazon or Glassdoor. You can ask the platform for written permission to use the review (or all your reviews) in writing. This is a viable substitute for written permission from the reviewer if the platform has stated in their terms of use that they have rights to use content submitted on their platform. Most review sites do this. If a platform has rights to the review content, they can grant that right to you as well. When this is done, the reviewer, the platform and you would now all have legal rights to use the review in advertising.

All the explanations shared here regarding FTC regulations are for your convenience and simplified understanding. Additional legal summaries are provided in section 3.4 of this book as well. It is encouraged that you read the most current FTC regulations surrounding all things related to reviews directly from the FTC and consult legal counsel before taking action. As of the time of publication of this book, here are the most critical documents you should be aware of and from which these summaries have been created:

1. FEDERAL TRADE COMMISSION
   16 CFR Part 255
   Guides Concerning the Use of Endorsements and Testimonials in Advertising[16]

2. FEDERAL TRADE COMMISSION
   The FTC's Endorsement Guides: What People Are Asking[18]

3. FEDERAL TRADE COMMISSION
   Consumer Review Fairness Act: What Businesses Need to Know[19]

Section 6.3: Maximizing your Marketing Efforts Using Reviews

How to achieve greater success using reviews in your marketing

The purpose of proactive marketing is to get potential customers considering your offering. You want them to pass through the consideration phase of The Review Cycle quickly and narrow their consideration with only your product in mind. Because consumers trust consumers more than brands, using UGC in marketing messages is highly effective. Tint, a UGC management company, found that digital ads have as many as four times the click-through rates than traditional ads.[20] A study by Yotpo, a review management company, found Facebook ads highlighting UGC also converted four times more than traditional ads, and at half the cost.[21]

You do not want to randomly select a positive review for an ad or mindlessly share that you have a 4.5-star rating. To maximize the power of your ads, you want to strategically select which reviews and stats you share. I'll share several variables you'll want to consider and optimize as you incorporate reviews into your marketing messages.

Incorporating quantitative review data in marketing

Quantitative review data is anything numerical. The most obvious numbers associated with your reviews include the star rating and the total number of reviews. When these numbers are favorable, referencing them strategically in ads can be highly beneficial.

First, you want to avoid advertising review-centric numbers that can change in static ads like flyers, billboards, signs and packaging. Why? Because the moment the number changes, your ad becomes inaccurate and you look like an uninformed fool. This applies to your star rating, total number of reviews, or any other number or percentage displayed on your listing or profile.

If you're thinking that your star rating and total number of reviews can always change, you are correct. For that reason, you don't ever want to use either of those numbers in a static ad. That means you should never print: "4.5-stars on Google! Come check us out!"

So what can be used? You can reference minimums that won't change. For example, you could print: "Over 1,000 5-star reviews on Google!" Of course, this would need to be a true statement at the time of printing. As new reviews are posted on your profile, it will still be accurate. As more 5-star ratings are posted, "over 1,000" is still true. Even if the star rating drops to 3 stars from a ton of new negative reviews, the statement "over 1,000 5-star reviews" is still true.

Another thing you could do is print an open invitation to read your reviews. Your printed statement might say: "Check out our reviews on Google" or "See what others are saying about us on TripAdvisor." Pairing a statement like this with an image of 5 stars and the respective platform logo would strengthen the message.

If you are delivering this message in a digital format, make it even easier for consumers to find your reviews by adding a hyperlink directly to the listing or profile where your reviews are found. To do this for your Google profile, login to your Google My Business admin account and copy the link for sharing your profile. Use that URL for your hyperlink of the text: "Check out our reviews on Google." That sentence can then be incorporated in an email, text, banner pop up or other digital ad.

Inviting others to read your reviews builds consumer trust. It's an act of transparency. You're stating that you have nothing to hide and you're comfortable with consumers looking up your ratings and reviews. They'll do it anyway, but your invitation makes consumers that much more comfortable with your company.

Some review sites make it easy to link to your review profile by providing you with hyperlink images and badges. Glassdoor does this. I can login to my company's admin account and copy the code for the badge seen in figure 6.5. This badge will then display the live star rating from our company's Glassdoor profile on our website where the code is added. This is an acceptable way to reference a star rating because it will always update for accuracy.

Just like Glassdoor provides a way to display your current star rating on a webpage of your choosing, many review management companies do this for product-specific review info found on ecommerce sites. Take the

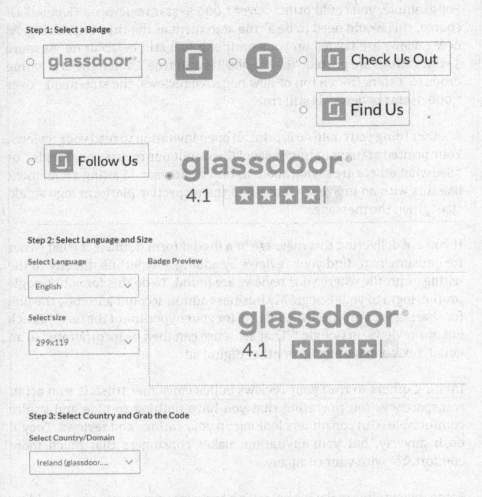

glassdoor ⚪ 🔲 ⚪ 🔲 ⚪ 🔲 Check Us Out

🔲 Find Us

🔲 Follow Us

glassdoor®
4.1 ★★★★★

Step 2: Select Language and Size

Select Language

English ⌄

Badge Preview

Select size

299x119 ⌄

glassdoor®
4.1 ★★★★★

Step 3: Select Country and Grab the Code

Select Country/Domain

Ireland (glassdoor.... ⌄

Figure 6.5: A dynamic Glassdoor badge can be
added to your own website using code provided from
Glassdoor's company admin portal[22]

screenshot in figure 6.6 for example. This is a Google search result for the term: "Cotopaxi backpack". The current star rating and number of reviews (labeled here as "votes") are both updated live from the review data on the product page for this item. Cotopaxi is able to attract more consumers to their product page from Google search because the star rating and total number of reviews are accessible from the search view.

Google   cotopaxi backpack   ✕ 🎤 🔍

https://www.cotopaxi.com › products   ⋮

Allpa 35L Travel Pack - Cotopaxi
The Allpa Travel Pack is a rugged, 35-liter **backpack** system built for adventure travel.
This pack is perfectly sized for carry-on convenience, ...
★★★★★ Rating: 4.6 · 799 votes · $200.00 · In stock

Figure 6.6: A Google search result for the term:
"Cotopaxi backpack" displays a star rating and total
number of reviews. These two review stats update
live with the use of review management software
from Yotpo and help drive more traffic to the product
page[23]

Referencing any form of quantitative review data is leveraging the benefits of social proof at scale. You are highlighting the collective voice of the online community and encouraging individual consumers to listen to them, even more than they should listen to you.

Incorporating qualitative review data in marketing

Highlighting the size and positive nature of your total pool of reviews (quantitative review data) is pushing the entire collective voice of the online community on consumers. Weaving individual review quotes, (qualitative review data) evokes emotion and showcases relatability.

Put simply, data convinces, stories persuade. There is a time and a place to convince a consumer that you are the obvious option with your impressive review numbers. But behind each number is a person sharing their individual experience. Since most consumers will only read six or less reviews on a listing it's your job to mine out the absolute best reviews and let them shine for your audience.

What makes the best review to spotlight in an ad? I'll show you how to identify specific reviews that will be more influential.

Deductive filtering

You need to find a short, powerful review that will drive traffic to your product. How do you find it? First, you need access to all your reviews.

Export your reviews from your review management portal or profile admin account. Once you have your reviews in an excel spreadsheet, freeze the top row and add filters to the top row. Next, add a new column and label it "Character Count". Add the formula: =LEN(cell) and enter the cell of the review body text. This will measure the length of each review by number of characters. Now you can deduce which of your reviews match all the attributes you want for your perfect ad.

On the column header "Character Count," sort from shortest to longest.

Next, filter all reviews by 5 stars.

Now you are looking at only 5-star reviews, filtered from shortest to longest. Having supported paid advertising campaigns, I learned that text in banner ads must be short. I had a colleague recommend using text 90 characters or shorter on Amazon banner ads. This seemed like a good rule to follow based on performance, so I adopted it. If you want to do the same, your next step is to read all the reviews, starting at the shortest all the way down until you hit reviews with 90 characters.

Attributes to look for in a stellar review for advertising
Now that your reviews are filtered and ready to read, you'll want to highlight each review that you feel could perform well in an ad. Here are the things I consider in this process:

- *Grammar: Is the review free of grammatical errors that could distract?*

- *Legal compliance: Does it meet FTC legal requirements from section 6.2?*

- *Message: Is the message in the review positive?*

After highlighting all your 5-star reviews that are 90 characters or less and also meet these three criteria, chances are, your list to choose from will be much more manageable. Pro-tip. If you have few reviews, go ahead and read ones that are longer than 90 characters. You can use a quote from a longer review without using the entire review itself. If you do this, keep the quoted text to 90 characters or less.

Reverse-engineer your focus

If you want to take this deductive process to the next level, follow the perception matrix reasoning we learned about in chapter 5. If you've previously conducted an audit of your reviews, you should have identified the experience drivers, both positive and negative. As you read through your 5-star reviews that are 90 characters or less, look for ones that specifically highlight your most positive experience drivers. These messages are more likely to attract customers also looking for that positive experience driver, which in turn is more likely to result in a positive experience after a sale.

It may be obvious that filtering your reviews by 5-star ratings is the best way to find reviews for your marketing efforts. I would agree with you. But with a little creativity, you may want to consider other reviews and how they could be applied to support your efforts.

Snowbird, a ski resort in Utah, is known for deep snow and long technical runs. They are not known for having the best training grounds for beginners, and that isn't their goal. Some negative reviews they received over time were clearly from more entry-level skiers and snowboarders.

Thinking back to the perception matrix, some perceived experience drivers can be both positive and negative. Oftentimes, these drivers are preference based. This was the case for Snowbird. For some, the higher difficulty of the terrain was the reason they kept coming back. For others, it was a complete turn off.

In 2017, Snowbird and their advertising agency came up with an ad campaign highlighting 1-star reviews citing difficulty of the terrain. One 1-star review from Greg, Los Angeles, CA read: "Too Advanced. I've heard Snowbird is a tough mountain, but this is ridiculous. It felt like every trail was a steep chute or littered with tree wells. How is anyone supposed to ride in that? No fun!"[24]

As seen in figure 6.7, the Snowbird team had fun highlighting these negative reviews. Using these and similar 1-star reviews, they made digital and print ads and even did some apparel.

Figure 6.7: Snowbird advertises the difficulty of their ski resort by highlighting 1-star reviews[24]

Was this a crazy move? Some would call it more risky, but for Snowbird, it worked. Sure, they ostracized some potential customers who would fall in the beginner bracket. But they really didn't want their business. They knew beginners were more likely to have a bad experience and consequently leave more negative reviews.

While pushing the beginners away, this campaign pulled in the more avid skiers and boarders. The playful scoffing at beginners' complaints resonated with them and drew them to Snowbird as a place to find a true challenge.

Match personalized review attributes with your audience

So long as you have legal permission, you can incorporate all attributes of a review in an ad. Beyond just the star rating and the actual text, this would include:

- *Pen name of the reviewer*
- *Location of the reviewer*
- *Age, gender, ethnicity, etc. if available*

If your advertising strategy is sophisticated enough to include demographic targeting, you could look for additional attributes in your reviews that align with your audience, making the message that much more relatable and influential.

The text that you incorporate in a more personalized UGC ad could reinforce the demographic alignment you are targeting. For example, let's say you're running a paid ad campaign on Facebook in a specific state. Your header text could say "See what [company name] customers are saying about [product name] in [name of state]." You could have several handpicked reviews (5-stars, 90 characters or less) that clearly indicate the reviewers live in the same state.

Visual review content

When filtering and sorting all your reviews for consideration, you may have some visual reviews with photos or videos. If these images and videos reflect a message you want your audience to see, these may be good pieces of content to consider.

Humor

Like the three-wolf moon shirt, some products will attract more funny reviews than others. If while sifting through your reviews you find a funny review, it may be a good one to use. From my experience, the safest bet when using funny reviews is to do what Snowbird did. Find negative reviews that complain about positive drivers. Reviews like this are simply a mismatch between the customer and the product. They aren't your target user and clearly proved it by the negative experience they had. Your target audience may find it funny to see negative reviews complaining about the very thing they like.

In 2020, Amber Share started the Instagram profile @subparparks highlighting comically negative online reviews of national parks.[25]

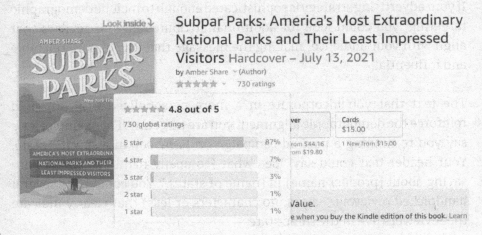

Subpar Parks: America's Most Extraordinary National Parks and Their Least Impressed Visitors Hardcover – July 13, 2021

by Amber Share ˅ (Author)

★★★★★ ˅   730 ratings

★★★★★ **4.8 out of 5**

730 global ratings

5 star		87%
4 star		7%
3 star		3%
2 star		1%
1 star		1%

ver
i

rom $44.16
rom $19.80

Cards
$15.00

1 New from $15.00

Value.

e when you buy the Kindle edition of this book. Learn

Figure 6.8: The book Subpar Parks by Amber Share became a New York Times best seller in less than six months. It highlights comical negative reviews of national parks[26]

Within months, the profile had over 100,000 followers. By the summer of 2021, she published a book featuring all the natural parks she had covered up to that point. Fast forward six months and the book became a New York Times best seller with 4.8 stars and over 700 reviews. It's clear people enjoy a good laugh at the unreasonable dissatisfaction of others.

A/B testing

The best marketers know that results are king. If your creative vision, for whatever reason, failed to increase sales, the campaign was a flop. The best marketers also know this is possible and they don't let a failed campaign stop them. Having a process to measure performance, reiterate, and measure performance again is critical.

A/B testing, also known as split testing, is a process in which you track the performance of two variables. In marketing, this could be comparing two ads against each other. With each test, you learn what worked and what didn't. The process of continually refining your efforts and testing approaches will lead to improvement over time. There are various ways to measure campaign performance. If you're testing digital ads, there are software tools available that will track your click-through rate and other key performance indicators for conversion.

As you begin incorporating reviews and other forms of UGC into your marketing efforts, be creative, thorough and have fun. Get feedback from your peers and teammates. Try something, see how it goes, and improve from there.

Section 6.4: Employer Branding

Engage employees and use employee reviews to build an award-winning employer reputation

Employer branding

Employer branding is brand management for your company's employer reputation. Leveraging employee reviews in your employer branding should follow the same principles of influence and strategy used for customer reviews with consumer-facing marketing. This is exactly what I did to get Malouf ranked in the top ten Glassdoor best places to work out of over one million employers.

I started working at Malouf in 2014. At the time, there were about 35 employees. My job was to manage all the product reviews on ecommerce sites. By 2016 we had a good system in place for managing and improving product reviews, and the company employed over 100 people. I started considering how we could expand our efforts. This led me to evaluate brand and company reviews. We started actively soliciting and managing reviews on Facebook, Google and other brand/company review sites. Having used Glassdoor for my personal job seeking efforts while in college, I also proposed that we open a company profile on Glassdoor.

I began proactively soliciting employee reviews from co-workers. With a brand-new profile, there were no old negative reviews to worry about. Our rating hovered around 4.9 stars for well over a year. The second year, we dropped just a bit to 4.8 stars, which was more of a normalization. I didn't even know there were "Best Place to Work" awards at the time. As I consistently asked for reviews from fellow employees, we hit the minimum requirement of reviews to be eligible for Glassdoor's award and in 2018, Malouf ranked the eighth best place to work in the U.S. on their small/medium business list.

We planned a company-wide celebration with cake, streamers and a sincere thank you to the employees from our CEO, Sam Malouf. People liked working at Malouf the day before our award was announced. After the award, there was a tangible increase in excitement, pride and engagement. Because someone else said Malouf was that incredible, everyone started believing what the leadership had been preaching all along. We went on to win eight significant national employer awards between 2018 and 2020. Each award cemented the credibility of Malouf's reputation as a top workplace. We saw average applications per job posting climb from a couple dozen to literally 100 applicants per job.

Winning awards is a part of employer branding. You want to share good news like this and you want your employees to do the same. However, there's more to employer branding than winning an award. You need to showcase your company culture and get your employees involved in sharing it as well. Below I'll share four additional areas of focus that I would recommend building into your employer branding strategy.

Placement:
Where does employer branding take place? Here are the online locations I believe are most important for your employer branding efforts.

Career page: This is a page on your company website. It's often labeled as "careers" or "jobs" in the website navigation. Here, you have full control of the content. You'll want to tell the story of why the company exists with a mission statement and/or vision statement. You'll want to catch the attention of job seekers that share the same values you do by inviting them to drive the mission forward together.

You'll want to highlight the employee value proposition. Why work here? What's in it for the employee? What are the benefits and perks like? How will the job seeker's life be improved as a result of joining the team?

Add in social proof. Spotlight smiling faces of current employees with testimonials. Feature anonymous review quotes from employees. Highlight links to your employer review profiles and encourage job seekers to validate their decision to apply based on their own research.

Including job openings and instructions to apply is critically important. Everything on this page should lead to applying for a job. This is the equivalent to a consumer buying from you.

Employer review profiles: Section 3.5 has a full list of all employer review sites. My favorites include Glassdoor, Comparably, Indeed and InHerSight. Ensure that the content strategy for each of these profiles is consistent with your career page. Each may vary slightly, but a lot of the items these profiles let you control are the same. Be consistent, accurate and up-to-date.

Secondary review profiles: As we read in section 3.1, there are primary and secondary review sites. For a consumer looking to buy something, a primary review site is where the transaction occurs. For job seekers, the "transaction" is submitting an application. Glassdoor, Indeed and the other employer review sites allow you to mirror your same open job list from your career page to their website. This allows job seekers to apply for a job on any of these profiles. For this reason, your employer review sites are your primary review sites for employer branding efforts.

So where are the secondary review profiles found? For consumers, your employer review sites function as a secondary review site. How you treat your employees may give a customer purchasing confidence. For a job seeker, how you treat your customers may give them confidence to apply for a job. This makes your consumer review sites, like Google, Facebook, Consumer Affairs, and any product review sites like Amazon and Walmart.com secondary review sites for job seekers.

Ensuring that your review management strategy is all encompassing, covering both the consumer side of your reviews and the employee side benefits both scenarios.

Social media: Although not specifically tied to online reviews, your social media presence should be tied to your employer branding strategy. , is important for these efforts. The type of content you have on your company profile should be consistent with your career page and employer review profiles.

Some companies choose to blend their content strategies on social media, highlighting consumer and employer-focused messages. This works for many organizations. Others will segment out employer branding content on designated profiles. Adobe is a great example of this approach. They have an instagram account @adobelife for all things employer branding. There, employees are spotlighted, employer awards are shared and many things related to their people strategy are posted.

Audience:

Who is your audience for employer branding? Although your employer branding messaging is focused on job seekers, you must realize there are additional audiences. These include current employees, past employees, investors, customers, partners, the community and others. Thinking back to chapter 4, who is your target audience when writing review responses? It's not the reviewer. It's everyone else. This same relationship dynamic exists with your employer branding efforts.

Publicly, you're speaking to job seekers. You're sharing why someone would want to work for you. You're talking about the benefits and perks, big news at the company and sharing what current employees say.

However, you may consider prioritizing what content you share to "job seekers" knowing that your goals are to influence current employees, investors and others. Like responding to reviews, you are on stage showcasing content to the job seeker, but the people watching the show (employees, investors) may matter most to you.

There are exceptions. For example, if you're desperate for new hires, perhaps your messaging genuinely is focused on job seekers above all others. Just realize that multiple audiences exist and be mindful as you build your content.

Content:

What do you share on your employer brand locations to engage your audience? All content used for employer branding should be employee-centric. Share known positive experience drivers from your employee feedback. Looking back at chapter 5, conduct a perception matrix analysis of your employee reviews and internal employee feedback.

At Malouf, I reverse-engineered our employer content by identifying the top five reasons employees like working there with a perception matrix analysis. We then build stories around those top five reasons, highlighting related company events, benefits, perks and employee quotes from anonymous reviews and internal surveys. By doing this, job seekers that aligned with those top five things we advertised were more likely to apply for a job and more likely to enjoy working with us.

Ensure that you are tactful when using employee quotes and stats. Unlike a customer that has relatively little impact on your business, employees work for you. They have access to your information and processes. Keep them on your side. I once saw a powerful example of how not to do this. Along the major interstate close to where I live a company ran many billboard ads highlighting their Glassdoor employer ratings. One of these billboards read: "97% of our employees recommend working at [company name removed] to a friend. How's that for a fancy marketing message?"

Other than the fact that they broke the six-word rule for billboard advertising, this message has two critical flaws: 1. The percentage referenced can change daily. As soon as it changed, their ad was no longer accurate. 2. The tone of the message could make employees feel exploited. Rather than being graceful and thankful for the feedback from employees, this message smears the positive ratings in other employers' faces.

Two years after this company ranked in the top 20 best places to work in the U.S., their ratings dropped from 4.7 to 4.0 stars with their "recommend to a friend" percentage dropping 26%. Is it now a horrible place to work? Judging by recent reviews, no. I believe they inadvertently encouraged the small disengaged employee population to write reviews by flaunting how awesome they were to the world in an egotistical manner.

Employee advocacy:

So far in this section, we've talked about what you as the employer should be doing and sharing for your employer branding efforts. If you want to supercharge your employer branding strategy, engage your employees as well. After you've built strong profiles on your employer review sites and your social sites, and have a great career page, consistently share content that your employees would want to re-share personally.

I have co-created two employee advocacy programs and built a third refined approach on my own. It works. The company shares employer-focused content on a regular basis. Executive leaders share employer-focused content on a regular basis. Then, when these two are in play, employees want to get involved. They also share, comment and like posts and news about you online and on social media.

LinkedIn is the platform to focus on, but it certainly extends to all online communities. Evaluate your own business situation to decide where to focus your efforts. I'll share three stats to remember about employee advocacy from "The Official Guide to Employee Advocacy" by LinkedIn:

- *Content shared by employees is clicked on twice as often than if the company shares it.*

- *People also believe employees' posts about your company three times more than posts shared by the CEO.*

- *Companies with socially engaged employees are 58% more likely to attract top talent and 20% more likely to retain them.*[27]

When building an employee advocacy program at your company, you want to sell employees on why it's good for them. Help them build and strengthen their own personal brands. Teach them the career building benefits of showcasing their best selves on LinkedIn and across the web. Then, make it easy for them to talk about your company as part of their personal branding. Comparably does an awesome job at this. With a paid partnership, you can easily create co-branded assets that highlight employee review quotes, company culture scores and employer branding awards. These can easily be shared by you to your employer review profiles and distributed to employees directly for re-sharing.

Know that there are software tools out there to gamify employee advocacy. You can build leaderboards for the best employee advocates, give awards and incentives to employees that re-share company content, and track the collective reach of your employees' network. I have not used any of them. I know they are effective, but it is an added cost. From my personal experience, having a leadership team that sets an example of proactively sharing company content does a lot to get employees involved.

The topics of employer branding and employee advocacy are deserving of entire books. I would recommend taking the time to research these topics, evaluate the current state of your employer branding and build a plan to expand. Simply start by reviewing where things are at now, then build upon your program day by day. You'll eventually build momentum that will propel your efforts forward almost on their own as your employees engage in sharing your content.

Chapter 6 Summary

Section 6.1: Crowd-Sourced Social Proof and Viral Potential

How reviews act as social proof and have viral influence potential

What is social proof?

Social proof is a psychological and social behavior of conformity. An individual who does not know how to act in a group copies the actions of those around them. Reviews, even when anonymous, function as social proof for shoppers making purchase decisions. The sum voice of the online community manifested in the form of online ratings and reviews drastically influences consumer purchase decisions.

Section 6.2: Legal Considerations of Using Reviews in Marketing

Understand which reviews can be used in marketing and how to use them

What legal considerations should be known before marketing with reviews?

The use of reviews in marketing must follow all laws given by the Federal Trade Commission. It is important to be very familiar with all current advertising laws as given by the FTC. Some of the most critical items to consider when using reviews in marketing include:

- *A statement of material connection must be included in reviews when applicable*

- *Claims made in reviews that you use in marketing must reflect the truth*

- *Claims made in reviews that you use in marketing must reflect typical user results, not atypical results.*

- *Claims made in reviews that you use in marketing must be verifiable*

- *Written permission to use a review must be obtained prior to use*

Section 6.3: Maximizing your Marketing Efforts Using Reviews

How to achieve greater success using reviews in your marketing

What is the best way to refer to ratings and reviews in static ads?

Any static ad, like print, cannot be updated with new information. It is created once, and remains. For this reason, any reference to reviews and ratings must be future-proof and accurate. Do not reference things that could change such as a star rating. Once your ad is no longer accurate, you look uninformed and untrustworthy. Instead, reference things that will always be true. For example, you could state that your company has over 1,000 5-star reviews, assuming this is true. You could also encourage your audience to read your reviews for themselves or quote a specific review that sends the message you'd like to deliver.

How do you identify an ideal review for an ad?

In most cases, you want to feature a 5-star review that is less than 90 characters long. Filter your reviews by star rating and sort by character count. Read these eligible reviews and find ones that are free of grammatical errors, meet all legal requirements, and match the message you are trying to send.

Why is A/B testing important?

A/B testing allows you to compare the performance of multiple ads against each other. As you incorporate reviews and other forms of UGC into your marketing, it is important to measure performance. This will allow you to customize your ad campaigns to your unique needs and improve them over time.

Section 6.4: Employer Branding

Engage employees and use employee reviews to build an award-winning employer reputation

What is employer branding?

Employer branding is brand management for your company's employer reputation. It is strategically showcasing your company culture and employee value proposition in order to attract job seekers. Highlighting your benefits, perks and what current employees like about working for you all support these efforts. Employer branding is primarily focused on your website's career page, your employer review profiles, like Glassdoor and across social media.

What is employee advocacy?

Employee advocacy is when employees share good things about working for you. Inviting employees to re-share company posts and updates on personal social media accounts increases the reach of your audience and attracts more job seekers.

Conclusion

The past five years creating The Review Cycle framework and book has been a discovery and refinement process. It started as a simple idea. Along the way, there were lots of drafts and concepts that were scrapped. It took three years and six iterations to uncover the final four-phase model now known as The Review Cycle. Many principles such as review DNA, the law of self-selecting extremes and the perception matrix also went through many iterations and proof-of-concept tests. Interestingly, more than 50% of the final text of the book was written in the final six months of the project.

It was tempting for me to think that earlier time invested was a waste. After all, so much of what I wrote didn't make the final cut. A fellow writer and friend of mine recently told me "All writing matters. None of it is waste. It is part of the creative process."

This changed my perspective. I recognized that the many drafts did contribute to the final copy. These seemingly discarded efforts were actually the building blocks of my learning and growth.

As you apply principles of this book in your own business, do not discount your attempts and failures. Embrace discovery and refinement. Every idea and every action can lead to something. Learn from it and try something new. I believe the same can go for career planning and life in general. This pattern is a great way to find what comes next.

I am continuing this discovery and refinement process today. Although I don't have perfect vision (I've been wearing glasses since 3rd grade), one thing is certain. I will write another book. My next book is already in progress. It will be focused on company culture and engineering employee experiences with feedback data. Originally, I had a chapter dedicated to this topic in The Review Cycle. I realized it deserved more detail than one chapter. My initial framework is in progress and now being refined. I look forward to sharing it with you when it is ready.

Until then, continue forward. Discover and refine.

REFERENCES

Chapter 1

1   No online customer reviews means big problems in 2017 [Blog post]. (2016, December 20). Fan and Fuel. https://fanandfuel.com/no-online-customer-reviews-means-big-problems-2017/

2   Frost, A. (2016, April 29). HubSpot. Only 3% of people think salespeople possess this crucial character trait [Blog post]. https://blog.hubspot.com/sales/salespeople-perception-problem

3   Murphy, R. (2018, December 7). Local consumer review survey [Blog post]. Bright Local. https://www.brightlocal.com/research/local-consumer-review-survey/

4   Perez, S. (2016, December 19). TechCrunch. 79 percent of Americans now shop online, but it's cost more than convenience that sways them. https://techcrunch.com/2016/12/19/79-percent-of-americans-now-shop-online-but-its-cost-more-than-convenience-that-sways-them/

5   Riley, C. (n.d.). Reviewing the reviews: How does TripAdvisor impact hotels and their bookings? [Blog post]. SiteMinder. https://www.siteminder.com/r/marketing/hotel-online-reviews/reviewing-the-reviews-how-does-tripadvisor-impact-hotels-and-their-bookings/

6   4.2 and 4.3 out of 5 stars rating images. (2018, February 20). Amazon.com [Screen capture].

7   Partner content program. (2018, April 26). In Bazaarvoice.

8   Yetis, Al. & Kavak, E. (2020). Analysis of customer behaviours on customer reviews and ratings. KTH Royal Institute of Technology. https://www.diva-portal.org/smash/get/diva2:1461817/FULLTEXT01.pdf

9   I-want-to-buy-it moments: Mobile's growing role in a shopper's purchase decision. (2016, July). Think with Google. https://www.thinkwithgoogle.com/marketing-resources/micro-moments/purchase-decision-mobile-growth/

10   Ramaswamy, S. (2015, April). How micro-moments are changing the rules. Think with Google. https://www.thinkwithgoogle.com/marketing-resources/micro-moments/how-micromoments-are-changing-rules/

11   Harbor Freight generator ad with rating. (date). Harbor Freight [Photo capture].

12   High-rise power straight jeans ad with review quote. (date). Old Navy [Photo capture].

13   Subwoofer tag with average customer rating. (date). Best Buy [Photo capture].

14   History of OOH. (2019). Out of Home Advertising Association of America. https://oaaa.org/AboutOOH/OOHBasics/HistoryofOOH.aspx

15   McDonough, J. (2012, August 29). First radio commercial hit airwaves 90 years ago. Utah Public Radio. https://www.npr.org/2012/08/29/160265990/first-radio-commercial-hit-airwaves-90-years-ago

16   Mertes, A. (2018, September 26). History of tv ads. Quality Logo Products. https://www.qualitylogoproducts.com/promo-university/history-of-tv-ads.htm

17   Market research. (2019, June 21). In Wikipedia. https://en.wikipedia.org/w/index.php?title=Market_research&oldid=902786395

18   Wood, C. (2012, July 27). Who really, really invented the internet? Government Technology. https://www.govtech.com/e-government/Who-Invented-the-Internet.html

19   Internet protocol suite. (2019, June 15). In Wikipedia. https://en.wikipedia.org/w/index.php?title=Internet_protocol_suite&oldid=901889428

20   ARPANET. (2019, June 19). In Wikipedia. https://en.wikipedia.org/w/index. php?title=ARPANET&oldid=902566571

21   History of the Internet. (2019, June 20). In Wikipedia. https://en.wikipedia.org/w/index.php?title=History_ of_the_Internet&oldid=902656709

22   Tech Musings. (2008, April 4). How we got from 1 to 162 million websites on the internet [Blog post]. Solarwinds Pingdom. https://royal.pingdom.com/how-we-got-from-1-to-162-million-websites-on-the-internet/

23   Lewis, P. H. (1994, August 12). Attention shoppers: Internet is open. The New York Times. http://www. nytimes.com/1994/08/12/business/attention-shoppers-internet-is-open.html

24   History of ecommerce. (n.d.). Ecommerce-land. https://www.ecommerce-land.com/history_ecommerce. html

25   Amazon.com, Inc. Form 10-K. (1997, December 31). http://media.corporate-ir.net/media_files/ irol/97/97664/reports/123197_10k.pdf

26   Del Rey, J. (2016, September 27). 55 percent of online shoppers start their product searches on Amazon. Recode. https://www.recode.net/2016/9/27/13078526/amazon-online-shopping-product-search-engine

27   eMarketer Editors. (2018, July 16). Amazon now has nearly 50% of US ecommerce market. https://www. emarketer.com/content/amazon-now-has-nearly-50-of-us-ecommerce-market

28   Consumer trust in online, social and mobile advertising grows. (2012, April 10). Nielsen. https://www.nielsen. com/us/en/insights/news/2012/consumer-trust-in-online-social-and-mobile-advertising-grows.html

29   SixDegrees.com. (2019, June 11). In Wikipedia. https://en.wikipedia.org/w/index.php?title=SixDegrees. com&oldid=901341796

30   Clement, J. (2019, March 18). Percentage of U.S. population with a social media profile from 2008 to 2019. Statista. https://www.statista.com/statistics/273476/percentage-of-us-population-with-a-social-network-profile/

31   Millwood, A. (2016, April 14). How to easily create effective Facebook ads with Yotpo. Yotpo. https://www. yotpo.com/blog/create-effective-facebook-ads/

32   O'Neil-Hart, C., & Blumenstein, H. (2016, July). Why YouTube stars are more influential than traditional celebrities. Think with Google. https://www.thinkwithgoogle.com/consumer-insights/youtube-stars-influence/

33   Chernev, B. (2019, March 15). Techjury. Influencer marketing statistics in 2019. https://techjury.net/stats-about/influencer-marketing/

34   Simonson, I., & Rosen, E. (2014). What marketers misunderstand about online reviews. Harvard Business Review. https://hbr.org/2014/01/what-marketers-misunderstand-about-online-reviews

35   Alcantara, A. (2018, July 16). New report shows just how significant Amazon's reach in ecommerce is. Adweek. https://www.adweek.com/commerce/new-report-shows-just-how-significant-amazons-reach-in-ecommerce-is/

36   Best-seller badge on chair listing. (date). Walmart.com [Screen capture].

37   Well Endowed. (2018, January 15). 11/10 product!!! Amazon.com [Screen capture].

38   Customer reviews featuring picture and video reviews. (date). Overstock.com [Screen capture].

39   Read reviews that mention. (2019, July 3). Amazon.com [Screen capture].

40   Pros and cons. (2019, June 1). Glassdoor.com [Screen capture].

41   The power of reviews. (2014). Power Reviews. https://www.powerreviews.com/wp-content/ uploads/2015/08/13185402/ThePowerofReviews-Report.pdf

42   Andersen, Isabella. (n.d.). How much are online reviews actually worth? [Blog post]. RevLocal. Retrieved June 10, 2019 from https://www.revlocal.com/blog/reviews/how-much-are-online-reviews-actually-worth-

43

Andre, C. (2012, December 11). Why do people continually write such extensive Yelp reviews without tangible reward [Online comment]? Quora. https://www.quora.com/Why-do-people-continually-write-such-extensive-Yelp-reviews-without-tangible-reward

BetterthanBings. (2007). Why do people write reviews for travel sites [Online comment]? TripAdvisor. https://www.tripadvisor.com/ShowTopic-g28926-i29-k735576-Why_do_people_write_reviews_for_travel_sites-California.html

Bjbert. (2007). Why do people write reviews for travel sites [Online comment]? TripAdvisor. https://www.tripadvisor.com/ShowTopic-g28926-i29-k735576-Why_do_people_write_reviews_for_travel_sites-California.html

Blumenthal, M. (2015, September 14). Survey: Why do consumers leave reviews? GatherUp. https://gatherup.com/ blog/survey-why-do-consumers-leave-reviews/

Chang, P. (2012, March 23). Why do people continually write such extensive Yelp reviews without tangible reward [Online comment]? Quora. https://www.quora.com/Why-do-people-continually-write-such-extensive-Yelp-reviews-without-tangible-reward

Daniels, M. P. (2012, December 11). Why do people continually write such extensive Yelp reviews without tangible reward [Online comment]? Quora. https://www.quora.com/Why-do-people-continually-write-such-extensive-Yelp-reviews-without-tangible-reward

DarthAnonymous. (2007). Why do people write reviews for travel sites [Online comment]? TripAdvisor. https://www.tripadvisor.com/ShowTopic-g28926-i29-k735576-Why_do_people_write_reviews_for_travel_sites-California.html

Dato, N. (2015, July 8). Why do people continually write such extensive Yelp reviews without tangible reward [Online comment]? Quora. https://www.quora.com/Why-do-people-continually-write-such-extensive-Yelp-reviews-without-tangible-reward

Decker, S. (2007, November 28). Why customers write reviews [Blog posts]. BazaarVoice. http://blog.bazaarvoice.com/2007/11/28/why-customers-write-reviews/

Garcia, R. (2012, January 17). Why do people continually write such extensive Yelp reviews without tangible reward [Online comment]? Quora. https://www.quora.com/Why-do-people-continually-write-such-extensive-Yelp-reviews-without-tangible-reward

Haden, R. (2013, December 26). Why do consumers write reviews [Blog post]. Haden Interactive. https://www.hadeninteractive.com/consumers-write-reviews/

Harel, T. (2018, February 5). The 6 real reasons behind why people write online customer reviews [Blog post]. Spectoos. https://www.spectoos.com/5-real-motivations-behind-people-write-customer-reviews/

HopSkipJump. (2007). Why do people write reviews for travel sites [Online comment]? TripAdvisor. https://www.tripadvisor.com/ShowTopic-g28926-i29-k735576-Why_do_people_write_reviews_for_travel_sites-California.html

Karr, D. (2012, June 18). Infographic: Why do people write online reviews? Social Media Today. https://www.socialmediatoday.com/content/infographic-why-do-people-write-online-reviews

Ledesma, J. (2017, June 20). Why do people write reviews? What our research revealed. [Blog post]. Trust Pilot. http://blog.trustpilot.com/blog/why-do-people-write-reviews-what-our-research-revealed

Levitt, S. D. (2005, July 22). Why do people post reviews on Amazon [Blog post]. Freakonomics. http://freakonomics.com/2005/07/22/why-do-people-post-reviews-on-amazon/

Macjack. (2007). Why do people write reviews for travel sites [Online comment]? TripAdvisor. https://www.tripadvisor.com/ShowTopic-g28926-i29-k735576-Why_do_people_write_reviews_for_travel_sites-California.html

Marsha w. (2007). Why do people write reviews for travel sites [Online comment]? TripAdvisor. https://www.tripadvisor.com/ShowTopic-g28926-i29-k735576-Why_do_people_write_reviews_for_travel_sites-California.html

Sickler, J. (2017, March 31). How to get Google reviews from happy customers [Blog post]. Reputation Management. https://www.reputationmanagement.com/blog/how-to-get-google-reviews/

Tet14. (2007). Why do people write reviews for travel sites [Online comment]? TripAdvisor. https://www.tripadvisor.com/ShowTopic-g28926-i29-k735576-Why_do_people_write_reviews_for_travel_sites-California.html

The unselfish reasons why people write online reviews. (2012, June 27). Visual News. http://www.visualnews.com/2012/06/27/heres-looking-out-you-kid-the-unselfish-reasons-why-people-write-online-reviews/?view=infographic

Wenzi, M. (2016, May 17). Why do customers post online reviews [Blog post]. ReviewTrackers. https://www.reviewtrackers.com/customers-post-online-reviews/

Why do people write reviews? (2009, March 12). Why do people write reviews? Freshminds. http://www.freshminds.net/2009/03/why-do-people-write-reviews/

44 Analysis of 7 million Amazon reviews: customers who receive free or discounted item much more likely to write positive review. (2016, June 29). ReviewMeta. https://reviewmeta.com/blog/analysis-of-7-million-amazon-reviews-customers-who-receive-free-or-discounted-item-much-more-likely-to-write-positive-review/

45 Five Stars. (2015, December 4). Amazon.com [Screen capture].

46 Just a very nice, durable product. Fit great!! (2016, July 12). Amazon.com [Screen capture].

47 Great, just a bit fragile. (2013, November 9). Amazon.com [Screen capture].

48 Frame is fantastic... hooks are horrible. (2017, February 13). Amazon.com [Screen capture].

49 Mattress still slips. Gave it 2 stars instead of... (2017, May 5). Amazon.com [Screen capture].

50 Removable caps are not so removable. (2017, October 10). Amazon.com [Screen capture].

51 Three stars. (2014, November 9). Amazon.com [Screen capture].

52 Four stars. (2015, June 22). Amazon.com [Screen capture].

53 Blumenthal, M. (2015, September 14). Survey: Why do consumers leave reviews? Retrieved June 10, 2019, from https://gatherup.com/blog/survey-why-do-consumers-leave-reviews/

54 Pleasantly surprised by quality. (2013, September 15). Amazon.com [Screen capture].

55 Not waterproof - at all. Find another mattress protector, this isn't it. (2014, May 28). Amazon.com [Screen capture].

56 Brad. (2015, August 10). Five stars. Amazon.com [Screen capture].

57 Brad. (2015, September 14). Worst fit and terrible!!! Amazon.com [Screen capture].

58   He loves to use a fan to make noise but this has a better, less whining tone. (2016, December 21). Amazon.com [Screen capture].

59   Three stars. (2016, December 21). Amazon.com [Screen capture].

60   Three stars. (2015, October 26). Amazon.com [Screen capture].

Chapter 2

1.   Purchase funnel. (2021, October 27). In Wikipedia. https://en.wikipedia.org/wiki/AIDA_(marketing)

2.   AIDA (marketing). (2021, October 27). In Wikipedia. https://en.wikipedia.org/wiki/AIDA_(marketing)

3.   Rosen, E. & Simonson, I. (2014, February). What marketers misunderstand about online reviews. https://hbr.org/2014/01/what-marketers-misunderstand-about-online-reviews

4.   Murphy, R. (2018, December 7). Local consumer review survey [Blog post]. Bright Local. https://www.brightlocal.com/research/local-consumer-review-survey/

5.   Laptop Google search returns filterable results. (2020, February 10). Google. [Screen capture].

6.   A view of a single product (laptop) page clicked on from Google results. (2020, February 10). Microsoft. [Screen capture].

7.   The review section on laptop product listing page. (2020, February 10). Microsoft. [Screen capture].

8.   Laptop checkout page. (2020, February 10). Microsoft. [Screen capture].

9.   Anderson, M. & Smith, A. (2016, December 19). Online reviews. https://www.pewresearch.org/internet/2016/12/19/online-reviews/

10.   Dean, B. (2019, August). Here's what we learned about organic click-through rate [Blog post]. Retrieved November 12, 2021 from https://backlinko.com/google-ctr-stats

11.   Saleh, K. (2020). The average website conversion rate by industry (updated by 2020). Retrieved November 12, 2021 from https://www.invespcro.com/blog/the-average-website-conversion-rate-by-industry/

12.   Hall, M. (2021, April 26). Elasticity vs. inelasticity of demand: What's the difference? [Blog post]. https://www.investopedia.com/ask/answers/012915/what-difference-between-inelasticity-and-elasticity-demand.asp

13.   Yetis, Al. & Kavak, E. (2020). Analysis of customer behaviours on customer reviews and ratings. KTH Royal Institute of Technology. https://www.diva-portal.org/smash/get/diva2:1461817/FULLTEXT01.pdf

14.   0.1-star rating change displays for Panera Bread and The Home Depot. (2021, October 15). Indeed. [Screen capture].

15.   Two products both display 4 and a half-filled stars. (2021, October 15). Amazon.com. [Screen capture].

Chapter 3

1.   Analysis of 7 million Amazon reviews: Customers who receive free or discounted item much more likely to write positive review [Blog post]. (2016, June 29). ReviewMeta. https://reviewmeta.com/blog/analysis-of-7-million-amazon-reviews-customers-who-receive-free-or-discounted-item-much-more-likely-to-write-positive-review/

2.   Asking for reviews from customers: The ultimate guide [Blog post]. (2021, May 24). ReviewTrackers. https://www.reviewtrackers.com/guides/ask-customers-review/

3.   Ham Radio. (2021, November 12). Example of syndicated review [Screen capture].

4.   About the FTC. (n.d.). Federal Trade Commission. Retrieved November 29, 2021 from https://www.ftc.gov/about-ftc

5.   FTC publishes final guides governing endorsements, testimonials. (2009, October 5). Federal Trade Commission. https://www.ftc.gov/news-events/press-releases/2009/10/ftc-publishes-final-guides-governing-endorsements-testimonials

6.   Update on customer reviews. (2016, October 3). Amazon. Retrieved November 29, 2021 from https://www.aboutamazon.com/news/innovation-at-amazon/update-on-customer-reviews

7.   Cheesman, J. (2017, October 17). Report: Candidates are bailing on you because of poor Glassdoor reviews. [Blog post]. https://www.ere.net/poor-anonymous-reviews-costing-employers/

8.   Arruda, W. (2019, September 22). Why online employer reviews are crucial to your branding. [Blog post]. https://www.forbes.com/sites/williamarruda/2019/09/22/why-online-employer-reviews-are-crucial-to-your-branding/?sh=56cc0a4c1f45

9.   Liu, J. (2020, January 6). 1 in 3 people have turned down a job offer because of a company's bad online reviews—but they're not always true. [Blog post]. https://www.cnbc.com/2020/01/06/1-in-3-people-have-rejected-a-job-offer-because-of-a-bad-online-review.html

10.   Chamberlain, A. (2017, February 15). Why do workers quit? The factors that predict employee turnover. https://www.glassdoor.com/research/why-do-workers-quit/

11.   Chamberlain, A. (2018, May 18). Metro movers: Where are Americans moving for jobs, and is it worth it? https://www.glassdoor.com/research/where-are-americans-moving-for-jobs/

12.   Website traffic statistics. (n.d.) WebsiteIQ. Retrieved September 25, 2021 from https://www.websiteiq.com/

Chapter 4

1   Online reviews statistics and trends: A 2022 report by ReviewTrackers. (2021, December 1). ReviewTrackers. https://www.reviewtrackers.com/reports/online-reviews-survey/
2   Murphy, R. (2020, December 9). Local consumer review survey 2020. Brightlocal. https://www.brightlocal.com/research/local-consumer-review-survey/
3   Sherri. (2015, October 9). Amazon.com [Screen capture].
4   Whale tale tea infuser. (2021, January 16). Amazon.com [Screen capture].
5   Passive voice. (n.d.). In Dictionary.com. Retrieved January 6, 2022, from https://www.dictionary.com/browse/passive-voice
6   Active voice. (n.d.). In Dictionary.com. Retrieved January 6, 2022, from https://www.dictionary.com/browse/active-voice
7   Anderson, C. K. & Han, S. (2016). Hotel performance impact of socially engaging with consumers. Center for Hospitality Research, 16(10), 7. https://hdl.handle.net/1813/71227
8   Power Reviews. (n.d.). How Q&A eliminates uncertainty and boosts ecommerce sales. Retrieved January 6, 2022 from https://www.powerreviews.com/insights/how-q-and-a-boosts-ecommerce-sales/?mkt_tok=NjUzLURNWi0xMDYAAAF__orSnveKaIvdREwdiKKqB3gGYb9WHrJeb_UFeRNQxublwtrmd6O8olC_osA-71xA6qFeNsrF1YM13jNsHFti2H8P0472rskivKabfN2UUTcEg
9   Glassdoor. (n.d.). How to respond to reviews. https://www.glassdoor.com/employers/resources/templates-for-hiring-pros-how-to-respond-to-reviews/

Chapter 5

1   A gray reading pillow. (2021, October 16). Amazon.com [Screen capture].
2   A gray reading pillow with dimensions. (2021, October 16). Amazon.com [Screen capture].
3   G. R. Carroll, D. W. Lehman, & K. O'Connor. (2019, June 27). The kind of authenticity customers will pay more for. Harvard Business Review. https://hbr.org/2019/06/the-kind-of-authenticity-customers-will-pay-more-for

Chapter 6

1   Social proof. (2022, January 14). In Wikipedia. https://en.wikipedia.org/wiki/Social_proof
2   Kelman, H.C. (1958). Compliance, identification, and internalization three processes of attitude change. SAGE journals. https://doi.org/10.1177/002200275800200106
3   Partner content program. (2018, April 26). In Bazaarvoice.
4   The mountain men's three wolf moon short sleeve tee. (2022, January 24). Amazon. https://www.amazon.com/Mountain-Three-Wolf-Short-Sleeve/dp/B002HJ377A/
5   Becerra-Fernandez, I. & Sabherwal, R. (2010, January 15). Business intelligence: Practices, technologies, and management. p. 273, https://books.google.com/books?id=T-JvPdEcmooC&pg=RA1-PA273#v=onepage&q&f=false
6   WMURg. (2010, January 27). State hopes to harness power of 'three wolf' shirts. https://www.wmur.com/article/state-hopes-to-harness-power-of-three-wolf-shirts/5161333
7   Our history. (n.d.) Federal Trade Commission: Protecting America's Consumers. https://www.ftc.gov/about-ftc/our-history
8   About the FTC. (n.d.). Federal Trade Commission: Protecting America's Consumers. https://www.ftc.gov/about-ftc
9   FTC overview. (n.d.) Glassdoor. https://www.glassdoor.com/Overview/Working-at-FTC-EI_IE38937.11,14.htm
10 Equal credit opportunity act. (n.d.). Federal Trade Commission: Protecting America's Consumers. https://www.ftc.gov/enforcement/statutes/equal-credit-opportunity-act
11 Careers at the FTC. (n.d.). Federal Trade Commission: Protecting America's Consumers. https://www.ftc.gov/about-ftc/careers-ftc
12 Contact the Federal Trade Commission. (n.d.). Federal Trade Commission: Protecting America's Consumers. https://www.ftc.gov/contact
13 Nordica Memorial Association. (n.d.) Nordica Coca-Cola advertisement, 1905. https://www.mainememory.net/artifact/17287/
14 125 years of sharing happiness. (2011). The Coca-Cola Company. https://www.coca-colacompany.com/content/dam/journey/us/en/our-company/history/coca-cola-a-short-history-125-years-booklet.pdf
15 Wheaties. (2022, January 26). In Wikipedia. https://en.wikipedia.org/wiki/Wheaties

16   Guides concerning the use of endorsements and testimonials in advertising. (n.d.) Federal Trade Commission. https://www.ftc.gov/system/files/attachments/press-releases/ftc-publishes-final-guides-governing-endorsements-testimonials/091005revisedendorsementguides.pdf

17   Citation removed

18   The FTC's endorsement guides: What people are asking. (2017, September). Federal Trade Commission: Protecting America's Consumers. https://www.ftc.gov/tips-advice/business-center/guidance/ftcs-endorsement-guides-what-people-are-asking#soliciting

19   Consumer review fairness act: What businesses need to know. (2017, February). Federal Trade Commission: Protecting America's Consumers. https://www.ftc.gov/tips-advice/business-center/guidance/consumer-review-fairness-act-what-businesses-need-know

20   Everything you need to know about UGC. (n.d.). Tint. 1-8.

21   Millwood, A. (2016, April 14). How to easily create effective Facebook ads with Yotpo. Yotpo. https://www.yotpo.com/blog/create-effective-facebook-ads

22   Glassdoor badge options. (2022, January 15). [Image, screen capture]. https://www.glassdoor.com/Overview/Working-at-iFIT-EI_IE3912.11,15.htm

23   Allpa 35L travel pack. (2022, January 17). Google. [Image, screen capture]. Retrieved from https://www.google.com/search?q=alpa+35L+travel+pack+cotopaxi&rlz=1C1GCEV_enUS921US921&sxs-rf=APq-WBtWXqq4aRbHhFmyGbBSjjxJFrt34Q%3A1644701240329&ei=OCYIYudE5PIkPIPyceWuA4&ved=0a-hUKEwjv2cPJjfv1AhUTJEQIHcmjBecQ4dUDCA4&uact=5&oq=alpa+35L+travel+pack+cotopaxi&gs_lcp=C-gdnd3Mtd2l6EAMyBggAEBYQHjIGCAAQFhAeMgYIABAWEB46BwgAEEcQsAM6BAgAEA06BggAEAoQHjoI-CAAQCBANEB5KBAhBGABKBAhGGABQrgZYhCRgjiVoAXABeACAAYECiAHoDJIBBTAuOC4ymAEAoAEByAEI-wAEB&sclient=gws-wiz

24   One star campaign. (2022, February 12). Snowbird. https://www.snowbird.com/one-star/

25   Subparparks [@ambershare_]. (2020, January 29). Please get a more sophisticated color palette and do something about all these tree, @yosemitenps. 1 star. [Instagram photograph]. Retrieved February 12, 2022 from https://www.instagram.com/p/B76ODJ-HoaQ/

26   Share, A. (2022, February 12). Subpar Parks New York Times bestseller example. [Image, screen cap-ture]. https://www.amazon.com/Subpar-Parks-Americas-Extraordinary-Impressed/dp/0593185544/ref=sr_1_1?crid=12VJS7GT6V605&keywords=subpar+parks&qid=1644700080&s=books&sprefix=sub-par+parks%2Cstripbooks%2C160&sr=1-1

27   Levinson, K. (2016, September 29). Introducing the official guide to employee advocacy. Linkedin. https://www.linkedin.com/business/marketing/blog/brand/introducing-the-official-guide-to-employee-advocacy

GLOSSARY

A/B testing- A process in which you track the performance of two variables

Active voice- When the verb of a sentence is in the active voice, the subject is doing the acting

Click-Through Rate (CTR)- Ratio of consumers exposed to your product in search results or in an ad to the number of consumers who click-through to the offering

Conversion Rate (CR)- Ratio of page views to purchases

Displayed star rating- The actual star rating displayed live on a listing or profile. Often, this rating is algorithmically calculated, weighing newer, verified and helpful reviews more.

Employer branding- Brand management for your company's employer reputation

Influencer- Social media user with a large following

Law of self-selecting extremes- A form of representation bias where negative reviews outweigh positives when no requests for sharing reviews are made by the business

Minimum rating standard- The bottom level star-rating threshold a customer expects in order to click on a product listing

Mirror messaging- A written form of active listening

Net promoter score- A ratio of customer loyalty and satisfaction. It is often collected through internally facing feedback mechanisms

Organizational-Generated Content (OGC)- Content or media produced by and derived from the ideas and concepts of an organization

Passive voice- A verb is in the passive voice when the subject of the sentence is acted on by the verb

Price elasticity- Responsiveness of consumers (demand change) to a price change

Purchase funnel- A marketing model that illustrates the progress a consumer goes through towards buying something

Qualitative review data- Any form of review data that is in word form and can be evaluated by reading and human reasoning

Quantitative review data- Any form of review data that is in number form and can be analyzed and evaluated with numbers and percentages

Rate of star rating change- The positive or negative rate of change to a star rating over a standard time frame

Raw average star rating- The calculated raw average rating of all reviews for a given time frame

Review DNA- The unique blend of a reviewer's motive for writing, method of rating, and trigger for posting a review

Review elasticity- Responsiveness of consumers (demand change) to a star-rating change

Review pace- The number of new reviews received over a standard time frame

Review rate % change- The calculated change in review rate compared to the previous time frame

Review Rate (RR)- Ratio of people who buy the item to the number of people who post a review

Review volume- Total number of reviews on a listing or profile

Shopping Cart Abandonment Rate (CAR)- Ratio of digital shopping carts used to number of completed purchases

Social proof- A type of conformity in which a person follows the behaviors of others when they are unsure of the correct way to act

Star rating- A rating indicated by stars (usually 1-5 with 5 indicating the highest quality or best features)

Star-rating change- Thes calculated difference in star ratings compared to the most recent time frame comparison

The Perception Matrix- A four-quadrant model for evaluating perceived and legitimate experience drivers across a positive and negative sentiment.

The Review Cycle- A four phase consumer behavior model illustrating the cyclical nature of purchase decisions informed by review data and the elements of influence a business can make on these behaviors

Translated quantitative data- Qualitative data turned from words to numbers for quicker analysis

User-Generated Content (UGC)- Content produced by a user or customer

About the Author

Matt R. Vance is a social innovator. His work and research center around human behaviors, perceptions and experience design. He has built consumer and employee experience programs at multiple global organizations, including iFIT and Malouf Companies and has consulted a wide range of other organizations. His work has been recognized with honors from Glassdoor, Utah Business, Comparably and The Stevie Awards. He received his bachelor's degree in Business Administration from Utah State University where he also ran track and cross-country. He loves to crochet and tell dad jokes. Matt lives in Logan, Utah with his wife and children.

Contact Matt R. Vance for consulting, training and speaking inquiries.
Email: mattrvance@outlook.com

You learned about reviews. Share yours of this book.

Learn more.
TheReviewCycle.com or at *MattRVance.com*

Follow Matt R. Vance.

linkedin.com/in/mattrvance

CPSIA information can be obtained
at www.ICGtesting.com
Printed in the USA
LVHW032109060722
722853LV00005B/417